Four Portraits of Jesus

Four Portraits of Jesus

Studies in the Gospels and
Their Old Testament Background

Elizabeth E. Platt

Paulist Press
New York/Mahwah, N.J.

Scripture extracts are taken from the New Revised Standard Version, Copyright © 1989, by the Division of Christian Education of the National Council of the Churches of Christ in the United States of America and reprinted by permission of the publisher.

Cover art: Christian epitaph with engraving of the Good Shepherd, found in the Basilica of Damous el-Karita at Carthago. White marble, late third/early fourth century. National Museum of Carthage, Carthage. Courtesy of Erich Lessing/Art Resource, NY.

Cover design by Sharyn Banks
Book design by Lynn Else

Library of Congress Cataloging-in-Publication Data

Platt, Elizabeth E.
    Four portraits of Jesus : studies in the Gospels and their Old Testament background / Elizabeth E. Platt.
      p. cm.
    Includes index.
    ISBN 0-8091-4204-X (alk. paper)
    1. Bible. N.T. Gospels—Textbooks. I. Title.

    BS2556.P57 2004
    226′.0071—dc22

                                  200302724

Published by Paulist Press
997 Macarthur Boulevard
Mahwah, New Jersey 07430

www.paulistpress.com

Printed and bound in the
United States of America

CONTENTS

PREFACE

"Who is Jesus *really?*" people ask.

They are likely to go on to say: "*Four* Gospels seem confusing. Why is there not just *one* story of Jesus? The combined account of events that were on TV at Easter time—isn't that basically the way it all happened?"

Those are logical and insightful questions about the main concern in Christianity, and these issues can open doors to fascinating studies in the Bible. The church has said for almost 2,000 years that to answer the question "Who is Jesus?" the believer needs to read all four Gospels under the guidance of the Holy Spirit. Then the *"fifth Gospel"* becomes truly the most important, and that is the unique Gospel the believer faithfully lives out in community in response to the question "Who is Jesus to *you?*" Or, in the words of Jesus to his disciples, "But who do you say that I am?" (Matt 16:15).

In order to get to the "fifth Gospel," it is necessary to see the perspectives of each canonical Gospel and to begin to understand their distinctive natures. The fact that Matthew, Mark, Luke, and John are in the Bible means that they are considered part of the "canon" in the sense of a "measuring stick." Using this measuring stick, our own response can grow into the question of who Jesus really is.

Many people today, as in other times, have come to the Bible initially and predominantly by hearing small single portions read aloud in worship. These narratives, sections, or verses are usually presented as isolated units appropriate to the hearer on momentary occasions. As welcome as each message may be, such a diverse and dotted collection creates a hunger for knowing the larger contexts of the four great Gospels. Each New Testament Gospel has a dynamic portrait of Jesus and his ministry; it tells of several disciples, and it holds up certain events, sayings, and teachings for view. As renowned commentators affirm, each Gospel originally served a particular church congregation to which it brought a message of hope, purpose, and call. Then, especially significant here, each Gospel can also be seen to rest on key aspects of the Old Testament that are central to Jesus' life and teaching.

This book is designed for adult education in the church. The Introduction, which follows this Preface, has responses to some basic questions about the Bible frequently asked by adult students. A course plan is suggested for five sessions one hour and fifteen minutes long each, with specific guidelines for the leader. The four main chapters (Matthew, Mark, Luke, and John) seek to explore issues of messiahship given in the Old Testament that each Gospel emphasizes.

The course plan gives prominence to beginning each class session with the passages of Scripture printed immediately under the section "Who is Jesus in...?" or suggested in the opening paragraph. For example, the actual study of Matthew begins with the passage Matthew 11:28–30. The new student reader is urged to start studying with their teacher exactly at the Scripture points for each of the Gospel sessions. Later, as the sessions get underway, the leader may encourage the reading of chosen sections in the Introduction or even in the Appendix. For this particular course plan, the focus is on reading and discovering the unique nature of each of the four Gospels *as soon as possible*. Even the introductory and summary sections found within the Gospel chapters are secondary to the doorway passages into each Gospel.

It is to the advantage of the teacher/leader of the Scripture study format suggested here to read *first* the Introduction that immediately follows the Preface. Those topics and questions prepare the leader for the underlying issues of the particular plan that is suggested at the conclusion of the Introduction. The design is intentional; further background on the history of biblical interpretation (in the Appendix) may interest the teacher, particularly those preparing for leadership in adult education biblical studies. It is also appropriate to have resources for continuing education that beginning students can access easily. Matthew's Jesus brings twelve new disciples to follow him in the call to teaching. Luke's writing prefaces the call to apostleship with the Gospel as a beginning handbook. There is precedent in Scripture for what is attempted here: beginners may be called to serve in times ahead as teachers.

There are many other ways the book could be used, of course; a single chapter on a specific Gospel could provide a preface to a month's study in itself. Background for a lectionary season on one Gospel could give initial grounding for individual passages. The chapter on the Gospel of Matthew could be used for a Christian introductory reading of the Old Testament starting with Genesis and Exodus. The chapter "On the History of Biblical Interpretation" (in the Appendix) could serve a class convened in the parish library.

Throughout the book the formatting is intended to aid the classroom presentation. Note that the Contents gives a schematic set of topics, which may aid the new student to find the exact chapter and place to begin. After the complete set of Gospels is treated in a course, the student may want to compose descriptive titles for Jesus for each of the four Gospel chapters. The suggested learning procedure is to have the teacher demonstrate how the conclusions are reached for such titles by reading and studying contextual Scripture passages. Then titles could be written workbook style in the student's own handwriting on the Contents. A sample list might include: Matthew—Jesus Christ, the Great Teacher (Who Shows How to Love God and Neighbor); Mark—The Crucified Messiah (Who Prefers to Be the Suffering Son of Man); Luke—Gentle Jesus, the Light to All Nations; John—the Divine Son, the Father's Passover Lamb.

The headings and subheadings in the body of each Gospel chapter are used because of the common understanding that one of the most effective ways of learning new information is with the question-and-answer method. The teacher may call attention to a section through its heading. The leader might write out ahead of time what questions in that unit are to come up for the next group meeting. As the reader considers the questions, he or she may want to underline a main point the textbook is discussing. The wide margins and blank spaces invite comments and reflections—either from class or in preparation times. Notes from other readings (especially those reviewed from recent Catholic biblical materials—see the Appendix) can be added in the margins. Sample topics for exercises are given with space to write or journal. Charts demonstrate key concepts but also encourage fill-ins. Daily Prayer Reflections are encouraged with sample formats and life-application questions for spiritual and communal growth.

Of the four Gospels, Matthew is presented for the first study because it has been the church tradition's choice as the most complete Gospel. Also, because Matthew is the first of the four in canonical order, people in congregations can expect it to be read first. Seminary students and others who have had more formal New Testament courses expect Mark to be studied first because it is considered to be the earliest Gospel by scholarly consensus. Reasons of preference could be given for any of the four Gospels to be studied first—for example, lectionary emphasis, favorite personal choice, or similarity to a hypothesized original congregation for whom it was written.

The short history of main events in Bible study through the ages (see the timeline in the Appendix) can aid the teacher's preparation or develop the engaged student's understanding of how church tradition has shaped interpretations of the Scriptures. Finally exegesis methodologies are summarized for use in preparing the message for church life and mission in contemporary times.

All Bible quotations come from the New Revised Standard Version translation unless otherwise noted. Shorter quotations appear in the text, set within quotation marks. Longer quotations appear as separate indented extracts. Quotations may also be used to indicate colloquialisms or twists on a word's meaning.

Every Gospel chapter in this study begins with a passage or two to lead into a key theme for that particular Gospel and moves out from there. Each chapter concludes with a fictitious portrayal that summarizes the unique setting or possible congregation to which the Gospel was addressed. Then, in the last section of each Gospel chapter, the Daily Prayer Reflections move from the study of the portraits of Jesus toward the question "How, therefore, shall we live?"

ACKNOWLEDGMENTS

My gratitude goes to teachers, especially in graduate school, seminary, and college, but also from earliest times in Sunday school and church, high school and grade school, because they taught students how to write their names and find them in the treasure houses of human culture. These teachers, knowingly or not, helped us to receive God's gifts and contribute them to others along life's pathways.

Most recently, for the pages here, I thank the faculty, the administrative staffs, the boards, and all the students at the University of Dubuque, but especially in the Theological Seminary; the colleagues in contributive projects, Kathy and Helmar Sakenfeld, Larry and Gillian Geraty, Larry and Denise Herr, Bob and Molly Dykstra, and Sue and Jim Lindsay; and my supportive Iowa neighbors. Technical skills and professional suggestions were given by kind teachers at the Paulist Press, Frs. Joseph Scott and Lawrence Boadt, and Paul McMahon, managing editor; masters at the computer, David and Debbie Lovett; and scribal assistants Tanya Fowler, the late Shirley Hickman, and Ruth Jeffries.

Finally I am grateful to the teachers in my family, to my brothers and sisters-in-law, and their children, but most of all my late father, Charles, and my beautiful mother, Mary Elizabeth, who first taught me by Word and deed about Jesus.

PART ONE:

Introduction

READING ABOUT JESUS IN THE BIBLE

A. *Why Read the Bible?*

The Bible in Western culture belongs to everyone because it is such an influential factor in our civilization—the common heritage of history, literature, music, art, and drama. Especially influenced by the Bible have been the ideas of right and wrong, the understanding of family and social relationships, as well as hundreds of concerns that make up the bundle we call "life." It is rare to come across a person in the West who has not heard of the Bible. Most significant to many, even if they claim not to have read much of it, is the way the Bible has guided peoples' relationship to God in the sphere designated "religious faith."

From the standpoint of the history of the human race, the study of religion and, in particular, the Bible can be designated as the oldest intellectual endeavor with the longest continuous tradition. There are libraries upon libraries of books and collections upon collections of material culture about religion. Numerous interpreters comment on its subjects, and there are many witnesses to the longings of the human heart for the Power beyond ourselves, yet dwelling within, usually called "God."

B. *What Is the Bible About, Basically?*

The ancient book called the Holy Bible (whose title comes from words that meant "the sacred scrolls") can be described as the account of God's relentless search to love human beings. The subject ranges from the creation of the universe and humankind to the divine choice of one group of people, the Jews, to be favored and called to share that blessing with "all the families of the earth" (Gen 12:3). Then, at certain junctures, the literature gives glimpses of the end of time when God promises a world yet to come in a community bonded together in love forever.

Pivotal in the scope of God's plan is the ministry and message of one working-class Jewish man called Jesus. He lived about two thousand years ago and traveled through districts of Galilee and Judea in the "land bridge" located between North Africa/Egypt and Asia Minor/Turkey and Greece at the eastern end of the Mediterranean Sea. At that time the Roman Empire, centered in the "boot" peninsula of Italy, ruled the known Western world.

The claims surrounding the man Jesus have been such that millions have come to believe that he alone most fully brought individuals and communities closest to God and that he, in a deeply spiritual way, continues to do so today.

C. *Where Is Key Information about Jesus?*

Among the many ways to learn about Jesus—such as through your friends; through help in difficult situations; through church worship, music, and art; by family tradition; and in formal institutions of instruction by learned interpreters and analytical scholars—the one of *reading the Bible's New Testament for oneself* has been the favorite way. The term "testament" means "covenant" or "bond" and came from words Jesus said at the supper just before his death. You can look up those words in the Gospel book entitled Matthew, in chapter 26, verse 28 (the abbreviation used here is Matt 26:28). The term "covenant" had been used by the leader Moses about 1,300 years previously when, at a mountain in the desert of Sinai, he brought words from God to bind together a group of escaped slaves (Exod 24:7–8). Some ancient Greek manuscripts of that Matthew text (Matt 26:28) use the adjective "new" to modify the word for covenant. The famous prophet Jeremiah, who lived many years after Moses but before Jesus' time, had said there would be a "new covenant" to come (Jer 31:31). So biblical followers of Jesus spoke of his ministry and message in these terms and of the heritage of Moses as "the Old Testament."

Of all the twenty-seven separate writings of the New Testament in the Bible today, the four Gospels or life stories of Jesus are studied most seriously. The term "Gospel" here means basically a biography with a religious message, and it comes from words indicating "good news." These four books seek to respond to the double question: "Who is Jesus? And, how, therefore, shall we live in God's love?" The "we" could refer to the people in Jesus' time of about 30 to 33 *AD* (Latin for "in the year of our Lord") or *CE* (English for "in the *common* or *current era*" of the Western dating system). Or the "we" could refer to the congregations for whom the Gospel authors wrote during the years ca. 70 AD/CE to 100 AD/CE. Most who have read and treasured the Gospels as holy writings or Scriptures would say the "we" refers to all readers who are followers in any historical period. Because Scripture study seeks to get *inside* the meaning of the Gospels, "we," "our," and "us" will be used often. That is not meant to serve any purpose other than to give the reader an interior perspective on the writings in three time segments—Jesus' ministry, the Gospel writers' circumstances, and what they could mean for today. The language of the Scriptures throughout both testaments characteristically invites readers to view themselves as the "we" from original times to their own.

D. *How Did the Gospels Come to Be Written?*

The four religious biographies that open the New Testament are not like books today whose dates and places of publication can be found easily, whose authors are named, and whose purpose for writing is stated clearly enough to make sense to every person or every time in which they are read. The four Gospels are considered hard books to understand. The religious organizations or churches who collected and preserved these writings translated them into thousands of languages and editions. The learned, the scientifically analytical, the skeptical, and the perplexed—as well as the faithful, the inspired, and the charitably concerned—have commented, questioned, and interpreted the Gospels for themselves and for others to understand. Scholarly scribes have meticulously compared the oldest handwritten copies (no signed-by-author originals exist) to make sets of the earliest texts. The names of the Gospels most likely came from those of disciples or apostles mentioned in the New Testament. These titles probably became attached to distinguish one from the others after a time of circulation among congregations. Undoubtedly people knew that the books were composed from four separate viewpoints for four separate churches, but the belief was strong that the message of Jesus himself to each person was of primary importance. The churches believed that God's Spirit among the readers would make the meaning clear for their special circumstances. Those who found help and peace for their own problems and crises were glad to aid others in study by putting information in writing.

There are many theories about possible individuals who put pen to paper. Here we are going to see more unified portraits of Jesus before entertaining the assignment of names of authors and stages of their editing processes. In the theoretical work of scholars there is consensus that disciple-like associations of author groups existed over a period of years—from the times of Jesus, the apostles, and churches in the first century. Nevertheless, from hints about people who appear in the Gospels during Jesus' ministry or during Paul's time, the present writer has ventured a few thoughts about the primary motivating authors and why they would have encouraged the writing-down process.

The views presented here of each Gospel's church and the hypothetical authors are not just fantasy, of course. They are based on research into commentary studies from the long "library traditions" of Judaism and Christianity (that is, about four thousand years). First and foremost is the use of history, especially as informed by archaeology, which has been key to this writer's training and lifetime academic and church career. Some of the influential resources, for instance, are the biblical languages that give meaningful names to characters in Gospel settings. "Jonathan" is a shortened sentence of praise that means in Hebrew "The Lord has given!" "Zedekiah" similarly means "Righteous is the

Lord!" Even today in the Holy Lands the middle name can refer to a member of the immediate family. If it is preceded by *ben* (or *bin*), it means "son of," *beth* (or *bint*) "daughter of": David ben Abraham, Rachel beth Nathan. After the child reaches a certain age, a parent can assume the child's name, particularly the firstborn, for example, "*av* (father of) Mordecai," and be called by that, as in the chapter on Mark. After a defining experience, like a new relationship with God, a name can be added to or changed—Simon to Peter, which could be translated into English as something like changing "Healthy" or "Prosperous" (Hebrew/Aramaic) to "Rock" (Greek).

Biblical settings with particular geographical locations can also reveal much about the subject of Gospel authorship. In the New Testament locales such as Galilee, Jerusalem, Rome, and Antioch have significance for the reader to recall for enriched understanding. Archaeology has provided information about city planning, such as fortification walls, temple courtyards, road pavings, monastic settlements, army camps, public gardens, subterranean caves, burial grounds, tent cities, prison complexes, and imperial capitals. A great deal is known about architecture and its designs for usage—synagogue meeting places, private homes and their decorations, furnishings for sleeping and eating, and, of course, pottery, utensils, metal work, and fine arts. Particular reference to significant Bible information has been published in periodicals, a few popular magazines, excavation reports, and documentaries on archaeological finds. We have evidence for crucifixion in Roman Jerusalem and for secondary burial of bones in ossuaries. Indeed, we also have manuscript collections like the Dead Sea Scrolls and their formulaic commentaries, such as the Pesher on Habakkuk. Ethnographic and anthropological studies give information on human ages from bones, causes of disease and deaths by weapons, as well as betrothal and marriage customs. Agricultural engineering for water sources in the ancient Near East, festivals for indigenous economic products, labor legislation for tenant farming, political history and military strategy from written records, remains from central cities and caravan encampments, tools of textile manufacturing and clothing for particular climates, complicated routes of trade, transportation vehicles from seaworthy vessels to war chariots and children's carts, coins with their inscriptions and depictions—all provide background for Bible times with documented issues by seasoned scholars. The challenge lies in choosing the details that might aid the reader in finding a deeper and more realistic interpretation of religious meaning in the biblical message of the four Gospels.

But even with as much as we do know, some difficult questions remain: Why are there four Gospels; why are there not more, or fewer? When there are differences in detail and in sequences of events and of teachings, which one is right? These questions sometimes have no satisfying answers. The approach suggested here involves thinking about each total portrait with its interwoven themes. Maybe we will find that they are all correct even though differences reside in several incidents or several interpretations of the same teaching or event. We are trying to see in what sense the writings are being true to God's revelation for contexts when the events happened and for the church communities for whom they were written.

It is of first importance to try to understand the references and hints in the texts about Jesus' own times and the issues he faced. As far as is known, Jesus himself did not write down any of his teachings or life story. Nevertheless, others at that period in history were writing varieties of literature in Latin, Greek, and Hebrew, as well as in the related language of Aramaic. Recent generations of scholarship hold that the final production of the four Gospels in everyday Greek forty-to-fifty years after Jesus' ministry came from gathered memories and followers' notes, probably done in one or more of the four contemporary languages.

E. *What Books about Jesus Were Already in the New Testament before the Gospels?*

The *evangelists,* Greek for "good news announcers," as the Gospel "authors" are sometimes called, were not the first to write books about Jesus. The letters of the apostle Paul to the churches he founded in the Mediterranean world were the first collections of writings that composed the New Testament. At least nine of the now twenty-seven books are ascribed to him. The letters (or epistles) are usually dated to about just twenty to thirty years after Jesus actually lived, and deal with the interpretation of Jesus' ministry in sermon-like essays. Paul, formerly a leader in Judaism, laid the foundations of what Jesus' life meant in God's plan (as known in the Old Testament or Hebrew Scriptures). Paul had experienced a dramatic conversion or call "on the road to Damascus" in Syria to spread Jesus' message. Paul's work is considered the first "theology" or "god-study" for the new churches he helped to found, and is shaped toward applications that could make individuals' lives more satisfying in their community settings. Subsequently the Gospel editors took up the task of collecting information attributed to Jesus and his early followers; Paul's letters undoubtedly paved the way for their work.

Readers ever since, who felt that Jesus came alive to them in these written accounts, could compare their situations and see how new understandings were still coming and growing from God's Spirit. In this sense "scripture," or that which was written down under the influence of God's Spirit, was like a set of lenses to make clear what God was and is doing anew in the everyday world.

F. *What Is the "Canon" and How Does It Function?*

The four Gospel lenses about Jesus, we could say, help people to select from the many things going on around them, and even inside of them, that are messages from God. The books in the New Testament are called the "canon," which means a "measuring stick," and part of what they help believers to measure is life occurrences in relation to what God's love must have in mind. Yet this measuring involves standards of selection. Each Gospel writer, or editor of material about Jesus, selected certain incidents and messages around a theme to meet the needs of the congregation who first read the collection. Clearly each writer also kept to certain basics, and in this way followers, too, have certain basics about Jesus. So with the four Gospels there are four themes that give four sides or drawn-out facets of the meanings.

Scores of books in the history of the church have sought to bring together as many parts as possible of the four Gospels into *one* picture of Jesus. In the nineteenth and early twentieth century, that was a very popular way to study Jesus. "After all, he was one person, wasn't he?" we would ask. The answer is "Yes, of course," but sometimes people would see only *one* picture of Jesus and it in itself would not be considered the canon from the Bible, for example, a TV movie at Easter, one religious leader's view, or one artist's painting. Such a portrayal could lead into reading the Bible, where the best approach would be for an individual or group to read all four Gospels and respond in words and actions to the double question: "Who is Jesus? And, how, therefore, shall we live in God's love?" If there were only one canonized Gospel, there would be too much limitation and, most likely, too much stifling conformity. People would think the revelation of God in Jesus could be understood and lived in one way only. The Bible throughout its pages wants readers to know basics—like the fact that we can love God, neighbor, and self, with some biblical examples as measuring devices. Then it is important to see how that loving can be creatively interpreted anew everyday by each individual. God's revelation of love in Jesus is alive and continuing by the Spirit in each member of the community as growth takes place, yet this growth is guided by the four Gospels in the canon of the New Testament.

G. *Where Do the Four-Gospel Lenses Come from in This Bible Study?*

The point of the study of Jesus in this book is to aid in understanding the distinct facets that each Gospel writer presents as the basic outline of Jesus' life is recounted. The distinct facets that are emphasized here are those that are not only from Jesus' biographical materials but are also selected from significant points in the Old Testament. The presupposition is that Jesus' life makes most sense when seen from Old Testament backgrounds of God's love present on earth from the creation of the world. Generally, for all the Gospels, Jesus is understood to "fulfill," make clear or complete, what was begun in the Hebrew Scriptures. At times he is portrayed as a creative innovator, but more often the view presented is in retrospect exactly what God really meant in the first place! This is what Matthew brings to the fore in the concept of "the higher righteousness" that we see in the first canonical portrait. In this sense Jesus is the faithful tradition personified. The Hebrew Scriptures then become a new revelation of God's Word through the Gospels' portrayal of who Jesus "really" is. Each Gospel writer knew this, but was led by God to choose and blend only certain aspects from the Old Testament to relate to the congregation who would be reading and hearing the story for their special times.

H. *Where Is the "Best" Starting Place for Gospel Bible Study?*

In light of all the consideration of how the Gospels came to be in the New Testament, where do people begin their study? In church worship the implication is that people need to hear first a small passage of a few sentences or paragraphs read aloud to them. Subsequently a commentary is given by the pastor on what the message meant in Jesus' time and what it might mean for today. That approach is an adaptation of the apostle Paul's presentation in his letters, and the Gospels show Jesus doing the same thing in his traveling ministry. From those models of Paul and Jesus, the present Bible study is designed.

Nonetheless, the reader here may feel as each major unit gets under way that he or she is being plunged into a very strange setting in the *middle* of the story. One might ask, "Wouldn't it just make more sense to start on page 1 of chapter 1, and read the entire book, page after page?" No one is keeping the reader from starting at the "beginning of anything." The problem is that, no matter where you start in the Bible, the feeling can be that of being thrust into the confusing middle of some quite unusual territory. For instance, many people make a promise to read the whole Bible "straight through." Confusion starts early on. In just the third book, Leviticus, which is set some years after the slaves have left Egypt but before they enter the Promised Land of Canaan, there is a vast amount of legal material. The Israelites are traveling through a desert, yet they are supposed to have ample amounts of grain and even fresh fruit to bring as offerings (for example, Lev 2:14)! Even sooner, readers come to the fifth chapter of the very first book, Genesis (Gen 5). There they read whole genealogies of named folk descended, matter of factly, from the only human couple so far created on earth. Who were the spouses for all these subsequent generations? How did the needed people arrive on the scene? Surely we are in the middle of something here, rather than at the beginning.

Other readers could have persevered through all the strange names, long lists of people (for example, again in Gen 10 and 11), and detailed laws (some even about pigeons and about pomegranate dangles on purple curtains) and arrived at the books of Joshua and Judges. It can be disheartening to find so many *wars*, especially coming after two closely matched versions of the Ten Commandments that say specifically, "You shall not kill" (Exod 20:13; Deut 5:17). Where in the Bible, one might ask, is the *beautiful* part about *God*?!

The Bible contains ancient literature from hundreds, even thousands of years of history, involving people in a variety of civilizations, who use languages no longer deciphered. It can be astonishingly difficult to comprehend what is being referred to even if we think we understand how to define each translated word. If we start in the first sentences of the first chapter of Genesis, we find that even before God actually did any creating, there was a lot of water (called "the deep"), there was "wind" from God, and there was "darkness." So there wasn't "nothing" at the beginning: there were phenomena that can be described! Who made them, and for that matter, who made God? Where is the *real* start of it all? And does that make a difference for people today?

On the other hand, new readers of the Bible are often advised to start in the New Testament with Jesus and move out in two directions from there. What led up to him, and what comes after him that could include us? This particular study guide says that one way to understand Jesus is to begin with a main point from each Gospel—one that makes a picture in words that might be familiar and understandable to most readers, first timers or not. Then, we will examine the background for that picture, and how the development of it is an introduction to the singular viewpoint of the Gospel under discussion. The Gospels are treated here as distinctive whole portraits that are primarily based on parts of the Old Testament selected by each author. Those Old Testament passages and perspectives make up the Gospel writers' lenses to see who Jesus really is. Each of the four lenses reflects on the writer's larger work as it focuses on Old Testament revelation or promise from God. In other words, before exploring the worlds and literature of the Old Testament, all the Gospel writers are saying, you and I must meet Jesus first!

I. *Is This an Agreed-Upon Way to Begin the Four Gospels?*

Not everyone would agree with the starting point of "meeting Jesus first." The choices of where to begin in the Bible are varied—some might start with Abraham, Father of the Jews, or with a genealogy from Genesis to summarize major events. Some might start with one of the great prophets like Isaiah to become properly "prepared" for the journey, or with an introductory narrative about an eminent priest who would take us into the religious tradition's hopes and dreams, or maybe with a psalm to be sung as a prayer for illumination. Today, in settings both secular and spiritual, teachers often first stress the complexities of the Old Testament with an elaborate curriculum of ancient Judaica. Many outstanding academic bodies, which credential brilliant research scholars of the wealthiest civilizations, affirm that it is better to keep the Old and New Testaments as completely separate divisions. University and seminary doctoral programs regularly divide biblical studies into Hebrew Scriptures with ancient Near Eastern studies, and Christian origins with theological emphases. To enter a Ph.D. program an applicant needs to choose one *or* the other but rarely a combination of both.

There can be many benefits from separating Old Testament and New Testament as divisions. One emphasis of New Testament studies has been to examine larger theological issues (for example, see Albert Schweitzer in "On the History of Biblical Interpretation" in the Appendix); another emphasis examines word-by-word vocabulary of small units and then puts the pieces together against the background of contemporary knowledge of the Greco-Roman times when Jesus, the apostles, and Paul lived. The resultant configurations of the person and teachings of Jesus as these elements emerge are conjectured to meet the needs of those in the first century's Mediterranean culture.

As you look over textbook collections in a college library for an introductory New Testament course, you will find a large section in each textbook on the Gospels, with commentary about four respective outlines on Jesus' life and teachings. There will be discussions of styles of language and charts of parallel columns printed on a single page to compare similar incidents and sayings. The unique features of each Gospel often relate back to the Greco-Roman world of the churches for which each was composed. This can be like hearing just one-half of a telephone conversation and conjecturing the other. All these emphases and others you might develop yourself are stimulating approaches for learning.

As you reflect on your own reasons for studying the Bible and how you communicate your findings, you have the enjoyable responsibility of deciding where you will begin for projects, classes, and discussions with particular people.

J. *Why Read the Bible at This Particular Time with Emphasis on Jesus and the Old Testament?*

The perspective here stresses precise information we have about passages from the Old Testament. These passages can give clues as to what Jesus' ministry meant then and now. The apostle Paul was leading in this direction with his letters and theology, which preceded the composition of the four Gospels. And you will be reading here about aspects of Jesus' own ministry that definitely imply, and are presented to substantiate, his Old Testament connections.

Because of the foundations laid in the *separated* disciplines of Old Testament and New Testament studies in the past century, the Jewish roots of the Gospels and sources involving Jesus' ministry are ready again for *combined* treatment. Notable scholars have begun the task, using research prompted by the Dead Sea Scrolls (see the Dead Sea Scrolls in "On the History of Biblical Interpretation" in the Appendix).

A fine example of this is by archaeologist Prof. Eric Meyers of Duke University, who demonstrates some common viewpoints that Rabbinic Judaism and early Christianity had from their roots in the Second Temple Period. (His findings were summarized in his opening lecture for the Dead Sea Scrolls exhibit at the Field Museum, Chicago, April 2000.) Another example comes from the massive research of Prof. James Kugel (Harvard and Bar Ilan University, Israel) in the history of biblical interpretation, third century BC/BCE to second century AD/CE. He also convincingly presents sources that Judaism and Christianity share. Kugel's collection of sample point-by-point biblical commentaries is remarkably accessible to the beginning student. See his book *The Bible As It Was* (Cambridge, Mass.: Harvard, Belknap, 1997), now in paperback. He gives an exhaustive contemporary bibliography and short abstracts of the primary source materials—from Qumran manuscripts, Targums, intertestamental pseudepigrapha, literature of the apocrypha, rabbinic tractates, and New Testament texts (567–646).

K. *Goal Summary of the Four Portraits of Jesus*

The present study invites exploration into authorship, church setting, and major organizing themes, using the basic historical-critical methods of biblical study. It seeks to honor each Gospel's presentation as a true account of Jesus' ministry. The major key here is to become acquainted with Old Testament passages that relate to Jesus' ministry. Eyewitness material, church needs, editors' and authors' interpretations, plus God's guidance all help the reader to see what "really" happened and what was "really" meant. We are looking to receive an inside experience of the same Spirit that brought into being these four Gospels and can inspire readers now as heirs of the tradition. This daring purpose seeks to know the revelation from God that will include readers once again in the company of God's people in ways that can be true for all humanity.

As we start out on these four pathways from Jesus into the Old Testament Scriptures, we may glimpse the profound wholeness of God's revelation. We might very well come to know anew the gloriously faceted single gem of Jesus, God's most magnificent gift to the entire world and the hope of all creation. The hope that emerges may be that each person, no matter what their situation and life story, can come closer to Jesus, to their neighbors, and to God in the holy community for which the Bible says all people are crafted to dwell forever. Knowing from Jesus and from the Bible's history of Israel's ordinary folks how God has worked to love human beings in the everyday events of this earth—age after age, place after place, family after family, individual after individual—can free all to affirm the unique divine gifts bestowed in blessing on ourselves and those whose lives touch and encompass ours.

Even so, the pages ahead are but a meager beginning of faltering first steps. There is only enough time and space to do limited parts of the Gospels and some of their Old Testament roots. The reader's process of going over all the Gospels many times and afterwards adding their own discerning of points is essential as the spiritual journey continues.

L. *Notes for Teaching*

For teachers and leaders of courses on the four Gospels, it is hoped that the basic presentation given here can be adapted with relative ease. Almost every class in Bible held in our culture has members with varying degrees of acquaintance with that "text": Some people have many years of formal pursuit, or a lifetime of serious private study and commendable social expression. Some are continuing their education for teaching and pastoring in the church; some are starting lay-pastor curricula. Others are taking introductory humanities courses in undergraduate years. New Christians are establishing first membership in a congregation. Seekers come for evening classes, and neighborhood friends join for devotion and prayer. All have questions and accept some parts or entertain certain perspectives for a while, then go on to their own seemingly appointed pathways. There is no doubt that the Bible presents a call to share what is written in its pages.

Each teaching setting needs to shape the material here in caring ways toward the people present. Students at a university have their special circumstances, usually to see the Bible as part of the essential "Liberal Arts," and to ask and "get inside" basic questions. Liturgists may want to have Gospel readings supported by Old Testament Scriptures that relate to the subject for the day. Homilists and preachers may want readings from both testaments that move them to a single interpretation for those in their weekly pastoring. Interfaith groups need time for voicing their presuppositions and past exposure to the Bible as they learn about each other's traditions. As the result of the approach here, people will be able to make informed identifications for passages read aloud in worship or study as to the Gospel or Gospels in which they are found. And their biblical knowledge has the opportunity to grow around unified themes, like Passover, Law-and-Covenant, and Mission. They can choose to memorize a favorite verse and tell others by word and deed how this represents their own portrait of Jesus. The four portraits discussed here can be adapted to a variety of purposes and levels of student background with creative additions and subtractions.

Nevertheless, it should be stated that the main setting out of which this book has been written is a theological seminary where students are preparing for ordination. The pages with wide margins for note-taking are designed for an adult education unit that seminarians might teach in their church congregations. For their own academic course in seminary, they have other required library resources and assignments but would most likely recommend for their church classes a companion reference volume of New Testament introduction such as Pheme Perkins' *Reading the New Testament* (New York: Paulist Press, Second Edition, 1988). It is essential for the reader to have a copy of the Bible at hand—there are many invitations to peruse chapters and passages. The New Revised Standard Version (NRSV) would be the easiest English Bible for them to use. It is universally available and accepted, and is the source of the quotations in this book. Even better would an "annotated" edition that has a description in the Preface of the translation goals of the NRSV. (See especially the third edition of the *Oxford Annotated NRSV*, 2001.) Or *The Catholic Study Bible: New American Bible,* edited by Donald Senior (New York: Oxford University Press, Inc., 1990) has excellent notes and general articles, and the translations are very similar to the NRSV.

No one body of material could be provided or summarized to satisfy "the majority" who conceivably might be studying the four Gospels and their Old Testament backgrounds. So what is between these covers is humbly offered as basic—to be shaped and expanded. My main advice in preparation is to say, "Come, say a prayer for illumination with those down through the centuries who have opened the Bible to read under the Spirit's guidance for the Church, and let us start just here."

A FIVE SESSION OUTLINE FOR USE IN A CHURCH ADULT EDUCATION BIBLE STUDY

Publicity and Announcements

Include notice of the Bible study program in church bulletins sent home with program announcements, in flyers with Sunday service orders-of-worship, and in oral presentations from the presiders at congregational events. This way all will have the opportunity to hear through customary channels about the Bible study. Nevertheless, it may also be helpful to extend *personal invitations* by an education planning committee and the teacher; so many people have said that they became interested in such a class when a particular person suggested it in a one-to-one conversation. A telephone call might simply say, "I was wondering if you'd like to come to a Bible class we're having on the four Gospels for five Wednesday nights, 7:15 to 8:30, at our church, and feel free to bring a friend." Information, written or oral, might include the request that members bring their favorite passage (one to four verses) from any one of the Gospels, and even two or three sentences written on a card explaining why this means something special to them. Nevertheless, do make it clear that assignments like this are not required. A letter could also be sent out as a follow-up to the personal invitation. The envelope should not look like "junk-mail" advertising, and the letter needs to have a handwritten note on it somewhere with the addressee's and writer's names. Targeting those whom the teacher believes might like the class is often welcome, if not compelling. In the Gospels, Jesus chooses a small group of twelve at a beginning point, and in Luke 6:12–16 it is after a retreat and a "night in prayer to God."

Announcements could make clear that people should bring Bibles, that the particular edition can be ordered ahead of time, and that a textbook (this one) is required (costs listed). Also note that some copies of the Bible, textbook, and resources will be available during office hours at church or a public library free for anyone to use. A few textbook copies should be set out for perusal at the church office in advance.

The Setting for Meeting

It aids expectations for the group to meet at the same place, room, and time for all sessions. Members have a sense of comfort about a common space for associations and will feel freer to judge travel time, casual dress, and study tools to bring to the setting. I suggest no food during the sessions; some may like to extend the fellowship and "go for coffee" at a local café afterwards.

The plans here for each session call for an optional extra twenty minutes for prayer and various concerns after the ending time. Some may want to stay to talk together with the teacher about matters that involve more intensive development. Here again, the teacher can initiate the offer on the spot in the main meeting when certain questions are raised, suggesting they be discussed in the after-session. We hear of a somewhat similar approach after Jesus' presentation of the Parable of the Sower in Mark 4:10.

The physical arrangements could be around a table. This is the best furniture for serious study with books, for note-taking, and for times of thoughtful discernment. A chalkboard (or newsprint, marker whiteboard, etc.) could be placed behind the teacher's chair, and an outline of the session with distinct topics in the teacher's presentation could be prepared ahead of time on the board. Alternatively, the board could be used for information as the session's issues are raised and clarified. In that case, a sheet of paper colored for each Gospel and sized to carry in the textbook could be put at each person's place, with printed opening devotions and closing prayer framing the distinct class topics. The topic list acts to keep everyone focused on the material, which is especially appropriate in a volunteer (or not-for-credit) milieu. If chairs with desk arms are used instead of a table, they might be set in a one-row horseshoe with a small teacher's table in front, the teacher's chair to one side, and the chalkboard behind the table. Good lighting to read by is essential in the evening, as is fresh air, but warm with no drafts. More people than expected may hesitate to say they cannot hear or cannot see to read, that they are too warm or too cold, or that they feel closed in so they cannot get out. So it is good to address these concerns from the start. Handicap accessibility is good for everyone.

Near the chalkboard on a pedestal, the kind used in the sanctuary for flower arrangement, could be a votive candle in a glass cup and a single flower in a small vase. A different color candle can be used for each Gospel. The lighting of the candle and the teacher's open Bible are signs for the session to begin. The implication of such furnishings would be that both teacher and students sit for Bible teaching (Matt 5:1); the light of the Word is put on a lamp stand (Luke 8:16); and the flower or stalk of wheat is a symbol of resurrection (John 12:24).

A Few Notes on Time

Central to the serious nature of our work is punctuality and efficient movement to cover the promised subject, as well as allocation for comments and discussion in a shared atmosphere. People come to church for things they can get nowhere else. The church tradition conveys a message through Scripture that it believes is the most important information in the world. This is the "hour that has come" (John 2:4 and 17:1).

The leader has the responsibility to be prepared, to be on time, to have the room arranged, and to start and finish on schedule. It may help to say that we start at 7:14 p.m. and finish at 8:29 p.m., and to have a large clock that especially the leader can see in the room. Using the same words, phrases, or sentences over and over can act as "clock chimes" to move from one part of the class session to another—prayers with "Amen" do this easily.

If the discussion section is slow in starting (after the teacher uses the two-sentence "chorus" each week to open the class-comments part of the session), the teacher or group leader can wait. We are encouraged by educational methodology to count silently to sixty while looking around the room for people whose body language indicates that they have contributions to make. It is a rare group that can keep quiet for that long. Someone gets embarrassed and makes a comment; others join in with "better things to say," so they rightly gain confidence. The teacher can find that people bring up on their own the very topics of questions listed or surmised—the Holy Spirit often works if given a chance! The teacher may guide the conversation at points and has the responsibility to elicit the ideas of shy members—with affirmation. It is not always easy to encourage shared and cohesive conversation on issues, but this kind of face-to-face community interaction is not available today on the couch in front of the TV. A summary statement at the end of the comment segment is appreciated (suggest this to a class member) and the leader's offer to continue for twenty minutes after the entire session ends is gracious.

The Teacher's Twenty-Five Minutes

The most difficult aspect of leadership for this kind of Bible study is the teacher's presentation and its timing. Usually, because teachers are educated on the subject and have prepared themselves with extra reading, they have a superabundance of "wonderful things to say." Limit it! Keep to the time constraints! Everything cannot be covered! Yet honestly portray gentle purpose and joy as you go. There are suggestions for presentation in the following outlines, but each teacher must make the unit their own.

Sometimes the teacher is aware that people in the class know the material quite well, or truly have prepared the readings from the Bible and textbook. Questions with *short answers* can then be posed to the class. After the response, the teacher can comment further to complete his or her outline. This can encourage other students to read the assignments and to be prepared. Of course, a major goal is not to embarrass those who do not participate or who do not wish to answer questions from the reading. The textbook here is designed with these short-answer questions in the text and the responses are often underlined to help people remember what they have read or where to look for the answers. If the teacher asks those very questions in the exact same words, class members can recognize what is appropriate to say, and they may be surprised that they can participate in that kind of learning experience.

There is one theme for each Gospel and the teacher needs to be satisfied when it seems as if the group has said it in the three sentences of their choice at least twice in the session. Something like, "In Matthew we lit a green candle because Jesus is pictured as _____. The church is _____ and the Old Testament background is _____. We are called to live as _____."

The final or fifth session is to be designed by the leader without written preparation here. There have been "blanks" all along in the material, such as chart columns, the topics to enter on the charts, the parable study in Matthew, the daily prayer reflections, and the study of the apostle Peter. Patterns have been included and suggestions are made. Class members can make contributions. If appropriate, the teacher might arrange for a closing eucharistic celebration. What do you think would draw the weeks together and yet encourage further, richer study? How do you see your class members using these four portraits of Jesus when they hear the Gospel read in worship? Give them casework to practice on in the last class so that they are confident about what they have learned—and encourage them to applaud one another.

> The Lord GOD has given me
> the tongue of a teacher,
> that I may know how to sustain
> the weary with a word.
> Morning by morning he wakens—
> wakens my ear
> to listen as those who are taught.
> (Isa 50:4)

Session I: Matthew

I. Opening Prayers at 7:14 p.m. for 7 minutes

People gather to sit around the table, chat a bit (3 minutes); teacher indicates start of session by lighting a small green candle in a glass cup, and opens the NRSV Bible to Matthew 11:28–30. Members open their Bibles to same passage and read from a green sheet with an outline of the session on it and the unison readings written out.

Leader says: Let us read aloud together Matthew 11:28–30.

Teacher gives a short prayer for illumination, such as:

May these words of Holy Scripture this evening come alive to each of us gathered here in these precious moments.

May all know the presence among us of the Great Teacher, Jesus Christ.

May our joy be like that of the Psalmist who says, our delight is "in the law of the LORD and on his law meditate day and night…like trees planted by streams of water which yield their fruit in its season…." (Ps 1:2–3).

In Jesus' name, Amen.

II. Teacher's Introduction to Course at 7:21 p.m. for 10 minutes

1. Teacher introduces self. With thick felt pen she or he has written the name they *wish to be called* in large letters ("ELIZABETH") on a 5″ by 7″ index card, folded lengthwise, and now puts it as a place card so that entire group can see it. Teacher distributes folded cards to everyone and two felt pens to pass around. Class members make similar place cards for themselves and set them on the table or desks. (This step is helpful if people do not know each other well.)

2. Teacher reviews basic information for the course—time, dates, etc.

3. Teacher passes out textbook and introduces it. He or she reviews the approach—a historical/literary study of the Bible summarizes briefly while turning to introductory chapters in the book, and mentions seeing the unique portraits of Jesus in the four Gospels with Old Testament backgrounds. Here three planned sentences from the introductory chapter (that is, Introduction) in the textbook can be read by teacher or volunteers.

4. Teacher asks if anyone has chosen as their favorite passage one from Matthew. Teacher asks someone to read Matthew 22:36–40. Then read two student passages only. Teacher invites class members to submit their favorite passage in the Gospels at the end of the session tonight. They could write it on the inside fold of their name cards or on a separate sheet of paper.

III. Teacher's Presentation of Matthew at 7:31 p.m. for 20 minutes

Suggested topics:

- Matthew—the church's Gospel—most complete—based on Mark plus a source that Luke shared and special material.
- Speak about opening passage and yoke.
- Have class read in unison Matthew 5:17.
- Teaching method—comparison and contrast, debate.
- Two definitions of law.
- Matthew presents Jesus' life as embodying Genesis and Exodus themes (members can "thumb through" Bible chapters Matthew 1—5 as teacher does this).
- More intensive debate and the Pharisees—how they are "good teachers" (turn to "Who Is Jesus to the Pharisees?" in the chapter on Matthew in Part Two).
- The theme of lawbreaking in Jesus' ministry—demonstrating "higher righteousness."
- Show how the questions in bold-faced type are often answered by italicized phrases and sentences in textbook.

IV. Class Oral Reading at 7:15 p.m. for 10 minutes

Class members one after another read aloud by paragraphs from Julianna's picture of Jesus on the hills of Galilee (see pages 68–70).

From the next section in the book, read the beginning of Psalm 1 together.

Explain that the color of the candle for Matthew is green for the green-growing tree and the Galilean hillsides.

V. Class Comments at 8:01 p.m. for 25 minutes

What general comments do you have? What was new or unexpected? Suggested questions.

- Why is Matthew called "the church's Gospel?"
- Where did the basic outline of Jesus' life come from that is common to Matthew, Luke, and John? What are the seven main parts of the outline?
- How does Jesus teach? (There are several answers.)
- What does Jesus teach? How does his life embody the Hebrew Scriptures?
- Why should "exceptions to the rule" be taken seriously according to Matthew's point of view?

- What did you understand that Jesus might be teaching you in your everyday world today, especially about the Old Testament?
- What situation were you in recently that you would like Jesus' opinion or example of how to love God or a neighbor?
- What people on the news this week, or in your town, seem to be doing the unconventional or to be involved in the exceptional?
- In Matthew 5:3–11 how does one category of blessedness speak to people you are especially aware of right now? Which categories could describe people in your church congregation today?
- If your group has read and studied the whole Gospel of Matthew and the entire chapter presented here, what do you think Matthew 10:34–39 could have meant to Julianna bint Nathan in Antioch? What does the passage mean to you? What might it mean to your church?

What questions would you add?

Teacher's closing words to the comments section:

Next time we will study Mark. To reflect on this week and to prepare for next week, you may want to—

- Read the Mark Chapter in the text.
- Compare Matthew and Mark.
- Read the whole Gospel of Mark.
- Read the intros to Matthew and Mark in the text, or
- Use the Daily Prayer Reflections on Matthew's Jesus on page 74.

(But be prepared and understanding—many people "do not have time" or do not like to do homework for adult-ed courses.)

VI. Closing Prayers at 8:26 p.m. for 3 minutes

Say the "Our Father" together.

Read from Matthew 6:9–13 and add NRSV footnote "j."

Blow out the candle.

Leader collects name cards and favorite passage information.

Invite people to stay for 20 minutes to talk more personally about their questions and faith experiences.

General dismissal at 8:29 p.m.

Session II: Mark

I. Opening Prayers at 7:14 p.m. for 7 minutes

People gather around the table, chat a bit (3 minutes).

Teacher gives out place cards with names. New people are given cards and pens; *addresses and phone numbers* can be written on cards tonight.

Teacher/leader indicates start of session by lighting a purple candle in a glass cup and opens the Bible to Psalm 23.

Read together these words of Psalm 23 (translation from NRSV, notes, and author):

The LORD is my shepherd, I shall not want.
He makes me lie down in green pastures;
He leads me beside still waters; he restores my soul.
He leads me in paths of righteousness for his name's sake.
Even though I walk through the valley of the shadow of death,
I will fear no evil; for you are with me;
Your rod and your staff, they comfort me.
You prepare a table before me in the presence of my enemies;
You anoint my head with oil, my cup overflows.
Only goodness and kindness shall follow me all the days of my life;
And I shall dwell in the house of the LORD forever.

Anointing Ritual:

Pass around a small dish of oil ("baby" or bath), put index finger in oil, and place on mid-forehead of next person saying:
"May God bless you, _____ (name)."

Leader gives prayer, such as:

We pray, Lord, for your anointing presence among us this hour as we study the Scriptures.

We remember Jesus' words from the cross in great suffering; how he knew the cry of King David in forsakenness and wrote the words for all who have felt that devastation.

May we begin to understand that when we, too, are in desolation, your Scriptures give us the ancient words to say, and the knowledge that

the poor shall eat and be satisfied;
those who seek him shall praise the LORD…
All the ends of the earth shall remember
and turn to the LORD;
and all the families of the nations

shall worship before him.
(Ps 22:26–27)

Thanks be to God!
In Jesus' name, Amen.

II. Favorite Passages at 7:21 p.m. for 4 minutes

Class member reads his or her favorite passage from Mark or two people read Mark 14:51–52 and Mark 16:5–8.

III. Teacher's Presentation of Mark at 7:25 p.m. for 28 minutes

Suggested topics:
- Turn to Mark 15 and the first page of the section "Who Is Jesus in Mark?" (page 81).
- Teacher reads the references to Jesus as "King of the Jews" (occurs several times): verses 2, 9, 12, 18, 26, 32. Mentions Roman Empire associations.
- Class members compare Mark 15 and Psalm 22, as teacher points out similarities (as noted in the textbook).
- King David, author of Psalms 22 and 23, prophesied the suffering of the Anointed One, the Messiah in his royal line.
- King David, Messiah, and Temple.
- God's words at Jesus' Baptism—Psalm 2, Repentance and Psalm 51. God's words at the transfiguration.
- Opening words of Mark's Gospel (Ch. 1:1); Old Testament definition of "gospel."
- Jesus' first title is: "Son of God," the title of the Royal Davidic Messiah.
- Jesus' first ministry is to people in desperate need: "Immediately!"
- The secret nature of his Kingship.
- The second title of Jesus is "Son of Man."
- Look at Daniel 7 and Mark 14.
- Apocalyptic literature and suffering.
- The historical setting of Mark's church—the Tenth Roman Legion.
- Use of the concept "Satan."
- The people in Mark's church, outcast and suffering, from the accounts of miracles.

IV. Class Oral Reading at 7:53 p.m. for 5 minutes

Class members read the vegetable farmer's picture story of Mark's congregation in war-torn Jerusalem (beginning on page 110), with each person reading one or two sentences aloud.

Explain that the color of the candle for Mark is purple for royalty and apocalyptic "clouds."

V. Class Comments at 7:58 p.m. for 26 minutes

What general comments do you have? What was new or unexpected?
Suggested questions:

- What is the mood of Mark's congregation in Jerusalem as portrayed by the vegetable farmer at the end of the narrative?
- Why is the crucifixion story in chapter 15 key to Mark's Gospel? Why is chapter 13 key as well?
- What do the terms "Messiah like David (or of the Davidic line)" and "Son of God" mean in Mark?
- What do the terms "apocalyptic" and "son of Man" refer to in the book of Daniel and in the Gospel of Mark?
- What basic double meaning could the phrase "kingdom of God" have in Jesus' life and message in Mark?
- Why do you think the portrayal of the strength and servanthood of Jesus might appeal to people suffering in situations described in Mark?
- When have you known of those who were suffering as Mark's congregation was?
- How do you think the words of Psalm 22:1 are characteristic of every believer's experience?
- Look over the weekly devotion topics: do any speak to you or people you know today? Exchange prayer requests among your group for people going through such circumstances.

What questions would you add?
Teacher's closing words to the comments section:
Next time we will study Luke. To reflect on this week and to prepare for next week, you may want to—

- Read the Luke chapter in the textbook.
- Look over the Gospel of Luke with the textbook outline and read what you like.
- Compare the three outlines of Matthew, Mark, and Luke.

- Read in the textbook about Cunningham's book on Mark and Rome (Appendix), or
- Read the intro to Luke in textbook.
- Use the daily prayer reflections on Mark's Jesus on page 114.

VI. Closing Prayers at 8:24 p.m. for 5 minutes

Use Psalm 23 from the beginning of this session as a group closing prayer.

Invite people to stay for a prayer session concerning the deep needs of suffering—20 minutes.

General dismissal at 8:29 p.m.

Session III: Luke

I. Opening Prayers at 7:14 p.m. for 7 minutes

People gather around the table, chat a bit (2 minutes).

Place cards with names are probably not necessary this time but can be distributed (after people are seated).

Teacher/leader indicates start of session by lighting a pink or rose candle in glass cup, and opens the Bible to Luke 10:1.

Read together Luke 10:1 and Luke 24:27–32.

Ritual:

Sing one verse of a familiar Christmas carol like *O Little Town of Bethlehem* or vss. 1 and 2 of *Silent Night*.

Leader gives prayer, such as:

Appoint us, O Lord, to be among your ambassadors that we may prepare the way for you to come to all the world.

May you be present with us at this table to interpret the things about yourself in these Scriptures.

Let our hearts burn within us as we journey with this open book.

In Jesus' name, Amen.

II. Favorite Passages at 7:21 p.m. for 4 minutes

Two class members read their favorite passages from Luke or two members can read Luke 15:4–6 and Luke 15:20.

III. Teacher's Presentation of Luke at 7:25 p.m. for 15 minutes

Suggested topics:
- Intro to Luke and Acts—*apostello*; Acts 1:8, Luke 24:46–47 and Genesis 10, the seventy others and the Twelve.
- Class read orally from textbook about the "successful mission" at Philippi on page 120—around the table, three sentences each member.
- "Where can we see the characteristics of successful mission?"
- "Who must have been in the first congregation at Philippi?"
- "Who is Jesus to the Philippians?"
- Pairs of Missionaries.
- Class read in unison the bold print of Deuteronomy 19:15.
- Christmas chapters and pairs.
- John the Baptist paired with Jesus.

- Death and martyrdom—John, Jesus; Stephen, Paul.
- Pairs of men and women in the Gospel, note especially miracles, parables, etc.
- Discerning how mission works or steps in mission.
- Use Luke-Acts as "mission manual":
  —importance of prayer;
  —finding the lost;
  —reading the Scripture and interpreting;
  —experiencing/watching the reversal or miracle;
  —receiving forgiveness, and (usually before!) repentance;
  —sharing the joy in celebration;
  —going out on the journey, paired with a new friend.

IV. Class Oral Reading at 7:40 p.m. for 15 minutes

Meeting the (Fictitious) Authors of Luke-Acts

Summarize some of this long section beginning on page 131, then have a few readers read aloud other parts of it, especially from the summary paragraph on life of Jesus to the end. How does the ministry of Mr. and Mrs. Luke illustrate the Steps in Mission above?

Explain that the color of the candle for Luke is rose for welcoming fellowship and friendship in love.

V. Class comments at 7:55 p.m. for 27 minutes

What general comments do you have? What was new or unexpected? Suggested questions:
- In light of the study of Luke here, explain what it means to say that Luke is a manual for mission.
- What is the book of Acts about? How does it continue the story of Luke's Gospel?
- Give examples of how the churches in Luke-Acts are more socially diverse than any other Gospel. Mention who the "Gentiles" are.
- Why does Jesus in Luke appoint seventy apostles? Why are these ambassadors sent out in pairs? How does the Old Testament, as read through the perspective of Luke, have support for social inclusiveness and mission?
- How does forgiveness play a central role in mission?
- What is "gentle" about the ways people are brought into the church in Luke-Acts?
- How have you experienced mission as a receiver and a doer?

- Who in our world do you think needs Christian mission most? Who are "the lost?"
- Why do you think that people who represent the many and diverse aspects of humanity (such as, those of another religious heritage, the elderly, children, women, strangers to a geographical area, those with unusual clothing styles, skin and physical features, etc.) have less credibility and acceptability as they move out of home settings into new social worlds? When have you felt rather shunned?

What questions would you add?

Teacher's closing words to the comments section:

Next time we will study John. To reflect on this week and to prepare for next week, you may want to—

- Read the John Chapter in the textbook.
- Look over the outline and read the introduction.
- Read in John's Gospel, especially noting chapters 6 and 13–21, or
- Compose the Daily Prayer Reflections on Luke's Jesus on page 142.

VI. Closing Prayers at 8:22 p.m. for 7 minutes

Leader will read Luke 11:5–13 first; then class members in unison will read Luke 11:1–4, and at the end all say in unison "In Jesus' name, Amen."

Invite individuals to stay at the end for private prayer—especially for those who need the mission work of Jesus.

General dismissal at 8:29 p.m.

Session IV: John

I. Opening Prayers at 7:14 p.m. for 10 minutes

People gather around the table, chat a bit. You go behind the chair of anyone who missed a session, welcome them by name, tell them personally that to review they might like to look over the concluding summaries of Matthew, Mark, and Luke in the textbook.

Teacher lights a gold candle and opens the Bible to John 6, then says:

"From John 11:28 'The Master is here and is calling for you.'

Let us read together in unison John 6:51 and 56."

Ritual:

Tell the basic story of the Last Supper in a few words, play recorded music, or show a painting (but do not use words from a liturgy or another place in the Bible).

Leader may say the following:

At the Last Supper, as recorded in the Gospel of John, Jesus prayed a long prayer to the Heavenly Father. Here are some of the intimate words (paraphrased from John 17) that the Beloved Disciple, who was close to Jesus on the memorable night, has given to us. Let us pray.

Father, glorify your Son so that the Son may glorify you, since you have bestowed on him authority to give eternal life. May all those you have given to him know you, the only true God, and Jesus Christ whom you have sent, in this life that leads to the eternal time to come. May they glimpse the glory Jesus had in your presence before the world existed.

We remember that Jesus also said: "I am coming to you, Holy Father, and I ask you to protect them so that they may be one, as we are one. As you have sent me into the world, so I have sent them. I am not asking you to take them out of the world, but I ask you to protect them from evil.

"I ask not only for them but for those who will believe in me through their word, that they may be one.

"May they become completely one, so that the world may know that you have sent me and have loved them even as you have loved me."

In Jesus' name we pray, Amen.

II. Favorite Passages at 7:24 p.m. for 4 minutes

Two class members read their favorite passages from John or have two members read John 3:14–17 and John 11:21–27.

III. Teacher's Presentation of John at 7:28 p.m. for 30 minutes

Suggested topics:

- Teacher may say: Open your Bible and look at the Last Supper account. Of the 21 chapters in this Gospel, look how many pages are devoted to the Last Supper! See chapters 13, 14, 15, 16, and 17—five complete chapters take place at the Last Supper. This is a key theme (especially in comparison to the other three Gospels). Note 13:1 and Passover association.
- What is Passover about in the Old Testament?
- Review Exodus 1—11 in a short summary. Mention the slaves in Egypt, Moses born and rescued by Pharaoh's daughter, when grown up Moses hears God's call in the desert burning bush, goes to Pharaoh's court and asks to take Hebrews into wilderness to worship their God (Exod 5:1–3; 7:16). Pharaoh vacillates; plagues sent by God; final plague, first-born sons will die.
- Exodus 12—prepare the Passover Lamb, protective blood on door post, roast, eat with unleavened bread and bitter herbs, with sandals on, ready to go, vv. 7–13.
- Instituting the festival (Exod 12:14–16).
    —Children's questioning (Exod 12:24–27).
    —The Great Event (Exod 14:5–9, 13–14, 21–23, 26–27, 31).
    —Later the people are hungry in the desert and God sends "bread from heaven" (Exod 16:2–4, 31).
- Review comments in textbook on John 6: "How is Passover a theme in John's Gospel?"
- The cross in John and Jesus as Passover Lamb.
- The function of John the Baptist, the words of Caiaphas.
- The "signs" in John as illustrated by the Wedding at Cana and the Feeding of the Five Thousand (metaphor of the contemporary theater "skrim").
- The Beloved Disciple
    —as author, as symbolic believer; Jesus' family; the disciple Peter and John 21.
    —The church of the Gospel of John (last paragraph of chapter).

No class oral reading.

Explain how the color of the candle for John is gold for divinity.

IV. Class Comments at 7:58 p.m. for 28 minutes

What general comments do you have? What was new or unexpected? Suggested questions:

- How is John different in general style from the other Gospels? What similarities are present?
- Why is it important for reading this Gospel to know about Passover as it appears in Exodus? How are food items and personal accounts of God's deliverance related to each other?
- Why is "gather" an important word to study?
- What is a "sign" in John's Gospel? What is a "scrim"?
- Who is the Beloved Disciple? Discuss several possibilities, the main one that is explored in this chapter, and your view.
- Why is the phrase "the Word became flesh and lived among us" from John 1:14 so important? What does it mean to you?
- How would you describe your most significant "experience of Christ"?
- What does the psalm-phrase "God is gracious!" mean for the Gospel of John? What does the phrase mean to you?
- How does community life around the Eucharist give us glimpses of eternity with Jesus? What would you like about Jesus' message in John to go on forever?
- How are you called, with Peter, to feed the lambs of Jesus?
- What might it mean for you as Beloved Disciple to "write a Gospel" with your life?
- Using the "Chart of Gospel Topics Compared" on page 180, discuss how the understanding of "love" in the Gospel of John can be viewed as the most "intense" of all four Gospels.

What questions would you add?

Teacher's closing words to the comments section:

Next time we will do a variety of things to tie together these four sessions. To reflect on this week and prepare for next week, you might want to—

- Read the concluding summary sections for each Gospel.
- Look at the chart with summary topics compared for each Gospel.
- Look at maps in a Bible atlas or a "Study Bible."
- Read in the Introduction to the whole textbook on basic questions about Bible study.
- Read in the Appendix the section on "Catholic Biblical Scholarship" about fourteen books concerning the four Gospels.
- Read in the Appendix the section on "Exegesis Methodologies" about methods of study in contemporary scholarship.

- Look at the four-Gospel study of the figures of Peter or Mary of Bethany using the approaches here.
- Compare the Parable of the Sower with lenses from Matthew, Mark, and Luke, plus the agricultural parable in John 12:24 and vine-and-branches metaphor in John 15:1–11.
- Use the Daily Prayer Reflections on John's Jesus on page 174.

Teacher might also ask the class for preferences on which of these or other topics to discuss in the last class. He or she might also ask if the class would like to have a traditional service of the Eucharist to end the course.

V. Closing Prayers at 8:26 p.m. for 3 minutes

Repeat the opening prayer, this time having the group read it out loud. Stay for 20 minutes for anyone who would like.

General dismissal at 8:29 p.m.

Session V: Conclusion

This session is to be designed by the teacher for the class, depending on class members' responses to suggestions in Session IV. Follow roughly the same sequence as the other sessions. If there is a Eucharist service at the beginning or end, omit the corresponding opening or closing prayers.

I. Opening Prayers

II. Teacher's Presentation

Select topics from the subject or subjects requested by class members at Session IV. If nothing appropriate was suggested, you might also use the workshop on the role of Peter, following this session.

III. Class Comments

IV. Closing Prayers

Jesus and his hearers. These stories, although not meant to be historical records, use events that "happen all the time," and the way Jesus uses them invites people to enter into their meanings with personal interpretations. Because of this, the parables have a quality that never seems to grow old; they are puzzles that are forever intriguing in their applications. In the lessons, Jesus' words come especially alive to everyday circumstances. When we are in similar settings, such as farms and gardens, it can be as if we ourselves were walking with Jesus and finding a message for our own times.

An Exercise in Parable Study

1. Who is Jesus in the Parable of the Sower? Read Matthew 13:1–9 and write your answer below.

2. How could this parable relate to the episode in Jesus' own life as recorded at the end of this chapter—Matthew 13:54–58?

3. How might these two passages above help disciples deal with concerns in their own ministries?

4. Read the Parable of the Mustard Seed in Matthew 13:31–32. Then answer the following questions in order:

a. What at first reading is the meaning of the parable to you?

b. What might be the meaning of the parable if the "mustard" plant in Palestine during the Roman period were a weed?

c. In light of the previous question, how might the writer of Matthew, with interests and themes discussed so far, interpret the parable? (Do farmers, for example, consider weeds to be illegal?)

d. Do any other biblical references come to mind (such as Matt 17:20 and Isa 55:10–11)?

e. What kind of added dimensions might these perspectives give to your meaning of the parable?

f. Who in your life might need to hear such a message? How could you communicate it?

Who is Jesus to the Pharisees?

Matthew's accounts of Jesus' teaching methods have several parallels to the teaching methods used by Moses, the prophets, and other leaders of the Old Testament, as well as other groups in Judaism of Jesus' time. The debate method mentioned at the beginning of this study is dramatically developed in Jesus' encounters with the group called the "Pharisees."

In Matthew 15, the debate with the Pharisees begins with a series of questions for Jesus that present their views on the issue of the disciples (and Jesus) *breaking the law*—their example is of washing hands. Jesus replies with questions about *their* conduct with reference to breaking a more serious law from the Ten Commandments, that of honoring father and mother. Jesus pursues the debate and deftly catches them "at their own game." He follows with a more intensive discourse on the issue they raise about clean and unclean, that is, defilement.

The most intensive debates with the Pharisees come in Matthew 23 with a series of very dramatic "woes" and hurled epithets against them. The opening summary makes Jesus' central issue clear: "Then Jesus said to the crowds and to his disciples, 'The scribes and the Pharisees sit on Moses' seat; therefore do whatever they teach you and follow it; but do not do as they do, for they do not practice what they teach'" (Matt 23:1–3).

Modern biblical studies of Palestine in the time of Jesus indicate that it was characteristic for teachers to draw groups of several students around them to study the Scriptures and apply them to everyday circumstances. Then the students would follow their teacher around day by day to see how the teacher carried out the Scriptures in real life. This is a vivid approach, but it can be difficult to make the leap from the familiar words of a traditional teaching to application because circumstances change and there are many variables in life situations. Yet to be able to see a variety of possibilities and to discuss them intensely on the spot surely makes a "class" alive!

The "scribes and Pharisees" were definitely among the crowds of people who followed Jesus and his disciples like students, hearing his teachings and watching his applications. The term "scribes" may refer to a specialized division of the Pharisees who attended to precise readings of the Scriptures and who carried on the written traditions. For example, the writer of the Gospel of Matthew could be considered the particular "scribe" for Jesus, the Teacher.

Teacher groups of disciples and scribes debated with each other. Debates, like the one on handwashing mentioned above, could often center on applications. Many, if not all, of the concerns expressed so dramatically in the "Woe to you" collection of Matthew 23 are from observable applications. It may be less divisive to debate the applications ultimately, than the core teachings—especially if the issues are so extremely characterized by the application examples that hearers who shared basic beliefs could not help but agree!

Do the issues with the Pharisees hint when Matthew's Gospel was written?

Matthew places the collection of the most vituperative language against the debating "students" of Jesus just before the section taken from Mark's Gospel that described Mark's congregation in their historical times. Matthew's text, because it remains tenaciously close to Mark's Gospel (closer even than to the Old Testament, its law and prophets, narratives and history), may now be divulging a perspective on the concerns of the church to whom *this* Gospel is written.

According to Matthew 23, Jesus and the disciples are in the midst of an agonizingly serious debate with "the scribes and the Pharisees" of their times, and the controversy sounds as if it is not over the root tradition, the law and the prophets. Instead, it is over the application, particularly the way it is lived out in Jesus' life. The opposition to Jesus finds that what Jesus does in his life to apply the teachings of the law and the prophets is wrong and breaks the law. What is it that is most unlawful? It is what happens in the key narrative section of both the Gospels of Matthew and Mark: the crucifixion.

Who is Jesus at the crucifixion?

At the crucifixion, Jesus is executed as an outlaw—according to the duly constituted religious-political authorities of the day.

As in Mark, when Pilate, the governor, asks Jesus if he claims to be the King of the Jews, which is treason, he says simply, "You say so" (Matt 27:11). When "the chief priests and elders" accuse him, Jesus says nothing, and they with the crowd call for crucifixion (the capital punishment for the crime of treason). We note that "the scribes and Pharisees" in this incident are *not* designated.

Matthew's addition is that Pilate responds to his wife's message to "Have nothing to do with that innocent man" (Matt 27:19). Pilate makes a gesture of his own personal innocence (handwashing), yet does turn over Jesus to be crucified (Matt 27:26).

Matthew's approach is to enter a massive debate and seek to demonstrate beyond the shadow of a doubt that Jesus really *is* the fulfillment of the law and the prophets as *the* Righteous Teacher. The goal is surely to win over the particular students called "the scribes and the Pharisees."

Can we learn about the Pharisees from another source?

After the fall of the Jerusalem Temple, a group began to form in a town named Jamnia (sometimes referred to as Jabneel or Javneh) on the far western edge of Judah, four miles from the Mediterranean Sea. According to the riveting story (given by Jacob Neusner in *First Century Judaism in Crisis*, Nashville: Abingdon, 1975, 146–7), on the eve of the great destruction of the Temple in AD 70, there lived a humble rabbi called Yohanon ben Zakkai. He was the youngest and "least distinguished" disciple of the famous Hillel. (Hillel lived about 60 BC to AD 20 and was perhaps a relative of Gamaliel, the apostle Paul's teacher from Acts 22:3). Yohanon had his own faithful disciples take him out of war-torn Jerusalem in a coffin. Upon arriving at the camp of the Tenth Roman Legion, as the disciples had been instructed to do, they asked for an audience with General Vespasian that very night. In the commander of the invasion's quarters, Rabbi Yohanon proceeded to get up out of the coffin, as a death-and-resurrection symbolic act.

His purpose was to ask to be allowed to go to Jamnia to have a "house of prayer" and to teach his disciples the Commandments. His Jerusalem was dying, but the Jewish faith would rise anew. Vespasian, whose reconnaissance had informed him months earlier of Yohanon's loyal statements about Rome, agreed to the request. Then, as if in passing, *Rabbi Yohanon reported that Vespasian was soon to become Emperor of Rome!* Yohanon believed that this was a divine revelation to fulfill a prophecy from Isaiah. The very next day, the account goes on to say, after the rabbi and his disciples left under military protection as per Yohanon's request, official emissaries arrived from Rome saying that Vespasian must go immediately to Rome to be crowned Emperor.

Jamnia, where Yohanon took his disciples, became the center of the rabbinic movement led by faithful heirs of the "Hasidim," whose roots back in the Maccabean Period had produced "the scribes and Pharisees" of Jesus' time. Although there is not a great deal of historical information about the early days of the rabbinic groups in Jamnia, by AD 100 they had produced in council a text and canon of the Hebrew Scriptures. This meant a more official break between traditional Jews and Greek-speaking Jewish Christians who were writing, collecting, and editing their New Testament. Christian "scribes" were using the earlier Greek edition of the Old Testament called the Septuagint, which had been produced by Jewish scholars about 250 BC in Alexandria, Egypt, and other Greek translations.

The years surrounding the destruction of the Jerusalem Temple (AD 70) were probably full of debate and strife between Christian groups and Rabbinic groups, as the Epistles in the New Testament do indicate. From the perspective of Matthew's Gospel, these main divisions had much in common.

The mission calls of Peter and Paul in Acts say that the apostles' focus will be on the worlds *outside* of what was later designated Judaism.

What is Jesus' mission according to Matthew?

Despite the mission call to the outside world given in Acts, Matthew's Gospel, where the disciples of Jesus go out exclusively "to the lost sheep of the house of Israel" (Matt 10:6), and in which there is strong emphasis on the debates over applications of the law and the prophets, bears witness to the massive desire to have God's people in one household. Matthew's Gospel is presented from the perspective that the disciples of Jesus want to meet their brother Jews on a common ground, using the Scriptures and rabbinic teaching methods common to both. The claim by Matthew's church is that Jesus truly is *the* Messiah because he fulfills, not abolishes, the law and the prophets. Behind the vituperative debates, Jesus passionately desires that his followers and all "the lost sheep" of Israel be in the same house. Along with Mark, Matthew sees the crucifixion of Jesus as the fulfillment of the Davidic Messianic prophecies, the first key act of the apocalyptic destruction of the Temple and the coming of the Eschaton, or the end of time. Here is the message for the most beloved neighbors, their closest family in the household of God.

Why must Matthew write a biographical "gospel" (and not a treatise on the Old Testament commandments or a collection of the sayings of Jesus)?

To show how Jesus' teachings of the law and the prophets, the whole Old Testament, are right in their application, Matthew, the Christian scribe, must write a Gospel in the sense of a biography. This Gospel scribe brings "out of (the) treasure" of the Old Testament the confirmation for "what is new" in Jesus (Matt 13:52). It is the *life* of Jesus (not just what he said) that bears witness to the central and total revelation of God as found in the history of Israel. On the surface, it looks as if Jesus died as an outlaw, because crucifixion is capital punishment for sedition. But Jesus on the cross, as Mark had said, was fulfilling what David really meant in Psalm 22, the great lament expressing the dire extremity of Israel's suffering across the ages. To present clearly why the crucifixion of Jesus is of key significance, Matthew must tell what led up to that death and what happened afterward. Matthew must show Jesus as the Righteous Teacher living the law.

How do the apocalyptic themes so important to Mark play a part in Matthew's Gospel?

Those who hold the belief that God promises rescue of the covenant people in the Messiah are called to see the seriousness of the claim that Jesus is the Davidic Messiah and, in an extended and more intensive way, the apocalyptic Son of Man who is promised kingship in the Eschaton. The endtime message focusing on the dreadful destruction of the Temple adds to the critical importance of recognizing Jesus as the Messiah. Matthew heightens the apocalyptic element by adding that, at the moment of the tearing of the Temple curtain (when Jesus died), there was an earthquake (27:51–54). Tombs of honored dead around Jerusalem contained the bodies of "holy ones," who were probably faithful followers of the law and prophets. Some of them could have been followers of Jesus who had died during Jesus' ministry. These could include commemorated rabbis whose appearances in Jerusalem after Jesus' resurrection would confirm the significance of Jesus (compare 1 Cor 15:20–26). The centurion and his Roman soldiers also confirm the occurrence of the earthquake. Their terror (apocalyptic) and proclamation of faith, "Truly this man was God's Son!" make clear the meaning of these events. Matthew calls his readers to recognize that the action of God in Christ is seriously related to God's ultimate plan for all of history—history that began in Genesis, is seen distinctively in Exodus, and continues through the ministry of Jesus to the Jews in Jamnia up to Matthew's day, and on into the Eschaton.

How does the crucifixion of Jesus carry out an extensive theme of lawbreaking in Jesus' ministry?

To see Jesus' crucifixion as at first a "breaking of the law" is part of the biblical tradition that includes David's breaking of the law when he took "the wife of Uriah," as was summarized in the genealogy of Matthew's first chapter. That incident with "the wife of Uriah" was one of several events (like those associated with Tamar, Rahab, and Ruth, also in David's lineage) in which God worked to bring deeper and more magnificent revelations of the divine saving power. The same is true for Jesus' very conception—on the surface it looks like a breaking of the law, but what is revealed is a deeper kind of revelation by the God who brought Israel out of Egypt.

The baptism of Jesus may on the surface also appear to be public confession to law breaking: John's baptism was ostensibly for repentance and forgiveness of *sins.* Matthew inserts a debate between John and Jesus. John's point is that *he* should be baptized by *Jesus,* not the other way around. But Jesus' side of the issue is that he is coming to John not out of repentance, but rather "to fulfill all righteousness," that is, to carry out and apply the law "perfectly." At a moment analogous to the event at the Reed Sea in Exodus, God's voice proclaims Jesus' Messiahship. The worst moment for the Hebrews in the Exodus experience was facing the Sea and either drowning or being killed by Pharaoh's troops. On the surface the situation looked bad, but it was actually the astounding moment of God's powerful action of rescue and deliverance.

Similarly, the cross looks bad in the account of Jesus' biography, yet the events took place at Passover when Israel reenacts the Exodus, and Matthew emphasizes the crucifixion as the moment for redemption that makes possible resurrection.

How is Matthew's account of the empty tomb different from Mark's? And how do the differences draw out Matthew's themes?

Matthew records the main narrative of the empty tomb with apocalyptic overtones: "suddenly there was a great earthquake" (Matt 28:2). The women actually see an angel coming down from heaven and rolling away the stone. "His appearance was like lightning, and his clothing white as snow" (Matt 28:3). The language is synonymous with, yet not slavishly identical to, Matthew's account of Jesus at the transfiguration, where commentators have found hints of God's appearance to Moses on Mt. Sinai (Matt 17:1–13). Even the tomb guards are afraid, "like dead men," and not just the women, as in the last line of Mark's account.

The angel in Matthew has a more heightened divine appearance than Mark's description of "a young man, dressed in a white robe, sitting on the right side" as a kind of official emissary of Jesus (Mark 16:5). The angel gives virtually the same message as the young man in Mark. But the women's response is not only "fear" but "great joy" as they "run" to be obedient (in discipleship fashion) to the instructions to tell "his disciples" (Matt 28:4–8). Matthew adds that "suddenly Jesus met them," and they respond by bowing down and taking "hold of his feet" (Matt 28:9). Jesus commands for the second time that they tell the others "to go to Galilee; there they will see me" (Matt 28:10).

In the following section we have a special explanation from Matthew as to why there is so much detail about the tomb guard in this Gospel version (see 27:62–66 and 28:11–15). It is because of a false story "still told among the Jews" claiming that the disciples stole Jesus' body; again Matthew is debating and countering the contemporary Jewish arguments against Jesus.

How is the "Great Commission" a climactic development of what Matthew reports as Jesus' greatest concerns?

The Gospel according to Matthew closes with a second commissioning to tell the message—the women had been obedient to the directive of the angel and the risen Lord. Now his "eleven" (Judas is missing) are in Galilee and on a mountain once more. They bow to honor him, as did the women, yet Matthew as a scribe faithful to realism records that "some doubted." Jesus seems to come closer to speak unmistakably, and *he commissions them in the legal language of the Old Testament characteristic of the teaching mode*. He commands them to "Go therefore and make *disciples*," "baptizing" and "*teaching* them to *obey* everything that I have *commanded* you" (Matt 28:16–20).

The striking difference between this and earlier commissionings of disciples during his ministry is that their own new disciples are to be drawn not just from "the lost sheep of the house of Israel" but from "all nations." The hope is that the Gospel (and especially this particular one of Matthew) has brought Jews and disciples of Jesus into the same household and now they can go out together to bring God's message to the world. This would reflect the prophecies from at least the time of the promise to Abraham that Israel's destiny is ultimately for all nations—"in you all the families of the earth shall be blessed" (Gen 12:3)—and is proclaimed so profoundly by the prophet Isaiah:

I am the LORD,
I have called you in righteousness...
[as] a light to the nations.
(Isa 42:6)

A View of Matthew's Church and Authorship of This Gospel

As a summary of the themes in Matthew surrounding Jesus, the Righteous Teacher of the Living Law, here follows a fictitious scene involving the authorship of Matthew. This illustrates one way Jesus' fulfillment of the Law might have been interpreted and spread, as well as become a divisive factor. Here we meet a church for whom the Gospel was written. At this point we are ready to ask ourselves how well we are learning to be disciples in the tradition of Matthew's church.

Julianna bint Nathan yawned in the close midnight air of the family bedroom as she lay on her mat listening to the raised and agitated voices from the room next door. She and her younger sisters had helped their mother and the women of the household serve dinner earlier in the evening as darkness fell. The leaders of the synagogue were meeting once again around the U-shaped table in their lovely new dining room. Their father, Nathan, managed a family-owned vineyard and was a ruling elder of the synagogue. Neither the pretty plaster wall paintings of vines and trees growing by green pastures and still waters, nor the abundant food prepared and set on the table, nor the cups overflowing with milk and honey seemed to bring any peace to the occasion. The arguments had gone on for months in house after house, night after night, in the prosperous dining rooms of Antioch, the third largest Roman imperial city, capital of Syria. Debate had always been vigorous in the synagogue, her grandfather told her, but now it had reached bellicose proportions. Men left the tables in anger and stomped out into the night. Would the people of God split irreparably over the message of the Righteous Teacher Jesus?

Julianna thought of Shukri, her dear fiancé, her promised young lad, her own nimble gazelle who bounded over the green hills and made blossom wreaths in the vineyards. They had been friends since childhood; in fact, they were distant cousins. Some of their Gentile Antiochian friends were surprised that, in the Jewish heritage since the times of Abraham and Sarah, Rebecca and Isaac, marriage partners could come from the same lineage. On a pilgrimage trip the families made to Egypt, then to

Jerusalem, her Shukri found an antique dish of delicate pottery with a vine-and-blossom design. He presented it to her as a gift for her own table someday. Tonight her mother said she could serve the fresh grapes in it to the guests, if she would like. Shukri's father was there, so Julianna especially wanted to please him.

She and Shukri had a great uncle in common who, around the time of the fall of Jerusalem twenty-five years ago and the tragic destruction of the Temple, became intensely involved with the Jesus Message. He was a specialist in the scribal tradition of copying the Torah scrolls. He learned this skill in the Beth ha Sepher, or School of the Book, as a member of a monastic brotherhood. His community was located on the creamy cliffs overlooking the western shore of the Dead Sea. He had even composed a special kind of commentary on the book of Habakkuk from the Hebrew Scriptures that demonstrated how their own Teacher of Righteousness had lived his life in fulfillment of what the ancient sacred writing had actually said.

When Uncle Ahiel ben Zedekiah, as the family told the story, knew that General Vespasian and the Tenth Roman Legion were coming, he and the brothers expected that the time was at hand for the celebrated final kingdom of God. But the soldiers just sat still in their campsite below every day, month after month. They calmly watched an occasional monastic figure leave, never to return. "What kind of army was this," the community asked, "that fought with peace?!" Uncle Ahiel encouraged the brothers with reassuring words that this was a sign—their dream had to change. By twos and threes they slid down the gravelly descent to the wilderness road with their belongings and leather bags of scrolls. Some went to branch communities, some left the brotherhood in disillusionment, and some sought other places of destiny.

Uncle Ahiel was the last to go after being satisfied that many scrolls were secure in tight-fitting jars and hidden among the myriads of caves. He had remembered visitors who came to the community; one in particular who wanted to study in their library. This visitor told of being a follower of a rabbi who by word and deed, in the ordinary business of everyday Galilee, brought new interpretation and fulfillment of the Hebrew Scriptures—and yet looked with assurance to the dramatic end-times to come. This scholar-visitor was a former tax collector who believed that he had been transformed by the Righteous Teacher of the Way. He had kept accounts of the rabbi's teachings as a disciple—a ma-they-téys, he said. Now Uncle Ahiel thought the visitor might be found at the school of disciples around the funny little rabbi called Yohanon ben Zakkai of the famous teacher Hillel. Rumor had it that the place would be Jerusalem where the little rabbi was weeping amid the sad times under Rome. Uncle Ahiel perhaps could help the scholar or his disciples with the writing about the Righteous Teacher of Galilee. And Julianna understood that he did do just that, and that she would grow up calling this Righteous Teacher who fulfilled the Scriptures of Israel and prepared for times to come:"Lord Jesus, the Messiah."

As Julianna continued her reminiscences, the arguing became more and more heated in the next room. The issue was the legislation about divorce: she knew Moses allowed for a certificate but the interpretation by Jesus drew attention to the blessing of marriage when "the two shall become one flesh."* If she and Shukri could not be wed, it would be as terrible as divorce. The suffering would be like that of the broken-hearted prophet Hosea; neither of them could ever forget.

Suddenly she heard from the next room a loud and furious voice followed by the hurling of a dish against the wall, then the shattering of broken pieces. Julianna turned over and wept into her pillow. She prayed and in the midst of the fury of that dark night, she pictured, with the help of Uncle Ahiel's scribal notes and stories, a happier scene of Jesus and his disciples. This is what she imagined:

I picture Matthew's Jesus as the Messiah, who is the Righteous Teacher of the Living Law and the prophets, sitting in a prominent place in the hilly region of Galilee near the Sea. It is spring and the hills are green and dotted with white, yellow, red, and blue wildflowers, "the lilies of the field." It is midmorning. His disciples are gathered around him listening, repeating, discussing, and debating; some are writing down his teachings and biblical references.

Not far away on similar hills are other rabbis with their students. Here at midmorning, the early chores of our pastoral life are completed, and it is a time for the short break from daily work now devoted to study.

Among Jesus' group are fishermen, farmers, vineyard managers, stewards, laborers, accountants, agents entrusted with errands for ruling estate owners, and merchants who deal in fine jewelry (gems and pearls especially) for royalty and elite. Women are there who have brought others in their care; some women work in the grain fields, some in the vineyard, and others in village businesses—such as baking bread and making pottery. Youthful and elderly shepherds are present. Little children are there, as well

*Matthew 19:5.

as older children accompanying their mentors or their parents as they learn a trade for the future. The crowd is intrigued with parables that relate their circumstances and life among the neighbors with "the kingdom of heaven." As faithful Jews they reverently refrain from using the word "God" (even in the prayer Jesus has taught them), so they do not say "kingdom of God," rather "kingdom of heaven." But they learn that the LORD's "realm" is already here with their teacher's presence, and yet much is still to come. In this time and place of peace, there is a chance to reflect on their full lives, its joys and sorrows, needs and bounties, the surprising and the customary, the legal and outlawed, their inadequacies and accomplishments, their families, friends, and enemies that make up the holy household; they remember the past with seriousness and look to prepare for the future ahead.

Some are remembering how God worked in a troubled past that came to seem so wrong, but turned out to have an amazing seed for good to blossom and bear fine fruit. Matthew, formerly a despised tax collector, was one of those disciples close to Jesus who could tell his own life story around that theme!

Today they are discussing the Parable of the Laborers in the Vineyard and how it perplexingly goes against what seems just. Nevertheless, the landowner cares for those who need and desire to work.

Soon the gathering will disperse and people will go back to their jobs and responsibilities, nourished for this day, to put into their actions gifts of love for their neighbor's good. Somehow each one feels cherished and blessed by the words of the Teaching—even if they came here downhearted or "poor in spirit," grieving and in need of comfort, or passionately hungry to know righteousness. Being together with an opportunity to exchange thoughts and experiences binds everyone into a household or an extended family. When it is time for people to get out their midmorning small meal, it seems that the presence of Jesus makes what they brought more delicious, satisfying, and abundant.

The breezes of Galilee are cool and refreshing; people can see the activities of village, farm, pasture, estate, seashore, and highway in the distance. Hearts are renewed for the time ahead, shalom has descended, encouragement has been received, and enthusiasm has been strengthened. All will return to work, and some will even go with Jesus to Capernaum this very day to heal and call new followers among the hungry, the thirsty, the strangers, the unclad, the sick, and the imprisoned. They will be looking for those who seem to be outside the fold, doing the unconventional or involved in the surprising or even unjust and downright illegal! And they might wonder if something will happen in the everyday miracles to bring closer the "end of the age."

Jesus closes the lesson with a favorite psalm and calls disciples to join in community to say it with faithful friends as they help one another with the burdens of this life.

> Blessed are those who take delight in the law of the LORD
> and on his law meditate day and night.
> They are like trees
> planted by streams of water
> which yield their fruit in its season....
> (Ps 1:1–3, author's translation)

Summary

We have been called into this study by meeting Jesus the Teacher, who offers comforting words. Under his teaching, human needs are to be satisfied. Jesus earnestly desires that students know there are choices. He portrays these choices vividly by short statements of contrast. The setting is one of debate concerning serious issues that demand our attention among the many matters of everyday life. Jesus speaks with structure and authority to present clearly his own direction.

The subject of teaching is the Law sent from God at the time of Moses and continually revealed and commented on throughout the Old Testament, especially during the time of Ezra. Even though there might be hundreds of rules, the Law is a set of commandments like the Ten (which were to be remembered, one on each finger) from the time of the escape of slaves from Egypt under the leader Moses. The commandments are guidelines of ways to love God and ways to love the neighbor, especially the needy neighbor. The core of the Old Testament and Jesus' ministry is here. But in Matthew there is a second definition of the Law and that is the *whole* Old Testament, *all* the books of the Hebrew Bible. They show a continuous story of God's love in action and the pathways God's people are grateful to follow.

Jesus claims that he has come to fulfill the Law, and Matthew proceeds to demonstrate precisely what that means by recounting Jesus' life—his teachings in words and deeds. Matthew organizes his information about Jesus to summarize the narrative of the whole Old Testament. Matthew begins with Genesis and its family trees, starting with the Patriarch Abraham but going through the names of an ancestral line up to King David, to whose house the prophets promised the great Messiah. Then the family tree goes on to the times of the Babylonian Exile and the Return to Israel, right up to Jesus' immediate family of Joseph and Mary.

At that point Matthew wants us to stop and consider a serious legal issue. It has to do with an unusual fact concerning the women in the Genesis-like genealogy: they all have in common the breaking of the very serious adultery legislation, or so it seems. Jesus, who claims to have come to fulfill the Law, has descended from a direct line of women whose offspring are the result of *breaking* the Law. But God was acting there to reveal a deeper law of higher or intensive righteousness and care for the people of Israel. So, too, is God's revelation coming in a special way in Jesus' birth.

The specific story of Jesus now has features that encompass the history of the Hebrew people in the first five books of the Old Testament. Joseph, the dreamer in Genesis, is compared to Joseph, Mary's husband, who hears God's rescuing call to go to Egypt in time of danger. King Herod is compared to Pharaoh, who decreed the massacre of Hebrew slave infants but God was there to save. The Reed Sea event where God separated the waters is like Jesus' baptism in the Jordan where God proclaimed the Divine Sonship. The temptation of Jesus in the wilderness is reminiscent of the people of Israel during the forty years of testing in the desert. The twelve tribes came into being as a community in the Sinai desert, just as Jesus formed his twelve disciples. The Sermon on the Mount was like the giving of the Law and commandments by God on Mt. Sinai to Moses with the people gathered to hear. Jesus claims the authority to intensify and extend the dimensions of the love commandments (such as to love the enemy). These are the gracious divine directives to help the people of God form a covenant community, therefore in this sense, he is honoring and fulfilling the Law, the heart of the Hebrew Bible. Jesus is seated "on the mountain" to teach his disciples Torah; the Twelve in turn will teach the continually coming crowds. The crowds will also have disciples, and Matthew's Jesus brings a heritage that endures down to today.

Subsequently, after covering many subjects, Jesus' method is to come down from the mountain and apply the teaching to life as it is lived out in the everyday world. This is how God has taught Israel from Genesis through the rest of the Bible. Jesus heals the sick, feeds the hungry, and cares for the needy in his immediate world. In this he fulfills the prophecy of Isaiah (ch. 53) bearing "infirmities" and carrying "diseases."

A favorite teaching device is the parable from the Old Testament traditions of Wisdom Literature and occasionally found in the messages of the Prophets centered around the times of the Assyrian and Babylonian Exile. Jesus uses parables in Matthew's Gospel presentation more than in Mark's. The point is to see the Teacher's ministry in action among the neighbors at their industries, businesses, and livelihoods. In this sense, especially in

Matthew's portrait, Jesus is the great entryway into understanding God's care for the people of Israel throughout the centuries of the Old Testament.

The writer of Matthew describes Jesus' ministry in terms of a trained, educated scribe of the kingdom who brings out of his treasure new and old. The old are traditions and memories of the Hebrew people, especially under Moses, the Prophets, and the Sages of Wisdom; and the new, the revelation coming from those roots by Jesus himself. The message is definitely that, among the convoluted events and waves of change in human history, God does keep his promises!

The Teacher uses the debate method, particularly in encounters with the group designated "Pharisees." Matthew emphasizes that Jesus agrees basically with what they teach but goes more deeply into certain matters. Nevertheless, Jesus characteristically calls attention to their attempts, or lack thereof, to make effective applications. In this kind of teaching method, Jesus seems very like other rabbis of his generation. It may be difficult for people in our times to understand the harsh competitive atmosphere of these debates, just as some who are not familiar with American sportswriters might find it shocking to see in tonight's newspaper the bold headline: *Saint Joseph Clobbers Holy Child*. Insight into cultural customs can be key!

The zealous language used to convince some rabbinical groups of Jesus' teaching may yield information about the date when Matthew's Gospel was written. The most difficult element in Jesus' teaching of the Law was surely the way his life ended in crucifixion. This was ultimate punishment for political *outlaws,* surely not to vindicate a Righteous Teacher! Yet the writer of Matthew takes this on as his final climactic message of who Jesus is.

A question remains, of course, as to who the writer of Matthew actually was. He was obviously one who knew the Hebrew Scriptures well and had great zeal for bringing "the lost sheep of the house of Israel" (Matt 10:5) into the fold of Jesus. He appreciated the teaching methods characteristic of the Pharisees in the Greco-Roman period in Palestine/Judea and Galilee and saw Jesus' ministry through those lenses. As a teaching disciple of the Teacher of the Divine Righteousness, he must have had access to written class notes and oral records which he evaluated and transcribed with seemingly precise accuracy. He might very well have had the aptitude for detail of an accountant such as Matthew, the tax collector (Matt 10:3), who was chosen with specific directness by Jesus to be his disciple (Matt 9:9). If this is the same person and incident as recorded in Mark 2:13–14 and whose name there is Levi, he was a Jew from a priestly family. Perhaps he was among those Levites who "wore the work pants" of the post-exilic Temple officialdom, but who were despised by other groups for their compromises and self-aggrandizement in finances and political power. In any case, the tax collector recognized Jesus' message as true for himself and as the fulfillment of the Jewish heritage according to the Scriptures we have before us today. If an early edition of the original tax collector's seminal work is here, the final work would be the result of his teaching and gathering at least one and maybe two generations of disciples who came after him and who preserved the Word and faithfully "bound up the testimony" (cf. Isa 8:16).

The years following the Roman destruction of Jerusalem were pivotal in the development of Rabbinic Judaism under Yohanon ben Zakkai at Jamnia on the Mediterranean coast. Seldom, if ever, were Christians more adamant in their desire to demonstrate to their Jewish family how Jesus the Righteous Teacher came to fulfill the Law—of love to God and neighbor—and the revelation of God in the Bible, Moses' Law, the Prophets, and Writings. These Christian disciples believed that the fulfillment came in the crucifixion and resurrection of Jesus. Matthew reports Jesus' resurrection from the empty tomb with a strong emphasis on refuting contemporary Jewish rumor. The resurrected Jesus concludes with the Great Commission: a call to the vocation of true discipleship. Now the goal is to become a righteous teacher oneself, who keeps the Law of biblical revelation by following in Jesus' footsteps—not just going to the house of Israel but to *all the nations of the world*, as Abraham's promise had originally meant.

In summary, we have been led into this study by a comforting call and restful promise of firm structure and guidance where everyday needs are satisfied. Jesus passionately desires students to know that there are choices, serious choices. As we come upon them in life, we are set in the midst of situations that demand attention, some especially because they seem to be aberrations. Jesus portrays striking contrasts for decisions; he offers strong bases on which to stand and decide. His life pattern, his biography, demonstrates how to make applications. This teacher is in earnest; he especially desires his house of Israel to know who he is. Probably the date is around 90 AD/CE when the separation of Rabbinic Judaism is being instituted. Disciples are challenged by examples to follow and adopt the teachings to their unique callings. Matthew presents Jesus as the embodiment and fulfillment of the whole revelation of God in the Old Testament. What God means by real righteousness is love responsive to Divine Grace and love that's given to needy neighbors, bound together as God's people in discipleship. This is plainly lived out in Jesus' ministry.

For the green growing trees and the teaching of the law on the green hills of Galilee, the candle lit during the session for the Gospel according to Matthew is colored *green*.

Daily Prayer Reflections for a Week with Matthew's Jesus

Suppose that we, too, are listening to Jesus on the green hills of Galilee. Learning that he is the fulfillment of righteousness, the Messiah promised by the whole Old Testament, we realize that we are called to a deeper discipleship. Our attention is first drawn to the unusual, to the exceptions, even the illegal and outlawed, for there God's righteousness may be revealed. After hearing these teachings, Jesus comes over to us to talk about certain phrases in our memories and about questions each of us has.

Read the Scripture quote here, as well as the full citation, and answer the question.

1. *"…just as you did it to one of the least of these who are members of my family…"* (from Matt 25:34–40).
   Who this day is a "family" member who needs something only I have to give?

2. *"And even the hairs of your head are all counted. So do not be afraid…"* (from Matt 10:29–32).
   What details of our lives occupy our most anxious moments right now?

3. *"…so that your alms may be done in secret"* (from Matt 6:1–4).
   What secret alms can I give today? How and why does the church sometimes need to give secret alms?

4. *"Lord, if another member of the church sins against me, how often should I forgive?"*
   (from Matt 18:21–22).
   Who in the faith just sinned against me (or someone close to me) once again? How can church members aid one another in the processes of forgiveness?

5. *"…are you envious because I am generous?"* (from Matt 20:1–16).
   How are we angry about what "the scorching heat," mentioned in the parable, means as it applies to us?

6. *"Truly I tell you, unless you change and become like children…"* (from Matt 18:1–5).
   What is childhood's most prominent characteristic?

7. *"Consider the lilies of the field, how they grow; they neither toil nor spin…"* (from Matt 6:25–34).
   Where has God's gift of grace made satisfying and beautiful some of the places where we are today?

MARK

Introduction

The Gospel of Mark has the shortest account of Jesus' biography, but given in it are the basic elements of all four Gospels. Because of features like this, scholars and commentators have conjectured that Mark's Gospel was written first. Of course, if it came to be honored as true, was the shortest, and was written first, others would tend to expand on the central elements—which is often more logical than condensing them. Key to Mark's presentation is the crucifixion. In the passion narrative there is a long passage that seems to refer to a contemporary audience (see Mark 13, especially verses 9 and following). Jesus is speaking to his disciples about the impressive masonry of the Jerusalem Temple that Herod, the ruler Rome had placed over Palestine, had commissioned to be rebuilt. Yet Jesus is describing persecution and conditions to come that sound particularly real, with detail so vivid that they could be happening at the moment. Because the description is very like what went on at the fall of Jerusalem during the time of revolt against Rome in 70 AD/CE when the Temple was destroyed, rather than forty years earlier during Jesus' ministry, the interpretation is that we are actually reading about the *writer's times*. Surely Jesus spoke of similar situations to come, but perhaps the writer at this juncture was compelled to add contemporary detail so hearers would not miss the point. The picture is one of persecution that readers must have known all too well in their own circumstances, and they would see the crucifixion Jesus was facing with deep understanding.

As the study here on Mark moves through the following pages, there is strong evidence of imminent suffering. The whole of Mark's Gospel can certainly be taken as a message for people in dire straits. With this in mind, we can imagine reasons why Mark's Gospel would be brief and basic to encourage those who were suffering. "Cling to Jesus who is strong during persecution because God is revealing a message and miracle for you!" We can imagine that, even if some people did not have the written text themselves, one member of the group could read the words aloud to the rest in order to tell the story of Jesus precisely—and with impressive words. Yet time was short and people were in great fear.

Another conjecture commentators make is that the author of Mark "invented" the Gospel form itself. The apostle Paul brought the message of the meaning of Jesus' life to people in his churches by means of sermons and letters with preaching (Acts and Epistles). Rabbis of the times were known to tell short vignettes of events with a final line to ponder. There were biographies in the Greco-Roman world of famous people. The combination in Mark, however, seems to be new, that of proclaiming the message from a dramatic life story, emphasizing certain historical circumstances that matched the hearers' lives. The biography was to bring them hope in an ancient divinity who came to this earth. As we will see, the term "gospel," or message of good news from the ancient tradition for today, as Mark is using it, fits well as a name for the new type of literature.

Here is an outline for the Gospel of Mark with basic parts in italics that are common to all four Gospels. The major divisions of Mark's biographical outline have Roman numerals.

Outline for the Gospel according to Mark

I. *John the Baptist's Message*   Chapter 1
     John is the prophet foretold by Israel's Isaiah
         who prepares the way for God as King.

II. *Jesus' Baptism*
     The Designation by Heavenly Voice as "My Son"

III. The Desert Preparation: Temptation by Satan for
     40 Days
     Jesus' Message of the Gospel: the Kingdom of God

IV. *The Choosing of Disciples* (or Cabinet Ministers)

V *Ministry Journeys*
     Miracles to Outcasts in Galilee (Unclean Spirit
         of Man in Synagogue, Fever of Woman,
         Various Diseases, Leper)
     Miracles Continue (Paralytic through Roof,
         Tax Collector Chosen)   Chapter 2
     Teachings about Associating with Sinners, Fasting,
         New Wine, David, and Sabbath
     Miracles Continue (Especially Man with
         Withered Hand)   Chapter 3
     On a Mountain *Twelve Apostles* Commissioned
         to Go Out with Message
     At Hometown Healing Unclean Spirits,
         Telling of His True Family
     Teaching *Parables*   Chapter 4
     Stilling the Storm on Lake Galilee
     In Transjordan Healing Demoniac   Chapter 5

Notes

The writer of the Gospel of Mark dramatically wants the readers to know that what happened with Jesus on the cross is the key to this man's true identity. Mark leads up to the climax of the cross from many corners or strands in the design of the Gospel. The crucifixion was at once the most perplexing and the most revealing event in the story of Jesus. It seemed to go against all that was good from God to have the "hero" die as a criminal in dreadful punishment and repulsive execution by a government and society that had brought such commonweal to so many fine people. Archaeologically speaking, never in history before or since has Jerusalem been more beautiful than under the generous government public building of Hellenistic-Roman city planning. The Temple complex as religious and social center of Jerusalem and Palestine during Jesus' ministry is a case in point. Rome provided a strong and elegant lifestyle with peace and justice far more comprehensive than the Mediterranean world had ever seen. Since then, Roman Law has left an enormous inheritance to all healthy and prosperous civilizations that care to make use of its legacy. The question Mark's Gospel must address could be stated as: "What happened that many nations for centuries have remembered of Rome only the hideous execution of a Jewish so-called traitor in Palestine who was tried and convicted of sedition against the state?"

Because this is Mark's task—it could even be termed his "passionate focus"—the appropriate starting place is with the first details of the tragic event. We will open to chapter 15, but, as is characteristic of this Bible study, just certain verses are emphasized and quoted so that the precise words stand out and are clear. Since we are working with the Old Testament Scriptures as background, the point is that Mark's key account of the crucifixion is highly influenced by what was available at that time. Mark chooses descriptions of only certain historical incidents to highlight the narrative of those hours. Following the biblical literary style as example, the larger contexts of the Hebrew Scriptures are often summarized here by specific short passages. Words and phrases are printed to show how precise the correspondence is.

Remember, however, that the language of the Jewish Scriptures is Hebrew. People in Jesus' time and Mark's time had translations or "Targums" written in the more common conversational language of Aramaic, which is from the same Semitic family. The author of Mark was writing the Gospel in conversational Greek of the Indo-European language family, and we have before us our Bibles in English. The goal of all written languages is to communicate (and preserve) clear meanings, but it is difficult to transfer identical meanings from one source or place to another. "Corn" in Britain means "wheat" in Kansas; "maize" in England means "corn on the cob" in Iowa. Also, in the Bible a word or phrase can represent or stand for a whole poem or story, just as "O Beautiful for Spacious Skies" is both a title and the first phrase of a song; or "Our Father" stands as the name of a prayer. In societies where fewer people have access to books, or in settings where books are not appropriate for the moment at hand, memorized first lines of well-known songs or poems or passages communicate more than just those few words. The writer of Mark knew well the Hebrew Bible and evidently the Aramaic translations. It is fascinating to see how convincing his case is that God's biblical revelation of old in Psalms to the people of Israel provides abundant clues to the meaning of the brutal crucifixion's tragic moments.

Who Is Jesus in Mark?

Part 1

> *The beginning of the gospel of*
> *Jesus Christ, the Son of God.*
> (Mark 1:1)

Are you the King of the Jews?

The time is the first light of dawn, and the night of purple sky is quickly fading. In Roman Jerusalem, a group of elegantly robed leaders have brought the bound prisoner to court. Beginning with Mark chapter 15, we have Jesus before Pilate who asks, "Are you the King of the Jews?" (v. 2). The highest representative of imperial Rome is asking if Jesus is a king who rivals Rome's authority in his (Pilate's) jurisdiction. Jesus' response is simply to say that Pilate has said so. The religious leaders, or Temple authorities duly constituted by Rome as having both political and religious authority, confirm Pilate's designation.

A second time Pilate refers to Jesus as "the King of the Jews" (v. 9) and compares Jesus with Barabbas, a recognized criminal guilty of a murder that took place during a political insurrection against the Roman government. Pilate for a third time refers to Jesus as "the King of the Jews" (v. 12), saying this is what the crowd calls Jesus. After Pilate asks the crowd for their judgment and punishment of Jesus, they shout "Crucify him!" twice, but there is no evidence for the crime of treason against the Roman imperial government. Pilate gives the order for execution.

The battalion (or cohort) of soldiers who attend to the personal protection and parade of the highest Roman political officer take Jesus to the palace courtyard, the precinct of highest office. In derision (and irony) they confer on him symbols of authority—a purple cloak and a plant-wreath crown. Then the full regiment, evidently two- to six-hundred strong, salutes Jesus in the customary military way of public acclamation, "Hail, King of the Jews!" (v. 18).

On the actual document of execution for the crime of political sedition against the Roman emperor, the legal statement of the charge reads clearly,

"The King of the Jews" (v. 26). Another royal acclamation of Jesus as King follows from the chief priests and scribes (v. 32).

So even though the protests are otherwise, the emphasis of the events of the trial and the crucifixion have the recurrent theme that Jesus is King of the Jews.

Who is Jesus in the words from the cross?

The title the religious authorities, the chief priests, and the scribes use at the crucifixion, "Messiah, the King of Israel," prepares the reader here for Jesus' own words from the cross, "Eloi, Eloi, lema sabachthani?" (v. 34). This is the first line from a psalm of King David, and it draws attention to other details reported here in the crucifixion of Jesus. The comparisons between Psalm 22 and Mark 15 are striking.

Psalm 22:18, "they divide my clothes among themselves, and for my clothing they cast lots," is strikingly parallel to the sentence in Mark 15:24, "And they...divided his clothes among them, casting lots to decide what each should take." Psalm 22:7, "All who see me mock at me; they make mouths at me, they shake their heads," is like Mark 15:29, "Those who passed by derided him, shaking their heads," and Mark 15:31, "In the same way the chief priests, along with the scribes, were also mocking him among themselves." The "chief priests" and "scribes" resemble the "many bulls" who encircle, the "strong bulls of Bashan" who surround in Psalm 22:12. Animal designations can signify the particular groups of leaders or noble houses that have admirable, strong animals as symbols and heraldry. The "ravening and roaring lion" may be implied in a similar way (Ps 22:13 and 21) when describing the Roman soldier "cohort" (Mark 15:16–20) who served under the insignia of the Roman eagle. In Psalm 22:16, the "dogs," on the other hand, are associated with the disreputable, such as in Mark 15:32, "Those who were crucified with him," that is, the two "bandits" in Mark 15:27, "one on his right and one on his left." The text says, "those who were crucified with him also taunted him." Even the criminals who were sharing his persecution derided him! These words and phrases indeed portray the rejection and ignominy of the event.

Other associations can be made with the general lament of Psalm 22. The first line, "My God, my God, why have you forsaken me?" is Jesus' cry of desolation in the worst moment of human history: the world has crucified on the cross the greatest gift ever sent. Because evil has now accomplished this devastating act, Jesus is crying to heaven in the dreadful words that describe the desolation.

That Jesus says the words at this moment on the cross is poignantly significant, yet they are words that the human race has uttered as soon as it left Eden in Genesis. In the midst of the extremities of suffering, biblical people

A View of Mark's Church and Authorship of This Gospel

As a summary of the themes in Mark surrounding Jesus, the royal Davidic Messiah who is also the Suffering Servant, the Son of Man, here follows a fictitious scene involving the authorship of Mark. This illustrates one way that the oppressed political atmosphere gave rise to and spread an apocalyptic message of hope. Here we meet a church for whom the Gospel was written. At this point we are ready to ask ourselves how we might wait in servanthood for the coming final kingdom as the result of studying Mark.

The man was glad that his white hair would give the impression he was older than his early 70s, and he practiced a wavering step with the aid of a walking stick to appear to steady himself. He was accustomed to blending in with the crowd as he went from the dock at Ostia toward a waiting cart of farm vegetables. "Sálūs, Papa!" said a welcoming farmer's voice in deference and respect. "Come sit on the cart bench as the donkey and I take you into the Eternal City—Rome awaits!" They greeted and kissed on both cheeks in the usual formal custom and were on their way. As soon as they were out of earshot of anyone, the old traveler said in a low voice, "The leaves of the book—liber—are sewn in the lapels of my robe. All are safe upon my heart. One can read aloud the words in two short evenings. It is the most precious treasure in the world." "Yes," said the farmer, "Blessed is our triumphant Lord, Jesus the Christ!" They spoke together in Aramaic, the language of Palestine, but occasionally added a Greek phrase from the ancient Scriptures, and a Latin term because they were on the road to Rome.

The traveler liked to be called av Mordecai these days, which meant Father of Mordecai. Mordecai was the wise adoptive father of Queen Esther, who called her to act in the royal Persian court to save her people from suffering and persecution, saying to her, "Who knows whether you have not come to the kingdom for such a time as this?"* That story and passage were most appropriate for this present trip, the traveler thought, but he also remembered with tears when his wife presented him fifty-three years ago with their firstborn. They decided to name him Mordecai because it sounded close to the fine Latin imperial name of Marcus. His wife had died

*Cf. Esther 4:14.

before Marcus was thirty, which was a blessing for her because she did not have to know the later tragedies of home and her Jerusalem. Yet she also could not hold her long-awaited and only grandchild either—he was born when Marcus was thirty-four. Although it had been a very difficult labor that left the young mother deathly frail, the infant Jonathan was a happy and handsome baby. Marcus and av Mordecai proudly believed he was true to his name—"The Lord Has Given!" Nevertheless, as the boy began to grow, his legs and feet would not hold him. So it was that Marcus and his grandfather made him a little cart he could push with his hands.

Young Jonathan became very skilled at managing his cart; in fact he liked to speed down small hilly roads with it. Marcus took him to the dirt-packed road in the Kidron Valley that went up the Mount of Olives by the Garden of Gethsemane. As long as the boy drove safely, Marcus would let him go by stages from the bottom, from the southern upper Gethsemane gate all the way down to Absalom's Monument. About that time Marcus encouraged Jonathan to bring some of the neighborhood children, a few at a time with their fathers, to share in taking turns. Jonathan's popularity with others his own age suddenly grew by leaps and bounds. But Jonathan noticed that his father never wanted him, nor anyone with them on these outings, to go into Gethsemane itself.

Jonathan also liked to traverse the chariot avenues. The flat-dressed stones made for a bumpier ride but he could make the cart wheels straddle one side of the chariot indentations and pretend that he, too, was a brave Roman soldier. At one stage his father took him up to the broad surface of the city walls, and if there were no people walking there to be bothered, he could drive in the breeze and feel as if he were on top of the mountain ridge of the world. The two of them would look over into the colonnaded, covered walkway that led to the side of the gate called Golden. This eastern part of the stoa marked the boundary of the Temple compound and the court that led to the women's precinct. It was known as Solomon's Portico and was the designated place for the apostle Peter's ministry when he was in Jerusalem.

The apostle knew Jonathan's father, but Marcus never spoke to the boy about how that came to be. One Sabbath Peter came to worship and lead the service commemorating Jesus' Last Supper in a place he called "the Upper Room." At the service Jonathan saw his father pull his mantle over his face to hide his weeping. The congregation was small and humble, one made up of people others thought were strange. They usually met in an old cave under the streets ("The Lower Room!" Jonathan thought, laughing to himself). Jonathan knew his father was ashamed of something—maybe it was his crippled son on his cart, maybe it was some of the worshipers in the cave. Some talked too much during the service, looked at other people, or moved around obsessively, and some even smelled funny in tattered clothes. Maybe that was why the two of them went to that synagogue—they belonged there rather than at the one held in the big house near the Temple that Grandfather knew about but did not really attend very often. Grandfather worked in the Temple complex, Jonathan was aware; because of the cart he was not allowed to go there, of course. But Grandfather also traveled a lot so he was often away from Jerusalem. Jonathan knew he worked for a banker whose assistants handled money that people brought to the Temple at festival times.

Av Mordecai's mind was often on Marcus and Jonathan during his trips. Now on the outskirts of Rome he was remembering the particular time when Marcus persuaded him to help carry Jonathan up all the stepped streets in the walled city of Jerusalem where the cart would not go. Marcus had made the unusual request that the three of them hear Peter's message that day in Solomon's Portico. Av Mordecai knew Marcus was greatly agitated and suspected that he was almost out of breath as they rushed up the Temple-area staircases with Jonathan supported between them. Peter preached eloquently to a riveted crowd. Av Mordecai heard Peter's words as if they were flames physically entering his very chest. Marcus and he discussed those things afterward; Marcus had an extremely retentive memory. They both wrote down certain sentences exactly and carried them in their robe pockets because they desired to keep the words safe:

"Beloved, do not be surprised at the fiery ordeal that is taking place among you to test you, as though something strange were happening to you."

"For to this you have been called, because Christ also suffered for you...."

"He himself bore our sins in his body on the cross, so that, free from sins we might live.... [B]y his wounds you have been healed."

"Cast all your anxiety on him, because he cares for you."

"The end of all things is near."

"Like good stewards of the manifold grace of God, serve one another with whatever gift each of you has received."

"And after you have suffered for a little while, the God of all grace, who has called you to his eternal glory in Christ, will himself restore, support, strengthen, and establish you."

"Yet if any of you suffers as a Christian, do not consider it a disgrace, but glorify God because you bear his name."*

*All quotations are from 1 Peter—4:12, 2:21, 2:24, 5:7, 4:7, 4:10, 5:10, and 4:16.

When Peter finished and had given the benediction, grandfather and father turned and embraced each other. Then they looked down at Jonathan who reached up between them, a hand for each. The boy's hands were warm and his eyes sparkled. Suddenly, with no pull at all, he stood up! He stood up on his own; his ankles and feet were strong, and he jumped a bit off the step and on to the floor! Peter was watching from a few steps away and came over to put his large fisherman's hands in blessing on the head of Marcus.

The bond between Peter and Marcus was evident in both their faces. Av Mordecai knew at last that the disgrace both of them had known was completely over and beautifully healed. Peter had told many of his denial of his Lord three times, as Jesus had foretold near Gethsemane, "this very night, before the cock crows twice."* And from this day forth, Marcus would be able to tell of the Gethsemane arrest in these words: "A certain young man was following him, wearing nothing but a linen cloth. They caught hold of him, but he left the linen cloth and ran off naked."*

Av Mordecai was known to tell, to add to the distress of Marcus, "His mother and I were very angry that night when our son arrived home. Although he had become Bar Mitzvah the year before, and was tall and mature of demeanor for his age, he was still so young! He had followed Jesus closely, at first because he was from Galilee and cared for the misbegotten. Then later Marcus sought him because of the claims he and others made about Jewish political leadership in opposition to Roman government. As parents we felt that he had no business being with such a volatile crowd during the Passover holiday in Jerusalem, especially where soldiers and Temple authorities were involved after dark! We found out that subsequent to the weekend, Marcus saw some of the followers privately, especially the rag-tag ones who had received miracles, and started a new Christian synagogue group. An underground cave meeting that he also kept hidden from his parents! Nevertheless, we appreciated his concern for his ailing mother, and his willingness to stay with her especially when I was away on business.

"My confidential work concerned investing Temple income in enterprises outside Palestine. For example, it could involve procuring the Phoenician shekel and half-shekel coins minted in the city of Tyre that were necessary for Jews to purchase for Temple tax payments. Rome would not allow Jerusalem Temple coins like that to be made in Palestine. Jewish leaders avoided such "tainted" matters for religious and political reasons. Our family members as residents of Upper Galilee had a long history in banking for commercial interest in Seleucid Greek times. That was why we were minimally proficient in the Greek language, although we always spoke our

*Mark 14:30 and 14:51—52.

native Aramaic and sometimes memorized translated Scripture passages in that Hebraic tongue.

"Due to political vicissitudes when Herod Antipas built Tiberius on the Sea of Galilee as a Roman government city (and married Herodias), our family moved south to Jerusalem. Marcus' mother and I lived as unobtrusively as possible on account of my travels and business concerns. After the Gethsemane incident, Marcus seemed to have a passing and intermittent interest in learning Greek from ways that I could personally provide. He was very subdued, often having silent periods of dark moods, as if truly possessed by a demon. He was preoccupied and lost in his own thoughts in those years. His mother and I hoped marriage might help as she faced her last days of a long illness. Then the birth of Jonathan was the greatest boon for Marcus and for me. And you know the story basically from then on."

The rest of the narrative concerning av Mordecai was found by archeologists in modern times on a document from an underground cave below a small church in Rome. It was signed in Latin by someone who referred to himself simply as a vegetable farmer. He noted that the leaves of the manuscript from Jerusalem brought by av Mordecai in his robe were given in honor of the apostle Peter to the humble congregation who considered Peter their holiest example in faith, and who met in a Roman cave used as a church. The cave had been a refuge for Christians who, in the chaotic years during and following Emperor Nero's reign, continued to be blamed for terrible crimes, as had been Jewish minorities at various times. In the wake of the massive fire that had brought disfiguring destruction to the imperial city (pathetically enshrined in Nero's ridiculous poetic arts and music), Christians had continued to be accused and martyred.

The document went on to recount the following events that av Mordecai shared one dreadful night with those who sought shelter from the rampaging patrols of a corrupt government. When General Titus' legions had actually attacked the Temple area in Jerusalem, av Mordecai's grandson Jonathan went that day to a place on the Herodian wall near Solomon's Portico and threw a large, rounded stone at a soldier. Jonathan's arms, strong from his many years of propelling his cart, aimed the missile forcefully at the soldier's lower neck, cracking collarbone and rib cage, and disabling the heart. The soldier died on the spot, but he had been covered by a charioteer with a spear who immediately responded in kind. Av Mordecai was able to retrieve the boy's body and place it in the loculus of a common tomb until it was ready for secondary burial. The tomb was a sizeable cave in the grave area of the Valley of the Hill Cleft that some months later similarly received the boy's father.

Marcus had been captured in a revolt instigated by Zealots and those of Jewish belief that the final kingdom was beginning. Marcus died by crucifixion (without a trial) but at his own request "with knees flexed," that is, nailed to a high foot support. Even though this posture prolonged the execution, Marcus believed that he as a servant was not worthy to die in the same position as his Lord and Master. Av Mordecai obtained a white limestone ossuary of about twenty inches in length, and at the proper time placed the bones of his son and grandson together in the church's multiple-grave site. The day before leaving Jerusalem for his last trip to Rome to bring the book, he himself scratched a meager engraving of the following words on the outside of the ossuary, the words he longed to have associated with his own name: "Jonathan, child of the Crucified."

So, I the vegetable farmer, whose cart bears a cross, have included my picture story to tell of the setting of the preciously treasured leaves worn in the robes of av Mordecai, servant of Christ, and placed in the hands of those who honored Peter the Fisherman.

I picture Mark's congregation made up of the outcasts who received Jesus' miracles or their relatives and descendants, huddled together in the early winter of the year AD 70. It is a cold night of stinging rain when they are gathered in their damp underground cave below the streets of Jerusalem. Through the one window-like hole near the ceiling, they hear the hundreds of marching feet of the imperial cohort from the combined forces of four Roman legions. These soldiers guard the war chariot of General Titus, son of Emperor Vespasian returning to the Antonia Fortress near the Temple precincts. In the palace courtyard of those precincts, Rome had clothed Jesus in a purple cloak, the purple of royalty and the color of the storm clouds containing the lightning and the fire of the final kingdom.

The members of Mark's church expect their own imminent executions to be somewhat like their Lord's some thirty-seven years before. They imagine that the women who anoint the bodies of Mark's church for burial will also see a man at their graves. The message will be of Jesus going forth by way of clouds above the Galilean hills to usher in the new age. Then, they, too, will tremble in terror and amazement and pray to soon be a part of the triumphant kingdom of the victorious Lord. What ecstasy it is this night to hear from a writer who thirty-seven years ago in Gethsemane fled in utter panic from Judas and the Roman soldiers, leaving his pale, earthly garment in their hands! Mark, the Gospel writer, reads aloud to them in the *achingly damp cave with a strong and courageous voice, the words they love and cling to more than any others:*

"The beginning of the good news of Jesus Christ, [the Messiah], the Son of God...."*

Concluding Summary

As the people around Jesus come to recognize the royal messianic themes in his ministry, Jesus himself draws away from the titles and their implications. It is as if messianic references begin the revelation, but then are considered inadequate because they are misleading or even dangerous and heretical. Doubtless here the issue concerns the kind of political power that corrupts the human heart and leads to tyrannizing others for selfish purposes, while causing agonizing suffering in this earthly world. Jesus boldly states that servanthood, the posture of a slave, is the significant royal role. Certainly in the overview of all of human history we can conclude that, even though we do not know exactly what the political ramifications of Davidic Messiahship were in the expectations of first-century Palestine, Jesus stood over against corrupt political control. The secret nature of his mission could better be understood now from a context in Old Testament Scriptures other than Davidic Messiahship—that of the revelation of endtimes, of a world yet to come. Jesus' reference to himself, his servanthood, his suffering, and his relationship to God has its biblical expression in the book of Daniel.

In Daniel's endtime (or eschaton) the Divine Emperor (God) bestows a new kind of kingship on a figure called the Son of Man or Child of Humanity. This is not a reference to an ordinary human being. This figure appears at God's throne after all evil in the universe is dramatically destroyed in cosmic disaster and cataclysmic holy war. This being, or individual, so strange to our minds that we can hardly imagine it, this Ben Adam, is what Jesus begins to speak about in reference to himself. He does it with "distancing language," not claiming identity by using words in the first person "I," but in pronouns like "he" and "him." Since the setting in Daniel 7 matches the situation Jesus describes in the apocalyptic passages in Mark, we can surmise that, at the eschaton, "the holy ones of the Most High" will be there among all nations and all peoples called finally to *serve* as well. Until that time occurs and all the servants are incorporated with Jesus into the kingdom, Jesus cannot refer to himself only as the Ben Adam—there is much more to be involved.

Yet even in the commencement of Jesus' ministry at the beginning of Mark, with his baptism and the apocalyptic element of the tearing apart of the heavens above to hear a divine voice, the eschaton is on the way! Other signs

*Mark 1:1.

of its coming are the miracles in the peoples' lives that happen under Jesus' commanding authority; the sending out of apostles to do the apocalyptic work of casting out demons; and the recognition of Satan even in Peter, the closest of "the Twelve." Included also are the apocalyptic signs of the opposition to Jesus in the Temple hierarchy and the imperial government of Caesar's Rome, the ripping of the Temple curtain at the crucifixion, the suffering of the persecuted church where there will be beatings by councils, abuse in place of worship, and executions like Jesus' own, now rampant among his followers. There will be the foreign desecration of the Temple and probably the destruction of Jerusalem, God's former choice of his earthly throne for the world.

With Jesus' ministry among the suffering and the events of Holy Week, and his use of the term Ben Adam, Son of Man, the endtimes *are* inaugurated and God's kingdom in servanthood for humanity is on the way, with the firm promise of eternal blessing forever!

The study of Mark's presentation of Jesus, which is shaped strikingly by Old Testament passages about Davidic royal messiahship out of which bursts the apocalyptic fervor of the suffering Son of Man, leads directly to the picture of a *church*. The hints in Mark of the people who need and respond to Jesus' ministry are those whose suffering separated them from the religious center of the Temple and consequently, ordinary human society. The immediacy of Jesus' zealous care brought healing and restoration into God's community as well as the defeat of evil causes, those signs of the incipient presence of the eschatological kingdom. From the baptism of Jesus to the crucifixion, his life story gave an applicable model to face the fierce times of AD 70 and the destruction of the Jerusalem Temple by the Roman government. But this is only a reassuring preface to the endtime, when God will defeat all evil and bring in the final kingdom where Lord Jesus and his servant people will reign in eternal glory.

Because this information arises out of words contained in Mark's Gospel itself, it is appropriate to look for a *possible early author* or redactor *within our Bible narratives*. Can we find someone who is described as feeling the terror of the crucifixion and perilous times but who was not counted among the Twelve? Is there someone associated with the Twelve, perhaps one too "young" for full responsibility or membership? Could the "certain young man" following Jesus in Gethsemane, who ran away leaving his linen garment (Mark 14:51–52), be a motivating author? His mood of fear and his status outside the Twelve would fit. He could have been about twelve years old then, and in his early 50s at the time of the destruction of Jerusalem. He could have known the stories of the miracles in Jesus' ministry from the people who experienced them. Perhaps he was with them as they formed a church group that traveled customarily with friends and relatives over the years from Galilee to Jerusalem for Passover and traditional pilgrimage festivals. Could he have left his anonymous "signature" in the few closing sentences at the terrifying end of the Gethsemane arrest?

What about the ending of the Gospel text, do any of the three final sections, noted after Chapter 16 in our Bibles, capture the general mood of those who were drawn to Jesus because of their deepest fears? Would the last words of the first ending of Mark be the original and truest: "for terror and amazement had seized them, and they said nothing to anyone, for they were afraid" (Mark 16:8)? Surely it is not that Mark's church denied the resurrection appearances or did not know of some of them as found in other Gospels, but their eyes were on the awesome visionary promise given to them by Jesus. Their Son of Man was now coming to meet them in the gathering purple clouds to transport them almost immediately into the kingdom beyond this world.

For the purple of royalty and of apocalyptic clouds, the candle lit during the session for the Gospel according to Mark is colored *purple*.

Daily Prayer Reflections for a Week with Mark's Jesus

In the mood of Mark's congregation, with fear and desperate need, let us pray with them in light of these passages.

1. *"Blessed is the coming kingdom of our ancestor David! Hosanna in the highest heaven!"* (from Mark 11:1–10).
   What do our times hope for in a leader who might be like ancient King David? How can I this day communicate to others that knowing you, O Jesus, begins the answer to that hope?

2. *"When Jesus saw their faith, he said to the paralytic, 'son, your sins are forgiven'"* (from Mark 2:1–12).
   Whom do we know whose excruciating sins may be paralyzing them? How can I in faith along with some fellow believers bring him, her, or them to Jesus?

3. *"My words will not pass away....But about that day or hour....I say to you: 'Keep awake'"* (from Mark 13:31–37).
   Show me how to expect your kingdom, O Lord. How do I let go of this world and envision the next, O Lord? Where might I find today glimpses of the eschaton in kingdom moments here in our world?

4. *"And he cured many who were sick and cast out many demons...; and he would not permit the demons to speak..."* (from Mark 1:32–39).

   What silent demons, Lord, are you casting out among us as signs of the kingdom here and on the way? How can I continue that ministry today?

5. *"But she [contributed] out of her poverty"* (from Mark 12:4–44).

   Where am I poor that you would want that for your treasury, O Lord?

6. *"What do you want me to do for you?"* (from Mark 10:46–52).

   Help us dare to join in your ministry, O Lord, by saying these words to a Bartimaeus "by the roadside."

7. *"So they...fled...and said nothing to anyone, for they were afraid"* (from Mark 10:46–52).

   I pray, O Lord, for all of us who are in fear and terror before your miracles. Give us in this hour the confidence of Psalm 23.

LUKE

Introduction

The Gospel according to Luke and its second volume, the Acts of the Apostles, clearly state their outline and purpose at several junctures: the Old Testament roots have their geographical locus in Judea of the Jews, particularly as represented by Jerusalem. First the author follows the ministry of Jesus in Galilee that fulfills what God's revelation began in the Old Testament, then the focus moves to Samaria, Transjordan, the Phoenician cities of Tyre and Sidon, and other places where Jesus went in Syria-Palestine. The goal, the Gospel "for all nations," is then spread to the "ends of the earth" by Jesus' apostles throughout the Roman Empire, as ultimately chronicled in the New Testament book of Acts.

The Gospel of Luke has interwoven references throughout Jesus' life and ministry to these three areas—Jerusalem, Samaria, and the whole Gentile world. Nevertheless, Luke's account also keeps the basic biographical outline as found in Mark and Matthew—the Galilean days, the final journey to Jerusalem, and Holy Week in the city. To suit the redactor's purposes Luke, like Matthew, prefaces the birth narrative; he does so by expanding the information on John the Baptist, especially concerning his Jewish roots. At the conclusion, Luke also has more development around the resurrection of Jesus to lead into the themes of Acts.

Scholars have been sensitive to the ways in which Luke more freely interpreted the Jesus tradition (than, say, Matthew over Mark). Luke's development is due to the changes in the historical situation of the church's spreading throughout the Roman Empire, but that fact now acts to position interpretation for the centuries ahead. The book of Luke itself functions appropriately as a manual of instruction for those commissioned to carry out Jesus' message. In Luke's presentation, the apostles who have known Jesus have a pattern to follow from his ministry. They have a living biography with examples of how gospel ministry works. Here is guidance about what to do, say, expect, pray about, and see unfold by the Holy Spirit. This pattern serves both their lives and the faith experiences of those who will come to join them on the journeys.

Here is an *outline of the Gospel of Luke* with basic parts in italics that are common to all four Gospels. The major divisions of Mark's biographical outline have Roman numerals.

Outline of the Gospel according to Luke

Birth Narratives of John the Baptist and Jesus   Chapters 1—2

I.   *John the Baptist's Message*   Chapter 3
      and Jesus' Vocation Confirmed by

II.   The Holy Spirit in *Baptism*

III. The Desert Preparation and Temptation   Chapter 4
      Jesus is led by the Spirit
      First Preaching in Galilee at Synagogue
        in Nazareth
        Reading Isaiah 61
        Description of His Ministry
        Dramatic Rejection
        The "Reversal Miracles"

IV. *The Choosing of Disciples*   Chapters 5—6:16
      Fishermen in Need of Fish Reversed
        to Abundant Nets
      Peter, James, and John Follow
      A Tax Collector Joins
      Prayer on Mountain Leads to the Calling
        of the Twelve Apostles

V.   *Ministry Journeys*
      Continue as Foreshadowed with Isaiah 61
        and Disciples' Demonstration
      Beatitudes Given "on a Level Place"   6:17–49
        (reversals of sufferings to blessings)
      The Roman Centurion's Slave and
        Other Miracles   Chapters 7—9:50
      John the Baptist's Disciples
      The Anointing by a Forgiven Woman
      Women Followers
      Parables Explained
      His True Family
      Stilling the Storm
      A Legion of Demons in Transjordan
      Jairus' Daughter
      The Twelve Sent out to Similar Ministry,
        Their Return
      Feeding the Multitude (5,000)
      Jesus' Identity and Mission,
        Messiahship and Suffering Son of Man
      Transfiguration on Mountain
      Emphasis on Rejection and Betrayal

Who Is Jesus in Luke?

Rejoice with me,

for I have found my sheep that was lost.

(Luke 15:6)

Truly I tell you, today you will be with me in Paradise.

(Luke 23:43)

Where do we begin with Luke?

To understand the perspective of the Gospel according to Luke in responding to the question "Who is Jesus?" we need to begin with the Acts of the Apostles, the fifth book in our New Testament. The first line of Acts tells us about the Gospel of Luke: "In the first book, Theophilus, I wrote about all that Jesus did and taught from the beginning until the day when he was taken up to heaven, after giving instructions through the Holy Spirit to the apostles whom he had chosen" (Acts 1:1–2)

The book of Acts goes on to chronicle the history of the Christian church as it first spread throughout the Roman world. *To Luke, that is the point of Jesus' life and mission—to spread the message of the kingdom of God to the world.* Acts, "the second volume of Luke," is about how this message was spread by his apostles in the first years after the earthly ministry of Jesus.

Where is the mission of Jesus to be spread?

As we have seen, Matthew's mission focus was mainly to the "lost sheep of the house of *Israel*" until the last resurrection appearance of Jesus on the mountain broadened that (Matt 28:16–20). The Great Commission includes the words, "Go therefore and make disciples of all nations," because "all authority in heaven and on earth has been given to me" (Matt 28:18–19). In the first chapter of Acts, just prior to the apostles' seeing the resurrected Jesus ascend into heaven, they hear Jesus' words outlining the "geography" of the mission: "…you will be my witnesses in Jerusalem, in all Judea and Samaria, and to the ends of the earth" (Acts 1:8).

This is a clearer and slightly more specific "map" than what was given in Jesus' last resurrection appearance in the Gospel of Luke: "repentance and forgiveness of sins is to be proclaimed in [the Messiah's] name *to all nations beginning from Jerusalem*" (Luke 24:47). The commission in Acts would indicate that the message should spread first from Jerusalem to the Jews ("Judea"), then to others who are closely related, like the Samaritans. The Samaritans traced their roots back to those of the biblical faith who were not taken with the leaders of Judah into the great Exile but remained in Palestine in the Babylonian (formerly Assyrian) province called Samaria. Ultimately, the message in its third phase would then go out to the "Gentiles" or "all nations," even to "the ends of the earth." At that time, "the ends of the earth" probably meant basically the Roman Empire, all the world that people knew.

The commission in Luke's Gospel gives a precise summary of this work's meaning of *Messiah:* "Thus it is written that the Messiah is to suffer and to rise from the dead on the third day (interpreting Hosea 6:1–2) and that repentance and forgiveness of sins is to be proclaimed in his name to all nations" (Luke 24:46–47). At the end of Luke, Jesus is the Messiah who has suffered and risen so that the message can go out "to all nations."

Who are the *actors* in Acts?

It is clear from both the Acts' commission and Jesus' last commission in Luke that those hearing and being sent out are designated "witnesses" (Acts 1:8 and Luke 24:48); the Greek word is *martures,* from which we get the term "martyr" in English. Acts records how the mission of those first "witnesses" sent out by Jesus resulted in the worldwide Christian church. The actors in this great drama were more frequently referred to as apostles, from the Greek word *apostello,* "to send out"——they were messengers, evangelists, missionaries, ambassadors, ones sent out with a charge. The book of Acts became a handbook for a religion that won an enormous number of members in world history: the handbook of lived-out, prime, tried-and-true examples of successful mission.

Where can we see the characteristics of successful mission?

One favorite narrative that has many elements of successful mission is about *the church at Philippi.* The founding of the Philippian congregation took place in the ancient Greek city built by Alexander the Great's father, Philip of Macedon. It had stood for at least four hundred years as a well-established, prominent, and influential metropolis.

According to Acts 16, two apostles, Paul and Silas, had been traveling in Asia Minor (modern Turkey), attempting to evangelize in Phrygia,

Galatia, Bithynia, and Mysia, where remarkably they were "*forbidden* by the Holy Spirit to speak" (Acts 16:6). At last, in the Aegean coastal city of Troas, Paul had a dream of a man standing before him "pleading with him and saying 'come over to Macedonia and help us'" (Acts 16:9). "Immediately" they set sail for the port Neapolis and went from there to nearby Philippi. After some days, they arrived and "[o]n the sabbath day we went outside the gate by the river, where we supposed there was a place of prayer; and we sat down and spoke to the women who had gathered there" (Acts 16:13).

At that place they met the renowned Lydia of Asia Minor's Thyatira. She was prosperous from her commercial enterprise in luxury goods for royal houses and the "carriage trade" of that strategic region. "The Lord opened her heart to listen eagerly to what was said by Paul" (Acts 16:14). After the subsequent baptism of Lydia, "seller of purple," and her household, she "prevailed upon" Paul and Silas to stay at her own villa as their base for founding a congregation. The two missionaries were not residents there long, however, before they were put in prison for healing the slave girl who belonged to some exploitative fortune tellers. The girl had persisted in following Paul and Silas while crying: "These men are slaves of the Most High God, who proclaim to you a way of salvation" (Acts 16:17). In prison, after they had been attacked by an angry crowd (incited by the slave girl's owners) and flogged and "beaten with rods," they were still "praying and singing hymns to God" at about midnight, when an earthquake occurred. The warden of the prison awoke to find the doors open, and in the dark of the night he assumed that there had been a massive escape. The text says that the warden "drew his sword and was about to kill himself" (Acts 16:27). Paul, who evidently could see him (perhaps by the moonlight coming through the outer doorway), called out passionately to the suicidal officer the words that, across the centuries, the church has desired to say to those at life's extremity: "Do not lay a hand on your life for *we are all here*!" (author's translation).

Remarkably the prisoners, though their "chains were unfastened," remained "stock still" in their places. They saw the warden, by the lights brought by guards, fall trembling at the feet of the two missionaries. The warden asked, "What must I do to be saved?" (meaning, to be rescued from this dishonorable predicament that has ruined my life), to which came the reply, "Believe on the Lord Jesus!" There followed a group baptism. Then the warden's household ministered to the prisoners with the washing of wounds, eating of a meal, and rejoicing in having become "believer[s] in God" (Acts 16:34). Paul and Silas soon returned to "Lydia's home, and when they had seen and encouraged the brothers and sisters there, they departed" (Acts 16:40).

Who must have been in the first congregation at Philippi?

The readers of Acts are informed by their narrator of the specific events that led to the founding of a notable congregation. And here was quite a socially diverse church, beginning with *an international trade magnate* and her *women peers,* who formerly met in a seekers' prayer group. In contrast was probably a recently deranged *slave girl* now abandoned by her owners. Even greater in contrast would be the *inmates* who had come to faith in a maximum security prison while listening in peace and awe to Paul and Silas "singing hymns!" Astoundingly, the prisoners did not even stir to make an escape after a mild but effective earthquake broke off their shackles! Definitely the *chief officer* of the penal facility was key to the new congregation—we know how his need in utter extremity of life was met. His family and household retainers, plus at least some of the *prison employees,* were in the baptized "household." Perhaps, too, some of the *city magistrates* came to be church members, the ones who released these "Roman citizens" with an apology for their scandalous treatment (Acts 16:35–39). Even *police officers,* who were the civil messengers, are mentioned (perhaps to put their charter membership in written record) in this astonishing state of affairs.

Who is Jesus to the Philippians?

Later Paul wrote a letter to this beloved congregation that is one of the most beautiful in the Christian canon of Holy Scriptures. Paul says: "I thank my God every time I remember you, constantly praying with joy in every one of my prayers for all of you, because of your sharing in the gospel from the first day until now" (Phil 1:3–5).

He teaches in the text of a hymn that Christ Jesus

…emptied himself,
taking the form of a slave,…
he humbled himself
and became obedient to the point of death—
even death on a cross.
Therefore God also highly exalted him…
so that at the name of Jesus
every knee should bend,
in heaven and on earth…,
and every tongue should confess
that Jesus Christ is Lord,
to the glory of God the Father.
(Phil 2:7–11)

And he leaves them with:

Finally, beloved, whatever is true, whatever is honorable, whatever is just, whatever is pure, whatever is pleasing, whatever is commendable, if there is any excellence and if there is anything worthy of praise, think about these things. Keep on doing the things that you have learned and received and heard and seen…and the God of peace will be with you. (Phil 4:8–9)

Who is Jesus to the apostles in Acts and to later missionaries?

The guideline that the apostles in the book of Acts and later missionaries followed in their evangelism would be a biography of Jesus Christ, namely the Gospel according to Luke. What they had "learned and received and heard and seen" about Jesus, as told in Luke's handbook, was considered the primary reference for their mission work.

A significant starting place for the mission theme of Luke, then, is when Jesus himself sends out apostles in Luke 10:1. "After this the Lord appointed seventy others and sent them on ahead of him in pairs to every town and place where he himself intended to go." Clearly the picture is that Jesus is the main missionary; the others are to go out *ahead* of him to prepare for Jesus' ministry.

Why did Jesus appoint *seventy* missionaries?

Seventy seems to be a large general number, a crowd, even an entire church congregation. But it may refer to the seventy nations listed in Genesis 10. This is one of the genealogies in Genesis that portrays all the nations of the known world as a family related to Noah after the flood; "from these the whole earth was peopled" (Gen 9:19). In a way it is a catalogue of place names spread out like a geographical map whose linkage is a family tree. With faithful Noah as their ancestor—"Noah was a righteous man, blameless in his generation; Noah walked with God" (Gen 6:9)— they were one family, all related, though now living in every known corner of the earth. If this is the meaning of the "seventy," it is markedly different from Matthew's instructions when sending out the Twelve: "Go nowhere among the Gentiles…but go rather to the lost sheep of the house of Israel" (Matt 10:5–6). Yet the Jews would definitely be included as descendants of Shem (Gen 10:21–31), specifically from the line of Eber down through Nahor, Terah, and Abraham (Gen 11:10–26).

What about the Twelve?

Luke's phrase "seventy *others*" obviously includes the twelve who are chosen and "named apostles" with the traditional first names of Peter, Andrew, James, John, and so on (Luke 6:13–16). It is interesting to note that Jesus designates the Twelve after a long night of "prayer to God" (Luke 6:12). And the seventy are sent out in "pairs"; this is not mentioned in Matthew, but it is in Mark, when Jesus begins to send out the Twelve with missionary instructions (Mark 6:7). Luke also has a sending out of just the Twelve (Luke 9:1–6). All these Gospel passages (except Luke 6:13–16) have similarities in directives—staying in one house as a base, curing the sick, and if not welcomed "shaking the dust off their feet." Luke has the Twelve designated and sent out twice (Luke 6:12–16 and 9:1–6), as do Mark and Matthew, yet Luke adds the larger crowd of seventy as a third "wave" of missionaries.

Why are missionaries sent out in pairs?

The pairs of missionaries, though specified with Mark's twelve, are of *key* importance to Luke. We read that Paul and Silas were the pair at Philippi. The book of Acts mentions pairs frequently and is structured around the two separate careers of the most renowned missionaries of the early church—first Peter, then Paul. In the Old Testament, the witness legislation is very clear that for serious confirmation in a court of law, at least two witnesses are required to testify for something to be claimed as true: "A single witness shall not suffice to convict a person of any crime or wrongdoing in connection with any offense that may be committed. Only on the evidence of two or three witnesses shall a charge be sustained" (Deut 19:15; cf. 17:6–7).

In a primarily oral society (without video cameras, recording devices, or today's plethora of written and photographed information), witnesses can be questioned separately, for example, for verification. If this is true for criminal cases, it is even more important for the kind of claims Jesus' apostles would make before the world. In a sense, they are dealing with the criminal case of Jesus' crucifixion, what led up to that, and what happened as a result. Consequently, as the Luke narratives are reported, two testimonies at least, and sometimes three and more, are plainly given.

Do other Gospels have pairs of testimony?

Although Matthew did not stress the mission of the Twelve going out in pairs, still, at a number of crucial points in his Gospel, two verifications were present. For examples, the two earthquakes in Matthew witnessing to a heightened apocalyptic dimension supplemented Mark's account of the tearing of the Temple curtain when Jesus breathed his last (Matt 27:51) and the angel's rolling away of the stone from the tomb (Matt 28:2). In Matthew's longer insertion into Mark's basic narrative of the women at the tomb, there was the double testimony of the command to go and tell the disciples about the journey to Galilee where they will see Jesus. One statement was from the angel and another from the resurrected Jesus (Matt 28:7 and 10). This was also an emphatic restatement of Mark's message to the women at the tomb. A dramatic example was the repetition of the Messianic title, King of the Jews, in both Mark's crucifixion narrative (Mark 15) and Matthew's (Matt 27), especially before Pilate who was conducting a formal, legal proceeding. In Mark, the named first witnesses of the empty tomb narratives were Mary Magdalene, Mary the mother of James, and Salome (Mark 16:1). In Matthew, Mary Magdalene and "the other Mary" (Matt 28:1) suggest careful attention to the legal requirements of the type of testimony demanded by Deuteronomy. (In John only one person saw Jesus at the empty tomb, but the Gospel of John has interests different from the technical legal confirmation.)

The very fact that Luke has more than two commissionings of apostolic missionaries in the body of the narrative (6:12–16; 9:1–6; and 10:1–12) suggests that this aspect of the work of Jesus is highly significant for Luke. Mission starts early in Jesus' ministry. This confirms that his own leadership focused on "going out" in mission at the foundation of what became a massive movement.

If pairing is so important, is Jesus paired with anyone?

Even before his commissioning of the apostles, Jesus himself in Luke is a missionary; not only that, but *even before he is born,* he is part of a paired witness team! The interwoven nature of the pairs in the opening chapters of Luke is emphasized and heightened by the miraculous: Zechariah and Elizabeth testify to a divine miracle pregnancy with their son John; Mary and Joseph come to know in a similar way of the miracle pregnancy with Jesus. The angel Gabriel appears to both Zechariah and Mary; the pair of Mary and Elizabeth confirm each other's miracles. Zechariah prophesies with what becomes a famous hymn/psalm for Christendom (the *Benedictus*), and Mary prophesies with the hymn of overwhelming popularity (the *Magnificat*). As Zechariah praises God at his son's birth, angels praise God at Jesus' birth. As Jesus is presented in the Temple, Simeon praises God with Messianic themes in what becomes the *Nunc Dimittis,* followed by Anna's arrival "to praise God and to speak about the child to all who were looking for the redemption of Jerusalem" (Luke 2:38). The child John "grew and became strong in spirit" (Luke 1:80), and the child Jesus "grew and became strong, filled with wisdom; and the favor of God was upon him" (Luke 2:40). John's father was a priest in the Jerusalem Temple when John was first heard of; Jesus as a young boy first started speaking of his Father among the Temple authorities in his "Father's house." And John begins his ministry as Jesus begins his, both with the same ritual of baptism.

What other pairs are there in Luke's work?

Throughout the Gospel of Luke, there are many "twos" (and sometimes "threes") that give testimony to the same or a similar message. Luke, carefully keeping Mark's order, has the first two healings of Jesus' ministry in Capernaum on the Sabbath—one of the man with the unclean spirit (Luke 4:31–35), the other of the woman (Simon's mother-in-law) with the high fever (Luke 4:38–39). Similarly the leper and the paralytic are together in Luke 5; coupled in Luke 7 are the centurion's slave and the widow's son. In Luke 8, the Gerasene demoniac (a man) is followed by the woman with the flow of blood and the raising of Jairus' daughter.

Among the parables, one of Luke's most well-known is the prodigal son, where there are two brothers of one father (Luke 15). The "prodigal" might be like the Gentiles and the second brother might represent the Jews. We can assume both are "lost" because the introduction to the double story is the placement of two parables—a shepherd who rejoices over finding a lost sheep and a woman who rejoices over finding a lost coin. It is worth noting that the first introductory parable portrays God as a man (a shepherd) and the second portrays God as a woman (a housekeeper). In the parables we are aware of mission work—finding the lost; we note the presence of women and another theme typical of Luke, the journeys.

Are missionaries always "successful"?

Jesus' own missionary work is not always successful. He begins his formal ministry after the temptation in the desert by preaching successfully in the synagogues of Galilee. Then follows a detailed example of preaching in his hometown of Nazareth on the Sabbath (Luke 4:14–30). Jesus reads aloud from Isaiah 61:1–2 and proclaims, "Today this scripture has been fulfilled in your hearing," a statement that is well received. He then claims that, like Elijah (and confirmed secondly by Elisha), he is not sent to do the kinds of miracles he has done elsewhere here in his hometown; the reason is that he is not "accepted as a prophet" by them. Jesus is sent, like Elijah and Elisha, to do miracles outside his hometown, that is, to be a missionary to Gentiles. The angry response of the attendees in the Nazareth synagogue is to drive him to a cliff in an attempt to kill him, "but he passed through the midst of them and went on his way" (Luke 4:30).

In Luke, the Isaiah passage is descriptive of Jesus' subsequent ministry and the accounts of the ministries of apostles "sent out" in Luke's Gospel and the book of Acts. Though rejected by "hometowners," probably the more unreceptive Jews, the ministries start in synagogues and move out where the teaching will meet the needs of people, as described in Isaiah 61, and there it "was praised by everyone" (Luke 4:15) in Galilee outside of Nazareth.

How is John the Baptist's mission like Jesus' ministry?

John the Baptist begins his ministry in "all the region around the Jordan, proclaiming a baptism of repentance for the forgiveness of sins" (Luke 3:3–4), and the words of Isaiah 40:3–5 are quoted. The implication is that John, like Jesus, is fulfilling a prophecy of Isaiah. John is "the voice crying out in the wilderness" who prepares "the way of the Lord." (The Septuagint or Greek Old Testament, which Greek-speaking Christians used, has the phrase "in the wilderness" referring to where "the voice" is "crying," rather than referring to "the way of the Lord" being in the wilderness, as in the Hebrew Scriptures and our present English Bible.) The picture is of John as a preliminary herald from the court of a king who is about to make a royal journey to see or meet the people of the realm. The herald's responsibility is to indicate or make ready the journey's route so that all the people will have access to the procession. In these verses it involves a series of reversals in the landscape. The normally hilly will be made even, the curves will be straightened, and the bumpy road will be smooth like a plain. *All this will facilitate travel for everyone;* missionaries move more efficiently on level roads. It is likely that the smooth plain also relates to Luke 6:17, where Jesus comes down from a mountain with his apostles to stand "on a level place" with the crowd from "all Judea, Jerusalem, and the coast of Tyre and Sidon." Here Jesus will deliver some of the Sermon on the Plain, which has the messages of Matthew's Sermon on the Mount (Matt 5, 6, 7), like the Beatitude "reversals."

After the Isaiah passage of prophecy, John's first message is a vivid one of calling to repentance and chastising the self-satisfaction of his hearers who are overconfident of their heritage as chosen in Abraham's Promise. This, too, compares with Jesus' bold chastisement of the Nazareth synagogue in his first sermon in Luke. In response to the people's questions, John goes into more detail about the "fruits worthy of repentance." Again he uses "reversal" language to speak to people who evidently have power or abundance and who should give in order to provide for those in need. These reversals are like those of Jesus' message from Isaiah 61 of bringing "good news to the poor," "release to captives," "sight to the blind," and freedom to the oppressed. Both John's and Jesus' Isaiah passages are from the beautiful hymnic poetry that

Old Testament commentators assign to the Isaiah prophecies after the Babylonian Exile.

What are the Old Testament passages that provide background for Luke's mission concern?

In 539 BC, Emperor Cyrus of Persia encouraged the exiles to go home and rebuild their communities. The prophetic oracles of Isaiah 40—55 reflect this historical situation and interpret the good news of freedom and return to be God's blessing. During the Exile, the leaders of Judah (who were the main people taken to Mesopotamia, or present-day Iraq) learned to live, worship, and maintain their religious heritage next to neighbors from all over the known world, also exiled by the Babylonian deportation policy. The exiled Jews came to see more vividly than ever before that their God ruled over all, and that their neighbors could be the Lord's people as well. The Isaiah passages and their refrain in Luke use phrases like "all flesh/all people shall see" the "glory of the Lord"/"the salvation of God" (Luke 3:6 and Isa 40:5); and for Israel, "I have given you as a covenant to the people, a light to the nations/Gentiles" (Isa 42:6). This latter verse precedes a section that is very like the Isaiah 61 passage Jesus reads in the Nazareth synagogue: "A light to the nations/Gentiles"

> to open the eyes that are blind,
> to bring out the prisoners from the dungeon,
> from prison those who sit in darkness.
> (Isa 42:7)

In Luke we have met the language of "a light for revelation to the Gentiles and for glory to your people Israel" (Luke 2:32) in Simeon's prophetic hymn to Jesus as Messiah, the *Nunc Dimittis,* at his presentation as a firstborn in the Jerusalem Temple.

The Old Testament prophetic theme of missionary—to the Gentiles/ the nations—is also present in reference to *Jonah* (Luke 11:29–32). Jonah was sent as a missionary to the Assyrian capital of Nineveh (the Mesopotamian empire that preceded Babylonia) to call them to Israel's God in repentance. Jonah's name in Hebrew means "dove" and may have associations with the missionary dove that Noah "sent out" from the ark after the devastation of the flood, the dove that returned with "a freshly plucked olive leaf" (Gen 8:11). The Jonah context in Luke 11 has strong apocalyptic overtones of judgment (v. 31), as does John's message of the Coming One who "will baptize you with the Holy Spirit and fire," the fire of apocalyptic harvest (Luke 3:16–17). At Jesus' baptism Luke strongly emphasizes the presence of the Holy Spirit and is unique among all four Gospels in vividly describing the Spirit's descent upon Jesus "in bodily form like a dove" (Luke 3:22).

How do the deaths of missionaries compare to Jesus' death?

Luke tells of the specific historical circumstances with Herod Antipas that led to John the Baptist's imprisonment. But the events surrounding the death of John are not given in detail; in Luke we hear only after the fact the report from Herod himself, who fears that in Jesus "John had been raised from the dead" (Luke 9:7). Referring to Jesus' similar ministry, Herod says, "John I beheaded, but who is this about whom I hear such things?" (Luke 9:9). The information about John's ministry, death, and continuing presence hint at the parallel witness of Jesus' ministry, crucifixion, and resurrection. Yet John the Baptist is definitely cast in a preparatory and less-developed role.

Luke portrays many ways in which the witness of John and the mission of Jesus are parallel, comparable, complementary, and supplementary. Their combination begins a definite model for mission that continues through the book of Acts as the apostles go out in twos on their missionary journeys. Even still, the Gospel of Luke presents the life of Jesus without peer in the two-volume work. Paul, not John the Baptist, is the only near rival to Jesus. Nevertheless, although there seems to be knowledge of Paul's death in Rome (Acts 20:22–25, 36–38), Acts emphatically concludes with Paul in Rome "proclaiming the kingdom of God and teaching about the Lord Jesus Christ..." (Acts 28:30–31). There is no rival death account of Paul—if there were, the church might have been called Paulist, rather than Christian.

Throughout Luke and Acts the emphasis is on communicating the message in speeches, but always confirmed by narrative events in the lives of missionaries. Luke, therefore, has chosen to present not just didactic pronouncements but biographical events. Centrally the life and ministry of Jesus must be told in a Gospel that demonstrates the message, with Jesus' biography, especially his work in evangelizing, bringing transformations (by reversals) to people's needy situations, going to the cross in death, and then rising from the tomb in resurrected life. Jesus *is* the Messiah in Luke because he brings exemplary and characteristically needy people of the world into God's ever-expanding kingdom through what happens in his own life. The Jews and Old Testament tradition are the grounding because they witness to the proclamation and fulfillment of God's promises; in contrast, they also provide realistic accounts of how human beings can reject God and those called to be missionaries.

The focus in Jesus' life is on the call to be a witness: the world is a mission field and the purpose of human existence is to live out the witness as Jesus did. Even on the cross, Jesus is a missionary to those who are executing him: his first words are "Father, forgive them; for they do not know what they are doing" (Luke 23:34). These words occur only in Luke's crucifixion account and are obviously the precedent for the final words of Stephen, the first Christian martyr, "Lord, do not hold this sin against them" (Acts 7:60). And Jesus enters into the conversation and needs of the two criminals dying on either side of him in those final moments on the place "called The Skull." When one says, "Jesus, remember me when you come into your kingdom," Jesus answers, "Truly I tell you, today you will be with me in Paradise" (Luke 23:42–43). Then Jesus dies the martyr's death with a prayer, "Father, into your hands I commend my spirit" (Luke 23:46).

Who is Jesus on the road to Emmaus?

The most well-known resurrection narrative from Luke happens on the road to Emmaus. In characteristic fashion, *two disciples*—a man, Cleopas, and another unnamed person, whom commentators have often surmised was a woman—are on an apostolic journey when a stranger joins them and questions them about their immediate circumstances. They tell a basic outline of the events of the Jesus story, the prophet who was crucified, the hope "that he was the one to redeem Israel" (Luke 24:21), and the women's report of the empty tomb. The stranger talks with them about their concerns on this matter, and they respond by inviting him to stay at the place where they are going. "When he was at the table with them, he took bread, blessed and broke it, and gave it to them. Then their eyes were opened, and they recognized him" (Luke 24:30–31). Again, this event has exemplary elements of mission work. The two on the journey, whose "hearts burn within them" as the Scriptures are opened, probably understand themselves to be called to witness to the stranger who needs welcoming and hospitality. The real "reversal," however, is that *the stranger is the Resurrected Lord who ministers or witnesses to them* "in the breaking of bread" (Luke 24:35).

A View of Luke's Church and Authorship of This Gospel

As a summary of the themes in Luke surrounding Jesus, the Messiah who is missionary to the world's needs through divine compassion, here follows a fictitious scene involving the authorship of Luke-Acts. This illustrates one way that the apostolic movement carried out or applied the mission of Jesus. Here we meet a church for whom the Gospel was written. At this point we are ready to ask ourselves how we might follow on the missionary journey as the result of studying Luke-Acts.

It is more than thirty years after the Jewish revolts that resulted in the fall of the Jerusalem Temple. Now the Roman imperial definition of political peace and harmony has spread through the vast reaches of the Mediterranean world. Superb roads by land and sea facilitated trade of goods and ideas; along them military efficiency provided protection and confidence in the government. A basic foundation of civil law enabled commerce and communication to thrive; the two common languages of Greek and Latin drew people of many heritages together. Immediately impressive was the magnificent city planning that encouraged the dignity of public life against the dramatic backdrop of architecture in concord with nature and geographical setting. In the safety of the cities' daughter hamlets, agricultural and pastoral economic life have had time to grow and be appreciated for its seasons of human activity and patterned abundances.

The month is October with its comfortable weather and its harvests in planting, livestock, and fishing continuing to come in for marketing and provisioning. The place is the large and highly influential strategic island of Cyprus, a nation in itself, founded on timber and copper resources in the Eastern Mediterranean. The time is late afternoon moving toward a lavender and rose evening. Near the western-edge city of Paphos, a ship is sailing into a wide inlet of the Great Sea said to be favored in former times by Venus herself but soon to become known as Episkopi Bay. The vessel is docking at the Roman town of Curium. As it glides quietly and gracefully into the peaceful harbor, clay dish lamps placed from the harbor up the hillside road in two borders are lit to delineate a welcoming pathway up the bluff to the handsome villa of the prominent ship owner Eustolios. At the harbor now bathed in golden sunset twilight, a crowd sings with anticipation. A party of about a dozen old and new friends disembark after the several days' voyage from the port of the Syrian city of Antioch. A cheer goes up as people join the crowd from smaller fishing boats in the harbor; many exchange warm greetings and embraces.

As the gathering begins to move up the lighted pathway now led by torchbearers in the soft twilight, two elegant figures emerge. One is Valentinus Lukas, a tall man with aquiline nose and white hair like a classical statue. He is now a retired Roman army general, whose white linen toga with its finely woven narrow purple border indicates his present service as a senator in the Empire's capital city. He wears formal dress tonight to honor the Roman government whose administrative capital in Cyprus recently has been under the eminent Proconsul Sergius Paulus in nearby Paphos.

Valentinus is a man of many skills due to his service in the military and politics; these talents have been abundantly enriched, others would say, in the service of the Holy Spirit. Not the least of these skills is cartography for the movement of troops, especially for efficient march. He loves maps of the Empire and the history of its captains in the Pax Romana. He still carries with him the surgical tools and medical equipment he used in the military. As the chief officer, he was responsible for diagnosing wounds and illnesses in his troops in the field and administering precious healing medications.

Former Centurion Valentinus had great respect for Jewish religious healers and although he had never gone to one himself, he knew of their sincerity and effectiveness through synagogue elders. He gave charitable gifts privately to local congregations in support of their building funds (especially when they favored the classical architecture of the Empire), when he had been stationed with his soldiers on assignment. Knowing the Roman tactics of encircling a city during siege (in Latin, circumvallatio), he said of the Jewish war in Palestine: "When you see Jerusalem surrounded by armies, then know that its desolation is at hand."* And his engineering skills include maritime travel with military personnel, and materiel and dispatch of reconnaissance to leaders in command. He was trained in Roman law with its clear statements of the rights of citizens. He knows about precedents in political cases of treason and how to speak in imperial pronouncement before courts of justice to exonerate the innocent and formally declare the guilty. To describe the soldier at the foot of the cross, he spoke boldly: "When the centurion saw what had taken place, he praised God and said, 'Certainly this man was innocent!'"*

*Luke 21:20 (t) and 23:47.

When it was his turn, Valentinus had served as a military justice. Solidly and with full integrity he stood for clear delineation of government action in cases of the policy of state. With loyalty to the peace of Rome and its highest ideals, he honored the greatest and most just political order that had yet been seen on the face of the earth. But without question he looked forward in the leadership of his Lord Jesus the Christ to the time when God's kingdom would reach across all of the Roman Empire.

One memorable tour of duty with the legions was in the legendary city of Palmyra, whose name suitably meant Palm Grove. Palmyra, located about 100 miles northeast of Damascus, was an oasis watered by springs in the desert of Syria. Among the kings in tides of ancient empires who counted this with their treasured possessions was King Solomon of Israel. He called the dazzling queen of the desert in his language "Tadmor" or "Tamar." General Mark Anthony in 41 BC, the same year of his dalliance with the Greek Queen Cleopatra of Egypt, began the Roman hegemony of the beautiful palm paradise. Soon the caravan trade route from the northeast brought goods of the far Orient through Palmyra-the-Prosperous westward to the Empire.

Valentinus Lukas would never forget the elegant women of Palmyra who wore stunning golden jewelry and lavender and rose sari gowns. Forms of these regal women were even carved in their stone funerary sculpture. They reclined with their husbands as devoted couples celebrating a banquet in heaven. He could not help but remember the city of palm groves because it was there that he met the faithful companion and traveler at his side, his wife Phyllis.

Phyllis Lukas, whom he affectionately calls Tamar or Palma, smiles at him in the torchlight as they slowly move up the lighted path to the villa of Eustolios together. They greet dear ones with joyful laughs and warm touching of hands. A young girl from the happy group of welcomers places a bouquet of rosebuds in her arms. Phyllis beams in response, and her diaphanous gown flutters as a breeze touches the rose silk embroidered with shimmering gold and silver medallions. Her dress fabric matches the glowing sunset colors with the stars of heaven just beginning their shining display. As her husband looks at her, they both share the thought that this evening in Cyprus is a moment in the kingdom come to earth.

When they had met, Phyllis was a trade magnate in Palmyra, in common parlance a "seller of purple," who managed a business that reached into India, bringing to the West the wonders of Persian carpets and Indian spices for preserving foods and seasoning royal banquets. The caravans brought elephant ivories for carved and inlaid palace furniture, metals of gold and silver used in jewelry and ornately tooled, costly chests for international tribute, precious gemstones of ruby, sapphire, emerald, lapis lazuli, and a host of others for court diadems, emblems, and embroideries. There were lustrous fabrics, textiles for draperies, robes and jewelry for caparisons of horses with princely decor for chariots in processions.

The routes and roads of the Roman legionnaire and the merchant of majesty intersected at a tent meeting one indigo night lit by stars on the sky-curtains of the desert that fairly touched the sand. A tentmaker from Damascus was being entertained by a mutual friend whose title in our languages would be sheik or mudir—the head caravaneer of a desert nation with a multitude of camels and many tents to make and mend. In the firelight this visitor, who could do fine stitchery through seemingly half-blind eyes, told them news and blessed their hearts in ways that profoundly reversed and transformed their lives. Tamar received a new name that night—it was from her Greek heritage and meant the kind of love, philia, that was exchanged in the deepest friendships. It was from a song of praise to God for giving philia love in abundance to those in need and for graciously providing even the desire to give all that you have received to others.

This God was made known in the life, death, and resurrection of the Messiah named Jesus of Nazareth. Jesus was a Jew, born in Bethlehem, a town sacred to the most famous of all Israelite kings—David. He was baptized in the Jordan, and he ministered with servanthood to people of many needs and of a variety of life situations, high and humble, in Galilee of Palestine, even in the region of Samaria and beyond the borders of his native land. Then he was crucified in Jerusalem, but God raised him from his tomb. Astonishingly Jesus appeared to his followers, walked with two to Emmaus, and ascended into heaven before the very eyes of his apostles! The Christ, which is Greek for Anointed One, the literal translation of the Hebrew term Messiah, is forever walking ahead, beckoning toward the journey deeper and deeper into God's kingdom.

After that supper in the tent by firelight and the wondrous breaking of bread, in a deliberate but patient manner the lives of Valentinus and Phyllis began to change quite radically. As they grew in faith, their steady hands and hearts discovered pathways of a common call to apostleship. Each had to settle their career affairs, which involved learning to live in a variety of lifestyle circumstances and effectively dispersing their incomes and economic resources in new ways. Phyllis had been especially sensitive to the poverty and misery of the worlds into which the caravans traveled. She had been torn since childhood between the luxurious superfluity and *exploitation by the aristocratic classes, and the plight of tenant farmers, laborers, slaves, the outcast ill and deformed, the destitute, the poverty stricken, the brutalized, and, indeed, the women and children. As an adult she knew well how dehumanizing it was to be dependent on trying to please with trinkets the whims and volatile emotions of self-indulgent overlords. Now within the Christian mission there were concrete ways to help. Her heart was filled with gratitude for what God in Jesus had done for her. With Valentinus she felt the power of Rome, its law, and its strength to act as the dramatic vehicle for the fire of the Holy Spirit. When these two, the Roman commander and the Greek merchant, had committed their fortunes and futures to the Lord and had spent day by day all they had in time, influence, money, and energy—never had they felt so free, creative, alive, peaceful, and so full of joy!*

Their first mission call took them to Damascus, to Jerusalem, and then to all Palestine where they studied the Jewish tradition and the Hebrew Scriptures. At times Valentinus went on journeys paired with leading apostles—even the Tentmaker himself whom he came to care for and respect as dearly as he cared for many of the soldiers, sailors, and officers in the military maneuvers of his commands across the Empire. Upon his return, Phyllis would show him the written accounts she had carefully made in her Greek literary compositions, done in the traditions of her Macedonian ancestry. She had collected much from the women of the movement, who were storehouses of memories, especially of the more personal and spiritual dimensions of human life, which they, to a woman, had "pondered in their hearts."* She wrote down the confessions of souls who had experienced miracles of forgiveness in villages and hamlets, and whose renewed personhoods became filled with rejoicing, song, and festivities. Blind people received sight, lepers were cleansed, hungry were fed, children were made to feel secure, the disturbed and distressed were blessed with peace, outcasts became guests at banquets, the robbed received recompense, and the lost were found.

As the company walks up the hill to Eustolios's house in Curium, they sing together in confident prayer for the miracle that may come this very night at the gathering of almost "seventy times seven." A neighbor's son has just returned from the distant country of Britannia where he spent his inheritance and squandered his property in foolish investments, gambling, and dissolute living. He is to be a guest of honor, along with his older sister, who is gifted but resentful of her confined existence. There will be time for storytelling and parables. Perhaps new letters from the tentmaker Paul, which the Lukases have heard are being circulated in collections,

*Cf. Luke 2:19.

will be read. Maybe there will even be two baptisms, with sweet amazement over the reunited family, duets and choruses sung, and a great meal where the Master and Lord of all is made known in the breaking of bread.

As Phyllis and Valentinus reach the crest of the bluff, the doors of the house of Eustolios, the ship owner, are open wide. In their host's hands is a copy of the manuscript recently finished by the Lukases in two large volumes and dedicated to all who share in the friendship of God. Eustolios embraces the two ambassadors; he carries the double book to a table in the large banquet room and sets it open in front of a plain wooden cross. Valentinus takes from a leather bag a silver cup the size of his large hand. He whispers to Eustolios that it was sent by the brothers and sisters in Antioch. A torchbearer from the harbor procession lights an olive oil lamp set on a lamp stand by the table so that the light goes forth to all in the house. The crowd spills into the room and some continue into the atrium, singing words from the beginning of Valentinus's own manuscript:

> *By the tender mercy of our God,*
> *the dawn from on high will break upon us,*
> *to give light to those who sit in darkness*
> *and in the shadow of death*
> *to guide our feet into the way of peace.**

Phyllis and Valentinus see the banquet table spread with seafood, stuffed vegetables, Greek pastries, juice from the fruit of Cypriot vines, and the large flat loaves of Passover bread. The food display matches precisely the giant mosaic on the tile floor in front of the table. The inscription and artistry of the mosaic will be copied, added to, and renewed for many generations in the villa's family. And the honor of Eustolios will live on. The Greek words in the mosaic read:

> *Instead of stones, rocks, fair copper, diamonds,*
> *the foundation of this house is Jesus Christ.*
> *This house was built on piety, modesty, and temperance.*

The rooms are hushed; a small boy with a crudely crafted crutch under his arm and a young slave girl with bright eyes walk silently toward the table with the cross. The boy announces that the Tentmaker's first letter to the church at Corinth has now been passed around to other churches. The letter is crumbling from many hands and many readings, but the boy has memorized some of the words:

*Luke 1:78–80.

136

According to the grace of God given to me,
like a skilled master builder,
I laid a foundation, and someone else is building on it.
Each builder must choose with care how to build on it.
For no one can lay any foundation other than the one that
has been laid; that foundation is Jesus Christ.
Now if anyone builds on the foundation with gold, silver,
precious stones, wood, hay, straw—the work of each builder
will become visible, for the Day will disclose it,
because it will be revealed with fire,
and the fire will test what sort of work each has done. *

The young girl then says from memory another part of the letter:

Love is patient, love is kind....
It bears all things, believes all things,
hopes all things, endures all things....
Faith, hope and love abide, these three:
and the greatest of these is love. *

Summary

The studies in this chapter hold that the apostolic or missionary theme is key to who Jesus is in Luke. The same terms used in Matthew and Mark of Messiah and Son of Man are present in Luke but are put in service to the theme of mission. An encapsulated introduction to Luke's understanding of how the gospel message spread can be read in the book of Acts about the planting of the church at Philippi in Macedonian Greece. Another longer introduction, of course, would be to follow the seeds of mission in the accounts of Jesus' biographical ministry. The outline of Luke's Gospel summarizes how the chapters in the author's first volume of mission history are structured to present Jesus from birth to death and resurrection. The outline also shows general comparison with the organization of the other New Testament Gospels. Matthew, Mark, and Luke are traditionally "viewed together" to demonstrate their clear relationships of dependence and diversity.

One obvious issue to emerge for each of the four Gospels is the fact that a special community is being addressed. Each of these churches must have had a surprisingly cohesive understanding and use of the message Jesus' identity brings, and how his biography affects the members' way of life. Luke's call is

*1 Corinthians 3:10–13 and 13:4–13.

to see Jesus as the transforming missionary who comes upon or seeks out a person or group in need (as described programmatically in Isa 42 and 61). Then Jesus acts to reverse the need, encourages repentance by forgiveness, and shares in the resulting joy. For those who respond by becoming followers, they are assigned with one or two others for the journey (witness numbers in a court of law as prescribed by Deut 19:15, etc.), when they will be empowered by the Holy Spirit. They will learn of God's promises to Israel that are fulfilled reassuringly in Jesus, the bringer of God's salvation for people everywhere. Because Jesus fulfilled Old Testament hopes, believers can be confident that Jesus' own promises will come true. There will be happiness and sorrow, acceptance and rejection, demands and gifts, efficient sparseness and unheard of abundance, with rejoicing and peace to come when all nations have heard and Jesus returns for the kingdom banquet. The whole earth at present is a mission field for the great sweep of God's plan of salvation that began with Adam ("Everyman" at Creation) and was promised to Jewish Abraham in Genesis 12:3 ("...in you all the families of the earth shall be blessed"). At the very birth time of Jesus, his mother Mary's "family sister" bore John the Baptist to be God's prophetic missionary as witness to Jesus. Later Jesus proclaimed his family as: "My mother and my brothers are those who hear the word of God and do it" (Luke 8:21).

As we consider this witnessing community, this family of hearers and doers in Luke-Acts, we cannot help but wonder who wrote these particular New Testament books. Maybe there was more than one author—missionaries were paired just as miracles, parables, and sayings often are in this Gospel's structure. And there is clear pairing of their constituent people as men and women. Would envisioning two writers help to understand this ancient literature better? Could they have left humble traces of their personalities and spiritual gifts as they collected and edited their accounts to prepare the way for Jesus to come?

In the closing pages of this chapter, I have ventured a fictitious presentation of authorship based on hints in the biblical text and supplemented by archaeological research. It would be exciting to have for other New Testament writings as much specific data as Luke-Acts gives, for example, about Peter and Paul. It does seem that particularly Luke-Acts and the Gospel of John and possibly Mark want readers to know about the personalities and circumstances involved in the traditions through which their material came. Gospel writing itself provides biographical details of the person Jesus, after all, which is an amazing characteristic of biblical literature among other religions and philosophies. Perhaps those who read the following pages will be able in days to come to gather more substantial material for biblical authorship. Here the fictitious narrative is given to aid in drawing together and concluding our Bible studies of Luke.

For hints of the authorship of Luke we can start with names in New Testament epistles associated with Paul. The Letter of Paul to Philemon (ca. AD 50s) in verse 24 mentions the names Mark, Aristarchus, Demas, and *Luke* as Paul's "fellow workers" and is addressed to "Philemon our dear friend and co-worker, to Apphia our *sister*, to Archippus our fellow *soldier,* and to *the church in your house*" (vv. 1–3). In 2 Timothy 4:11 (ca. AD 100), Paul states that "only Luke is with me." In Colossians (ca. AD 70), just before the final verse, "I, Paul, write this greeting" (the classic passage reads "Luke, the beloved *physician,* and Demas greet you"). These passages tell us that someone named "Luke" accompanied Paul in paired or small-group missionary work, that a *woman,* Apphia by name, and a *soldier,* Archippus, also were part of the team with others at various times. We note as well that churches could meet in a host's own house. So it is from Paul we attribute the designation of Luke as a physician.

Nevertheless, scholars today and in the recent past have not stressed the designation of Luke as a physician for his primary profession. They reason that Luke is not mentioned as a physician in the Gospel or Acts; and also there is not any particular reference to healings or physician's medical information in Luke's Gospel to any significant degree more than in the other Gospels. Archaeological evidence of bronze surgical instruments from Roman times in Transjordan compares with surgical and medical equipment in field camp finds of chief officers in the Roman military. This suggests that Roman officers could be skilled in medical practice as part of their training in the responsibilities for group travel to a variety of settings—war, accidents, unfamiliar local diseases, etc. Other capabilities they would need to move troops on campaign are certainly efficient travel information, knowledge of government protocol and law, and diplomacy in human relationships. They would probably be skilled in networking with political leadership for passage and protection, and know historical data on rulers and changing geographical boundaries. They would need facts about transport availability, and realistic knowledge of deterrents—weather, terrain, negative hospitality, food and water sources, as well as having expertise in maps for military strategy. For Paul and the early Christian missionaries, all these skills from a soldier would be welcome and many are strikingly evident in the Luke-Acts special redaction. Even so, undoubtedly the most personable gift in times of illness when one's world becomes very limited would be that of the "beloved physician," who had had past experience with troops in the faraway military fields.

In recent years of biblical scholarship it has been surprising to find how clear it is that women contributed substantially to the Jewish and Christian religious movements in key historical periods. From names, to social functions, to specific associations with events in the Bible, we are gathering whole new bodies of factual data. These can give guidelines to readers today and for

4. *"Where I am, there you may be also"* (from John 14:1–4).
   How does the community life experienced at the Lord's Supper give us glimpses of eternity with Jesus after death?

5. *"After he received the piece of bread, Satan entered into him"* (from John 13:21–30).
   At the Lord's table, about whom do we need to be concerned?

6. *"'Cast the net to the right side of the boat'....Jesus came and took the bread and gave it to them, and did the same with the fish"* (from John 21:1–14). Where today in my most familiar setting is Jesus telling me to "cast my net"? How is Jesus feeding us from that "net?"

7. *"Do you love me?...Feed my sheep....I have other sheep that do not belong to this fold. I must bring them..."* (from John 21:15–17 and 10:14–18).
   Have I seen sheep from other than our fold that Jesus is bringing in?

PART THREE:

Supplementary Materials

Chart of Gospel Topics Compared

Gospel & Candle Color	Portrait of Jesus	Function of John the Baptist	View of Jesus' Baptism	Aspects of Jesus' Disciples	Purpose of Miracles
Matthew **Green** The Growing Tree of the Law of Love	The Great Teacher of (Higher) Righteousness (in God's Law), plus Mark's Messiah and Son of Man	He called people to repent of sins against God's law, as the Prophets had.	"To fulfill all righteousness," said Jesus in a debate with John the Baptist.	The Twelve represent the Tribes of Israel. Focus on Peter, James, and John.	They are demonstrations of God's revelation of the Law of Love, which disciples are called to learn and do.
Mark **Purple** Royalty and Clouds of Apocalyptic Times	The Royal Davidic Messiah = Son of God *and* The Apocalyptic Figure Son of Man	To prepare the way for the Messianic King as the prophet Isaiah, the royal herald, had announced.	It designated Jesus as the Davidic Messiah. God said of him, "You are my son..." as in Psalm 2.	At first they are the "King's Cabinet" but they do not understand. The real disciples are those who received the miracles of Jesus.	They are attestations to Messiah's power now on earth. They are battle evidence for the eschatological defeat of evil.
Luke **Rose** Welcoming Friendship in the Community	The Missionary Savior for the World	Jesus' first companion *witness* on a similar mission journey. He emphasized repentance.	John's missionary act was to be copied by apostles—a baptism for all people. It began Jesus' ministry of prayer and Spirit.	The Twelve are the first "sent out"; later many follow in their footsteps, such as the seventy. Apostleship is key.	They are demonstrations of reversals of need that missionaries are called to use to spread the gospel.
John **Gold** Gold of Divinity	The Divine Son of God, known especially as the Passover Lamb	He proclaimed: "Here is the Lamb of God who takes away sins of the world."	It authenticated John's role but subordinated him to Jesus. It was the sign of water and Spirit.	The Twelve are not as key as others in intimacy—like the Beloved Disciple at the Last Supper.	They are *signs* of love about which Jesus will speak. They lead to the Last Supper, and the feeding of Jesus' sheep.

Gospel & Candle Color	Significant Sayings	Theme: Words from the Cross	Theme: Resurrection Aspects		Who is the main fictional redactor of the Gospel?
			Empty Tomb	Resurrection Narratives	
Matthew **Green**	Sermon on the Mount and Parables that teach of the Law of the Kingdom	Mark's words from Psalm 22. Earthquake opens tombs of "saints"—rabbis who go to Jerusalem (to fulfill contemporary hopes).	Two Marys go; they see earthquake; angel descends from heaven to roll away stone; guards' fear, message for disciples, then Jesus comes to women.	Jesus comes to two Marys—message for disciples to go to Galilee. Chief priest's ruse of stolen body. At mountain in Galilee, the eleven disciples are commissioned.	A teacher in a church community about AD 90 struggling to keep Jews and Jesus' believers in same household.
Mark **Purple**	Apocalyptic discourse in Jerusalem before crucifixion. Parables emphasizing suffering. Royal *immediacy* of actions	Psalm 22—Davidic experience of suffering is transformed into victory. Other references to Jesus as king.	Named women find stone rolled away. In the tomb a young man in white robe on right. "Go tell disciples…in Galilee." Women flee in terror and say nothing.	None. Later additions are from other Gospels. Eleven are commissioned after repentance—needed sermon. Jesus ascends to right hand of God.	A "servant" in an underground church just before AD 70 as the Temple fell. Was he related to the lad in Mark 14:51?
Luke **Rose**	Parables in twos about men and women, lost and found, etc., to use in missions	Jesus cries, "…forgive them" and "today in Paradise." He dies a martyr's death.	"Women" find stone rolled away. Two men in dazzling clothes appear with message. Women tell but apostles think "idle tale." Peter goes and sees cloths.	On road to Emmaus two followers are on missionary journey; they meet traveler who witnesses to them. Jesus comes to the eleven when two tell. Thomas touches. Jesus tells of OT Witness, Messiah, and "all nations."	Two first-century missionaries, a Roman general and a Greek merchant.
John **Gold**	Discourses with words establishing intimacy; metaphors of close relationships, especially at the Last Supper	Jesus shows the intimate love of mother, and he calls the Beloved Disciple to be her son. His legs are not broken; he is the Passover Lamb.	Mary Magdalene goes first; Beloved Disciple next, then Peter. (Stone had been rolled.)	Mary Magdalene weeps outside tomb and Jesus comes. Jesus comes to disciple group. Jesus comes with Thomas there. Jesus comes to fishers—esp. Peter and Beloved Disciple.	The Beloved Disciple, near to Jesus at the Last Supper, was author of main core, others of similar devotion added.

Gospel & Candle Color	What are the opening chapters about?	Distinctive emphases of the miracles of feeding a multitude	Distinctive parts of seed parables that would stress each Gospel's theme	Old Testament passages important to each Gospel, and why	What does "LOVE" imply?
Matthew **Green**	A genealogy from Abraham to Joseph, husband of Mary; Joseph's marriage and visit of wise men to Bethlehem; trip to Egypt; baptism	Matthew 14:13–21 (for student comment)	Matthew 13 esp. verses 18–23 (for student comment)	Genesis and Exodus (student adds why)	Love is an attitude of willing the neighbor's good that results in an action done for God.
Mark **Purple**	John the Baptist's ministry, Jesus' baptism, temptation, choosing fishermen, doing miracles	Mark 6:30–44 (for student)	Mark 4 esp. vv. 15 and 17 (for student comment)	Psalm 22 Psalm 2 Daniel 7 (student adds why)	Love is an immediate response to a situation of suffering, a "gut-reaction." It is faith that Jesus will heal and his kingdom will come.
Luke **Rose**	(for student to fill in)	Luke 9:10–17 (for student)	Luke 8:4–15 esp. vv. 5 and 11 (for student comment)	Genesis 10 and 12:1–3; Deuteronomy 19:15; Isaiah 42:7; Isaiah 61 (student adds why)	Love is the prayed-for Spirit of friendship that reverses the need of one who is coming into Jesus' mission. It is expressed in joy and praise.
John **Gold**	(for student to fill in)	John 6:1–14 (for student)	John 12:24 (for student comment)	Exodus 1–24 Exodus 12 and Passovers recorded elsewhere in OT. (student adds why)	Love is intense intimacy experienced by being close to Jesus at the Lord's Supper. It involves the privilege of listening to Jesus—even his prayers. It binds those at the Supper together as "One."

Gospel & Candle Color	The setting of the fictional redactor's church	What is "the world" to each church?	How does prayer function uniquely in each Gospel? (for student comment)	[Student's Choice of Topics]
Matthew **Green**	(Early Summer) Hillside (near a lake?) teaching after morning chores (11 a.m.?) of working folks like those in Jesus' parables.	The world to Matthew's church is a SCHOOL for learning of Jesus' way to love God, neighbor, and self. This includes the legacy of God's revelation in the OT.		
Mark **Purple**	(Winter) Cave room under streets of Jerusalem after curfew at night. Congregation of "outcasts" from families whose members 40 years ago received Jesus' miracles.	The world to Mark's church is a BATTLE-GROUND out of which will come Jesus' kingdom.		
Luke **Rose**	(Fall) A house church on bluff in Cyprus for evening meeting and meal with visiting missionaries. Variety of classes and ages hearing Parable of Prodigal Son and Older Brother.	To Luke's church the world is a MISSION FIELD where all members are sent in twos to welcome everyone as Jesus leads.		
John **Gold**	(Spring) Gathered for Lord's Supper at Passover time as a fellowship of beloved family. They are somewhere in synagogue context (but separating to be a church).	To John's church the world is a SACRAMENT where the love of Jesus brings peace and eternal life.		

Passages to Read Especially

Matthew

Chapters 1—8:14
Chapter 10:1–15
Chapter 12:1–21
Chapter 13
Chapters 20:17—23
Chapters 26—28

Mark (all)

Chapters 1—16

Luke

Chapters 1—7:10
Chapters 8—10:17
Chapter 15
Chapter 19:28–46
Chapter 21:1–4
Chapters 22—24

John

Chapter 1
Chapters 2—4
Chapters 11—12
Chapters 13—17
Chapters 18—19
Chapters 20—21

Summarizing the Bible (Part 1)

Historical Time Line

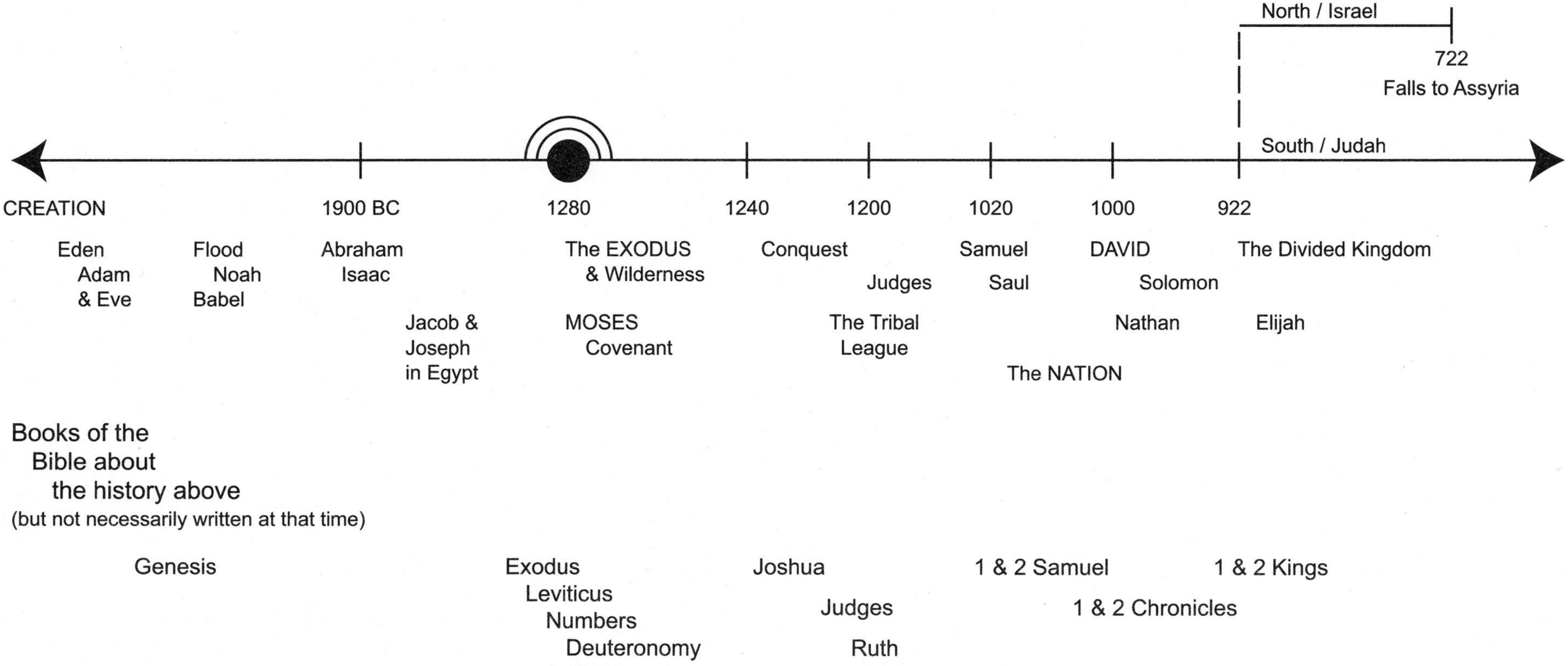

	1900 BC	1280	1240	1200	1020	1000	922	
CREATION								

CREATION

Eden
Adam & Eve

Flood
Noah
Babel

Abraham
Isaac

Jacob & Joseph in Egypt

The EXODUS & Wilderness

MOSES
Covenant

Conquest

Judges

The Tribal League

The NATION

Samuel
Saul

DAVID
Solomon

Nathan

The Divided Kingdom

Elijah

North / Israel

South / Judah

722
Falls to Assyria

Books of the
Bible about
the history above
(but not necessarily written at that time)

Genesis

Exodus
Leviticus
Numbers
Deuteronomy

Joshua
Judges
Ruth

1 & 2 Samuel
1 & 2 Chronicles

1 & 2 Kings

Summarizing the Bible (Part 2)

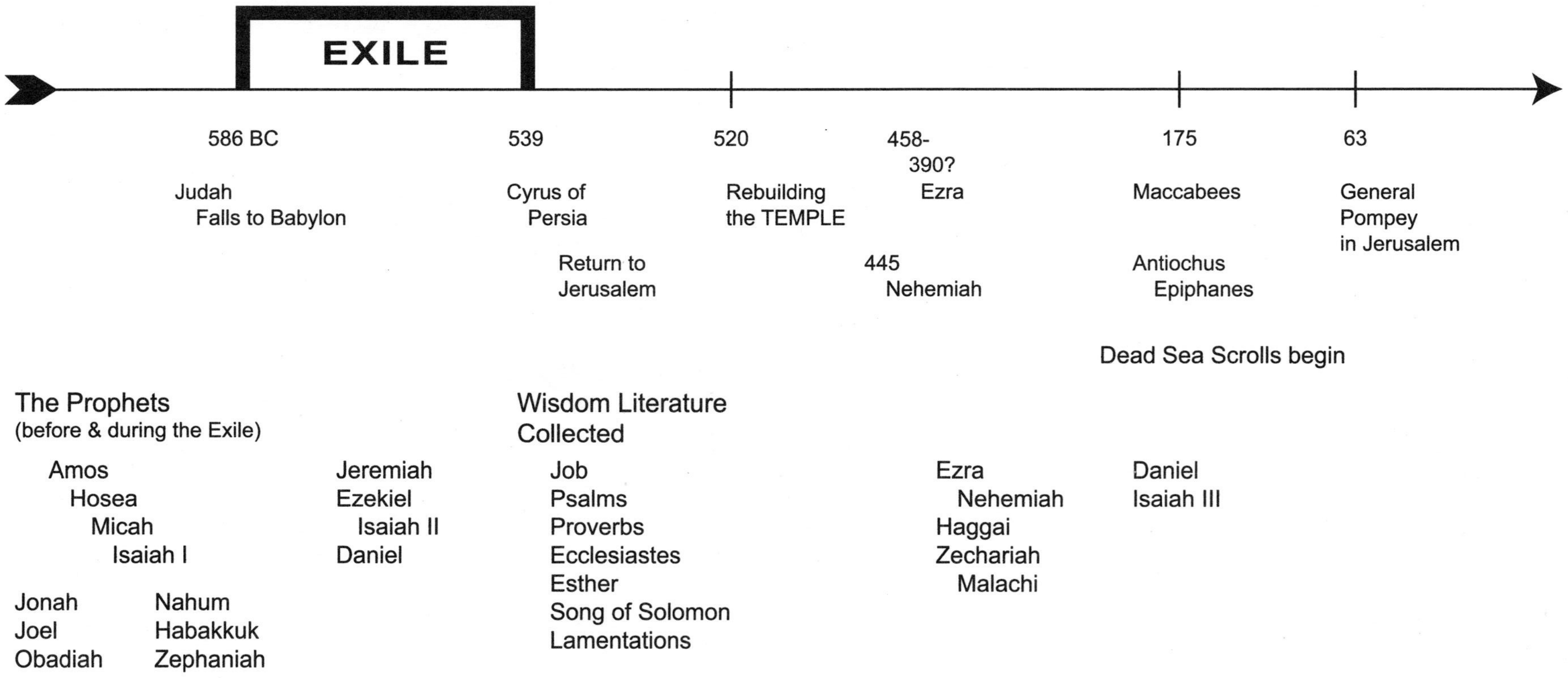

EXILE

| 586 BC | 539 | 520 | 458-390? | 445 | 175 | 63 |

586 BC
Judah
Falls to Babylon

539
Cyrus of Persia

Return to Jerusalem

520
Rebuilding the TEMPLE

458-390?
Ezra

445
Nehemiah

175
Maccabees

Antiochus Epiphanes

Dead Sea Scrolls begin

63
General Pompey in Jerusalem

The Prophets
(before & during the Exile)

Amos
Hosea
Micah
Isaiah I

Jonah
Joel
Obadiah

Nahum
Habakkuk
Zephaniah

Jeremiah
Ezekiel
Isaiah II
Daniel

Wisdom Literature Collected

Job
Psalms
Proverbs
Ecclesiastes
Esther
Song of Solomon
Lamentations

Ezra
Nehemiah
Haggai
Zechariah
Malachi

Daniel
Isaiah III

Summarizing the Bible (Part 3)

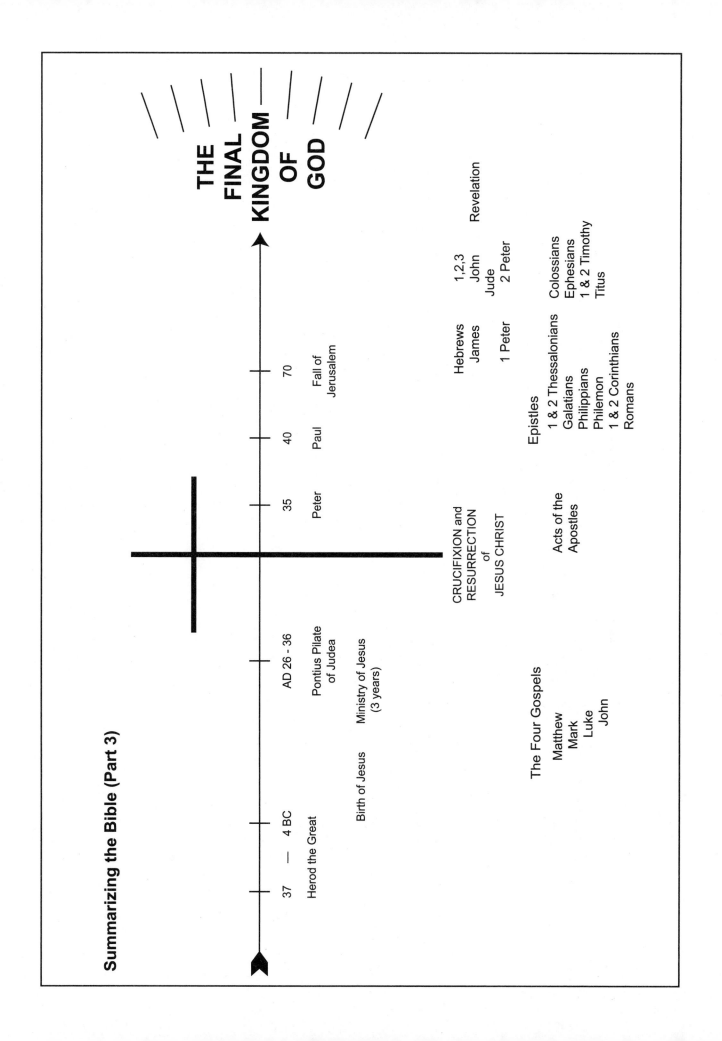

SELECTED BIBLIOGRAPHY FOR CONTINUING STUDY OF THE FOUR GOSPELS

Matthew

Raymond Brown, S.S., *The Birth of the Messiah* (Garden City, NY: Doubleday and Co., 1977).

Edwin D. Freed, *The New Testament: A Critical Introduction* (Belmont, CA: Wadsworth Publishing, Co., 2nd ed., 1991). See esp. ch. 1 "The First Three Gospels: Origins and Relationships," 53–96.

Jacob Neusner, *First Century Judaism in Crisis: Yohanan ben Zakkai and the Renaissance of Torah* (New York: Abingdon Press, 1975).

Pheme Perkins, *Reading the New Testament* (New York: Paulist Press, 2nd ed., 1988). See esp. ch. 13 "Matthew: Jesus, Teacher of Israel," 214–28.

Krister Stendahl, "Matthew," in *Peake's Commentary on the Bible,* ed. Matthew Black (London: Thomas Nelson and Sons, Ltd., 1962), 769–98.

———, *The School of St. Matthew and Its Use of the Old Testament* (Philadelphia: Fortress Press, 1968).

Mark

Donald Juel, *Messiah and Temple,* Society of Biblical Literature Dissertation Series 31 (Missoula, MT: S.B.L., 1976).

Werner Kelber, *Mark's Story of Jesus* (Philadelphia: Fortress Press, 1979).

Ched Meyers, *Binding the Strong Man: A Political Reading of Mark's Story of Jesus* (Maryknoll, NY: Orbis Books, 1988).

Robert A. Spivey and D. Moody Smith, *Anatomy of the New Testament: A Guide to Its Structure and Meaning* (New York: Macmillan Publishing Co., Inc., 3rd ed., 1982). See esp. ch. 2 "The Gospel According to Mark: Triumph Through Suffering," 61–96.

Luke

James L. Bailey and Lyle D. Vander Broek, *Literary Forms in the New Testament: A Handbook* (Louisville, KY: Westminster/John Knox Press, 1992). See esp. "Vice and Virtue Lists," 65–68; "Parable," 105–113; "Stories about Jesus," 147–55; "Hymn," 161–65; and "Speech," 166–72.

E. Earle Ellis, *The Gospel of Luke,* New Century Bible Commentary (Grand Rapids, MI: Wm. B. Eerdmans, 2nd ed., 1974).

Jack Finegan, "Philippi," in *The Interpreter's Dictionary of the Bible,* ed. G. A. Buttrick (New York: Abingdon Press, 1962), vol. K-Q, 786–87.

Robert A. Spivey and D. Moody Smith, *Anatomy of the New Testament: A Guide to Its Structure and Meaning* (New York: Macmillan Publishing Co., Inc., 3rd ed., 1982). See esp. ch. 4 "The Gospel According to Luke: Witness to Jesus," 133–65.

Leonard Swidler, *Biblical Affirmations of Woman* (Philadelphia: Westminster Press, 1979). See esp. pp. 261-281.

Robert C. Tannehill, *Luke,* Abingdon New Testament Commentaries (Nashville: Abingdon Press, 1996).

Gerd Theissen, *The Shadow of the Galilean: The Quest of the Historical Jesus in Narrative Form* (Philadelphia: Fortress Press, 1987).

John

Raymond Brown, S.S., *The Gospel According to John,* 2 vols., Anchor Bible Commentary (Garden City, NJ: Doubleday and Co., 1966 and 1967).

Luke T. Johnson, *The Writings of the New Testament: An Interpretation* (Philadelphia: Fortress Press, 1986). See esp. ch. 24 "The Gospel of John," pp. 469–500.

Robert Kysar, *John: The Maverick Gospel* (Atlanta: John Knox, 1976).

Gail R. O'Day, "John," in *The Women's Bible Commentary,* eds. Carol A. Newsom and Sharon H. Ringe (Louisville, KY: Westminster/John Knox Press, 1992), 293–304.

Elizabeth E. Platt, "The Ministry of Mary of Bethany," *Theology Today* 34 (April, 1977), 29–39.

General Subjects

Paula Fredriksen, *Jesus of Nazareth, King of the Jews: A Jewish Life and the Emergence of Christianity* (New York: Alfred A. Knopf, 1999).

Daniel J. Harrington, *Who Is Jesus? Why Is He Important? An Invitation to the New Testament* (Franklin, WI: Sheed and Ward, 1999).

See also the bibliographical list of books reviewed in the Appendix on the final pages of the chapter on Catholic biblical scholarship, pp. 209–10.

PART FOUR:

Appendix

ON THE HISTORY OF
BIBLICAL INTERPRETATION

People often ask in New Testament study, "Who is the real Jesus; what was Jesus really like in his ministry? How does that relate to the church, to us here right now, and to me?" When we turn to the Bible that the church has given us down through the ages, we find that there has been a long tradition of people who have asked and discussed exactly those questions. Biblical scholar Lawrence Boadt has written, "...the New Testament proclaims the life and message of Jesus Christ as 'good news' for all peoples, and sees in Jesus the continuation and fulfillment of the Old Testament hopes of a Savior and Messiah...." Boadt also states that "it is faith in this Jesus that makes the crucial difference..." (Boadt 1984, 14).

We can say that in order to understand "faith in Jesus" we need to study the New Testament in light of the Old Testament especially. One of the earliest ways Christians did this, as New Testament writers show, was to point to certain vibrant Old Testament themes in the life and message of Jesus. This approach was already characteristic of interpretive reading in the Hebrew Bible itself. One example would be from Isaiah 48:20–21. The prophet viewed the wonderful return of Israel from Babylonian Exile, as initiated by King Cyrus of Persia in 539 BC (under the Lord's command, of course), to be another great Exodus like that of old (1280 BC) from Egypt.

Isaiah of the Exile reminded contemporaries of when God took care of the thirsty Hebrews in the Sinai desert and water came "out of the rock" as Moses hit it with his staff (Exod 17:1–7). Now in Persia a similar, even more dramatic, miracle was happening right then. Words and phrases reminiscent of Exodus themes appear in Isaiah in chapters 40–55:

40:3	In the wilderness prepare the way of the Lord, make straight in the desert a highway....
40:29	He gives power to the faint and strengthens the powerless.
41:18	I will open rivers on the bare heights, and fountains in the midst of the valleys.
42:6	I have taken you by the hand and kept you; I have given you as a covenant to the people.
43:2	When you pass through the waters, I will be with you.
43:20–21	...for I give water in the wilderness, rivers in the desert, to give drink to my chosen people, the people whom I formed for myself....

51:10   Was it not you [Lord] who dried up the sea,
         the waters of the great deep;
         who made the depths of the sea a way
         for the redeemed to cross over?

51:11   So the ransomed of the Lord shall return,
         and come to Zion with singing.

When this kind of interpretation is used, scholars have designated it technically as *the method of typology*. The reader or hearers are being informed by bringing other more familiar passages forward as clues to what is "really being said." Characters, incidents, and events from God's former revelation in the Bible serve to make the present meaning clear. The circumstances and accounts of the well-accepted past have established God's presence and care. Here are familiar lenses or *types* to see divine salvation dramatically present "before our very eyes."

The interpretive method of typology can be discerned readily in all four Gospels as the writers present the significance of Jesus' ministry and message. Two examples are from John and Matthew. In John, referring to the Old Testament book of Exodus, Passover themes in particular are vividly present at the Last Supper. Then, in the opening baptism scene and ultimately at the crucifixion, Jesus is identified as the Passover Lamb of God. In the Gospel of Matthew, Exodus typological themes are present in King Herod's massacre of infants, the Holy Family's trip to Egypt, Jesus' baptism in the river, and the Sermon on the Mount remembering the Sinai covenant.

During the patristic period of the early church in the two hundred years after Jesus, and subsequent to the writing of the New Testament epistles and gospels, a strong tradition developed of emphasizing the *literal and historical method* of interpreting the Bible. It was centered in the sophisticated Hellenistic-Roman city of Antioch in Syria where at its founding (by the Seleucid Hellenistic ruler Nicator in 300 BC) Jews were free to worship in the ways of their heritage and in their synagogues, where they welcomed interested Gentiles. Christians fled there from Jerusalem after the martyrdom of St. Stephen and evangelized Gentiles without requiring circumcision as symbolic of their theological perspectives. It was here in Antioch that members of their congregations were first called "Christians" (Acts 11:26). Of note among the later Christian fathers who used Antiochian interpretive methods was St. Jerome (AD 347–420). He was translator of the Vulgate, the Latin Bible, from Greek (and some Hebrew) into the "vulgar tongue" of the people.

The "literal" meaning of the Scriptures, as translators would emphasize, was also characteristic of the Old Testament and Hebrew Scriptures. Manuscripts with exact copying of the Hebrew letters and exact word counts had preserved the holy writings for centuries. Great honor was placed on having the oldest exact words from, for example, the "book" that the Temple "excavations" produced during prophet Jeremiah's and King Josiah's time (622 BC, Josiah's "eighteenth year"). According to 2 Kings 23:1–25, the king himself held an assembly of all the officers and the people to "read in their hearing all the words of the book of the covenant that had been found in the house of the Lord" (23:2). Then he began a thorough religious reformation that included the reinstituting of Passover "as prescribed in this book of the covenant. No such passover had been kept since the days of the judges…" (2 Kgs 23:21–22).

Daniel J. Harrington, S.J., has summarized about the Antiochian school in this way: "A literal approach focused more on the historical realities described in Scripture, and taught that any higher or deeper sense should be based firmly on the literal sense of the text" (qtd. in Senior 1990, RG 18).

Emphasis on the Old Testament's pervasive sense of history is overwhelmingly obvious, of course, but this is particularly true in the passages and themes that use the years of kings' reigns for dating events, plus both extensive and shortened family genealogies, for example: "Josiah was eight years old when he began to reign; he reigned thirty-one years in Jerusalem. His mother's name was Jedidah daughter of Adaiah of Bozkath" (2 Kings 22:1).

The Hebrew Bible also pays close attention to place names as historical reference ("Bozkath" above) and monthly dating by days: "On the third new moon after the Israelites had gone out of the land of Egypt, on that very day, they came into the wilderness of Sinai. They had journeyed from Rephidim…" (Exod 19:1–2). And, in a number of sections in the Bible, historicity is established by precise geographical maps in words for landscape features, directions of the compass, and place names in appropriate (cartographic) relationships.

The four Gospels have used in many ways these interpretive literal and historical methodologies to follow the leadership of the Hebrew Bible as well. The purpose was to aid the reader's understanding of precise events and records. The emphasis was to affirm that "these things *really* took place; these exact words *really* were spoken." Examples of precise historical dating and context are particularly abundant in the passion narratives at the end of each Gospel. For example, all four Gospels mention that the Roman official related to the crucifixion was Pilate and that the date was the time of Passover. For use of literal words, one vivid incident given by both Mark and Matthew is Jesus' quoting the first line of Psalm 22 while on the cross. The words in the surrounding narratives are in Koiné Greek or people's spoken language (rather than classical literary Greek). But for this particular phrase, the Greek alphabet is used to transliterate Jesus' actual words, just as in our English Bibles "English" letters are printed so that we might sound out Jesus' exact words. The terms for "God" are spelled slightly differently (Mark has an "o" inserted) but both represent Aramaic grammatical forms. Scholars have determined that these words are the first line of Psalm 22 in Aramaic versions of the Hebrew Bible. These versions are called "Targumim" or "Translations," which represent the Bible's long history of being put into the common language of the people. Commentators generally agree that the people around Jesus in his ministry spoke Aramaic in their everyday life in first-century Roman Palestine, which is a language related to Hebrew, and there are many manuscripts of Targumim still existing today for contemporary knowledge of the language.

It is also interesting to note the suggestion by scholars that Abraham, the ancient ancestor from Ur (ca. 1900 BC), spoke a Mesopotamian language of the Akkadian type, and that biblical Hebrew was *not* his native tongue. When biblical Hebrew began to be spoken generally by Israelites, then Abraham's words would have been *translated* (as *literally* as possible) into the Hebrew language and alphabet. So translating the Bible, and the task of interpreting it into the common reading and speaking language of the people, has surely been around throughout its entire history. For hundreds of years in the tradition of Christianity, the church has said that the languages to be considered "original" for the Bible, or primarily basic for interpretive study, are the Hellenistic Koiné Greek for the New Testament, and for the Old Testament, Hebrew, a member of the ancient family of Northwest Semitic languages, with some passages in biblical Aramaic. The New Testament seems to quote Old Testament passages from Aramaic and/or Hebrew texts only on occasion, and more generally from the *Greek* Bible. The main Greek Old Testament translation (but not the only one used) is called the Septuagint, whose name refers to seventy or seventy-two Hebrew translators gathered and commissioned by the Hellenistic King Ptolemy IV in the years around 250 BC in Alexandria, Egypt.

Another influential interpretive methodology came from the Christian church in Egypt during the second and third centuries AD. It is designated the *allegorical method*, and its most illustrious proponents were the church fathers Clement and his prominent student Origen of Alexandria. Origen did produce a textual study edition of the Old Testament, giving the literal Hebrew but in Greek alphabetic letters, and at least four parallel columns of Greek translations now known only through quotations in other ancient writers' works. But Origen became most known for his philosophic Christian dogmatics and his theological foundations for the allegorical interpretation of Scripture. This interpretive approach allowed for multiple-level meanings to be drawn from authoritative passages to fit philosophical positions. So Origen, when in an Egypt that was not under a slave-master pharaoh but having a peaceful government allowing travel, could write, "of the *soul* as it leaves the *sensual world* (Egypt) and journeys toward the promised land of *blessedness* (Canaan)" (Newsom 2001, 486, author's italics).

Apocalyptic vision in the Old Testament book of Daniel could be called "allegorical" when the dream of fierce animals attacking the "host/army of heaven" (Dan 8:1–14) is narrated and then interpreted. Gabriel comes to explain that the ram with two horns represents the kings of Media and Persia, and the goat is the king of Greece, all of whose political power shall be broken, though "not by human hands" (Dan 8:15–26).

In the Gospels of Matthew, Mark, and Luke, the story of the sower, designated a "parable," is interpreted by Jesus as an allegory of the various faith stances of people who have heard the Word of God.

The classic allegory in the Bible for many centuries of interpretation for Christians and Jews is the Song of Solomon. Perhaps being influenced by the theology of the Old Testament prophet Hosea, it is read as the description of the covenant love between God and Israel, Christ and the Church. In the Jewish lectionary setting, it is to be read at Passover; and certainly in the Gospel of John the language of intimacy and the vine-and-branches is characteristic of the Last Supper. St. Augustine (AD 354–430) used both the literal/historical *and* the allegorical methods for struggling with some passages, but also commented, "If it seems to anyone that he has understood the divine scriptures, or any part of them, in such a way that by that understanding he does not build up that *double love of God and neighbor,* he has not yet understood" (*Confessions* 5.11.21, author's italics).

During medieval times biblical scholars in the monasteries continued with the foundations from patristic writers, especially Jerome and Augustine. The favorite way of approach was to determine four "senses" of the biblical text: *literal-historical, allegorical, mystical* or "heavenly" (anagogical), and *moral* (leading to human behavior). The cathedral schools which grew into the first universities of the thirteenth century emphasized more of the literal-historical as led by the theologians of Scholasticism. The most influential was Dominican Thomas Aquinas (1225–1274), who sought to bring the rational thought of ancient Greek philosopher Aristotle to bear on biblical truth. Also influential was Rabbi Solomon ben Isaac, or Rashi. As Jewish interpretation had influenced Christian interpretation in Alexandria and Antioch in former times, now in the twelfth and thirteenth centuries in France, Rashi focused the larger collections of midrashic commentaries for Hebrew Bible.

As the Renaissance began with its revival of classical (Greek and Roman) culture and languages in Western Europe, so did interest renew in biblical languages. Johannes Reuchlin from Germany became famous for his language tools in Latin and Greek, but especially after 1506 for the publication of a grammar and lexicon in biblical Hebrew (influenced by his Jewish studies) for Christian students. And the incomparable scholar Desiderius Erasmus, born in the Netherlands and sheltered by the Augustinians, presented a renowned "critical edition" (i.e., a single text based on the comparison and evaluation of many recently acquired manuscripts) of the Greek New Testament in early 1521. This was the first time in history that the Greek New Testament had appeared as a book in *print* (Professor Gary Hansen, University of Dubuque Theological Seminary, personal conversation, July 6, 2001). These two, Erasmus and Reuchlin, officially remained within Catholicism during the turbulent Reformation period, yet their biblical studies greatly influenced key elements in the Protestant movement and the debates among its various fragmenting groups throughout Europe in the succeeding centuries.

In December of 1521, Martin Luther, protected and hidden in Germany's Wartburg Castle by his territorial ruler, Frederick the Wise, began his translation of Erasmus' Greek edition of the New Testament into the language of his common-folk neighbors, so they could know what the Bible *"really"* said. Brother Martin, the son of a peasant-miner family, had also been sheltered under the auspices of the Augustinians as he had begun his religious life. He had graduated from the University of Erfurt in 1505 in preparation for further study in the legal profession so desired for him by his ambitious father. Nevertheless, deep spiritual concerns after the death of a friend and being caught in a lightning storm compelled him to join the Augustinian hermits in Erfurt on July 17, 1505, a monastery known to historians as providing medieval religious life at its best. Reading the New Testament book of Romans had been the instrument by which he had experienced the most satisfying sense of God's grace for spiritual salvation. In the midst of the tumultuous debates that followed with church leaders, who Luther hoped would see the theological import of biblical study as he so easily and profoundly had, he met a companion in the faith—Philip Melanchthon. The summer of 1518 at the University of Wittenberg, where Luther himself was teaching (and lecturing on Romans), marked the installation of young scholar Philip as professor of Greek, a grandnephew of (ever-Catholic) Reuchlin.

French Reformer John Calvin, whose father also had determined that his son should enter the legal profession, desired as well to work within the Catholic church. Sometime during the period from spring of 1532 to the winter 1534, Calvin had an experience of conviction and obedience that God spoke to him through the Scriptures. The Scriptures, he claimed, set before believers the law of God which acts as proof or measuring stick for the works that confirm the deep and saving union with Christ in God's grace. This experience of assurance makes chosenness or election, predestined from the foundation of the world, a doctrine of Christian comfort: Romans 8:38–39: "…neither death, nor life, nor angels…will be able to separate us from the love of God in Christ Jesus our Lord."

Because Calvin's legal training was concerned with understanding Roman law in its original historical settings with the writers' intentions, Calvin's biblical approach placed similar emphasis on the literal/historical method. He stressed the literary contexts, the cultural settings, and the rhetorical forms that biblical passages use. But Calvin—and followers in Geneva, and soon Scotland, England, and America—also emphasized the importance of education in language and historical settings for every student of the Bible. This led to the democratization of literacy and public education on a grand scale in church and society.

For *The Catholic Study Bible* (Senior et al., 1990), scholar Daniel J. Harrington, S.J., begins his summary survey on "The Bible in Catholic Life" (RG 16–30) with an astonishingly transparent statement:

One of the great achievements of the Second Vatican Council (1962) has been the renewal of interest in the Bible among Catholics. How dramatic this renewal has been can be grasped by

comparing Catholic practice around 1950 and the situation in the closing years of the twentieth century.

> At midcentury the Scriptures were read in Latin at Mass. There were few selections from
> the Old Testament, and a rather small number of New Testament passages dominated the one-
> year cycle. In response to Vatican II we now have a three-year cycle of Sunday readings and a
> two-year weekday cycle....The Old Testament is very prominent, and almost the entire New
> Testament (Gospels and Epistles) is represented. The readings, of course, are in the vernacular
> (English, Spanish, or whatever is the dominant local language)....Now the texts of the Bible
> form the primary resource for Catholic religious education at all levels,...(are) popular in adult
> education...(and compose) a major component of the seminary curriculum (for
> clergy)....Students in Catholic seminaries assume that much of the preaching and teaching in
> the future will be devoted to the Bible....The language of Catholic prayer in almost every
> instance (from sacraments to spirit-filled small groups) derives from the Bible....The
> Scriptures have also been a major element in the ecumenical movement...(where) the most
> progress has been made (when) the different church groups have focused on the Bible as their
> common heritage.... (RG 16–17, author's parentheses)

Can't we just hear the "Hallelujahs!" of the sixteenth-century reformers and their heirs from the last
four hundred years?! But should we really be so surprised; have we not just reviewed the workings of the
"descent of the Dove" in the first fifteen-hundred years since the visits of the ev-angel Gabriel to Mary, then
Joseph, in Nazareth—and surely the brooding Spirit of God *(rûah Elōhîm)* before that?

Certainly a key moment was the publication in 1965 of the official statement from the Vatican II con-
ciliar deliberations commonly referred to as *Dei Verbum*. In paragraph 12 the historical context in biblical
study is confirmed with the words "...the interpreter of sacred Scripture, in order to see clearly what God
wanted to communicate to us, should carefully investigate what meaning the sacred writers really
intended." Also, with reference to literary observations, "...the interpreter must investigate...contempo-
rary literary forms in accordance with the situation of [the biblical writer's] own time and culture...and
the customs [people] normally followed at that period in their everyday dealings with one another" (quoted
in Branick 1998, 11–12).

Harrington draws attention to the document's next sentence, which distinguishes the Bible as God's
Word (in contrast to "strictly human books" in our world).

> But since sacred Scripture must be read and interpreted with its divine authorship in mind, no
> less attention must be devoted to the content and unity of the whole of Scripture, taking into
> account the Tradition of the entire Church and the analogy of faith, if we are to derive their true
> meaning from the sacred texts. (in Senior et al., 1990, RG 20)

For the Catholic church these statements described what the study of the Bible needs to be about,
that is, endeavoring to understand Divine Revelation coming through the Scripture by means of human
words written and treasured by the community of believers down through the ages. These statements
become vehicles to propel the Catholic communion (under the continuing presence of the Holy Spirit) into
a new era of biblical interpretation. This is the era of the last thirty-five years of the twentieth century, with
fuller lectionary readings from the gospels, epistles, and Old Testament in Catholic education from early

years to seminary and university graduate schools, and in adult education in the church, as described previously here by Father Harrington. The *Dei Verbum* statements confirmed the use of biblical study tools or methodologies largely, but not exclusively, developed by Protestant scholars in the post-Reformation era, particularly in the nineteenth and twentieth centuries, called literary-historical "criticism" (or "research").

Since the Reformation period had drawn on the Christian (i.e., "Catholic") church's use and understanding of the Bible so profoundly and had emphasized the *personal reading* and *interpretation* by *individual* believers, one of the most difficult results came to be the fragmentation into groups and denominations that based their disagreements on Scripture passage interpretation. The process of dealing with these issues fell to seminary and university professors who were given time and financial support to hone skills in biblical research. Of course, many factors led to this—such as the intellectual tenor in other university studies like the sciences of the physical/natural world, and the freedom in developing democracies that separated doctrinal religion from state government to pursue new avenues of knowledge. Then there was the financial inability of small congregations and their aggregates to support academic institutions for clergy education, so larger university settings chose to "adapt to the market." And very important were international wars that turned up archaeological and ethnographic finds to decipher.

What the Catholic Church contributed to a fragmented Christendom tired of disputes over biblical implications was a *simple statement* that few denominations could disagree with, about what was important in Bible study in line with God's revelation in Christ. *Dei Verbum*'s effects, whether consciously realized or not, initiated a new era of friendship, cooperation, religious sensitivity, and human understanding among diverse sections of the Bible-believing public. In the Reformation movements of the sixteenth century, it did not take long for the most avid advocates of personal Bible reading to realize the perplexing results of individual interpretation and to see the need for reflective guidelines and theological leadership. Every group and denomination articulates its lenses—from manuscript preparers to "original language" translators, to full-canon determiners and selectors of key "salvation" passages. Yet underneath is a great longing expressed in the prayer of John 17:21 "that they may all be one." To do that in the complicated arena of ecclesiastical leadership, it is appropriately satisfying to have a large body of long-term-tradition "rememberers" make some simple statements to aid the greater household.

Following the leadership of the 1965 *Dei Verbum*, for example, two years later the General Assembly of the Presbyterian Church (U.S.A.) passed this statement in its *Confession of 1967*, paragraph 9.29:

> The Bible is to be interpreted in light of its witness to God's work of reconciliation in Christ. The Scriptures, given under the guidance of the Holy Spirit…[were] conditioned by the language, thought forms, and literary fashions of the places and times at which they were written. They reflect views of life, history, and the cosmos which were then current. The Church, therefore, has an obligation to approach the Scriptures with literary and historical understanding.

Traditions and guidelines in Bible study can be the work of the Spirit through church statements, councils, assemblies, institutions of higher learning, scholar's books, and systematic theologies that speak effectively to a historical setting, as well as in congregational endeavors where even just "two or three are gathered in my name" (Matt 18:20). Nevertheless, there is one vehicle of tradition that is hardly ever presented in formal ways and rarely mentioned except occasionally as a unique phenomenon: the faithful human ("genetic," we would say) family, which somehow over the years and generations is a remarkable locus for contributing significant leadership to the church. In the years of the influence of Protestantism

197

with its many-faceted political divisions and its strong insistence on foundational Bible study for the church, *clergy families* have now and again raised up pastors, officers, and teachers who have kept a balanced ministry going with centered and adaptive Scriptural guidance. Many have come to be names in history books—like Samuel and Susannah Wesley, parents of John and Charles; or, in our times, the Martin Luther Kings, the Robert Schullers, and the Billy (Ruth, Franklin, and Anne) Graham family. New Jersey's Princeton can list the Hodges—Alexander, Charles, and Caspar Wistar. Union Seminary in New York during the post-World War II years had Reinhold Niebuhr, son of Rev. Gustav Niebuhr (pastor in the St. Louis, Missouri, area), and Reinhold's spouse, Ursula Niebuhr, a professor of religious studies at nearby Barnard College of Columbia University. Gustav's daughter Huldah was well known in the field of religious education, and his other son, H(elmut) Richard, was a professor of theology at Yale. Then Richard's son, also Richard, was a professor of theology at Harvard.

There are many other family-related clergy and teachers of the church who are known within smaller subcultural "tribal circles." Their distinction is that they received their education in biblical interpretation in *lived-out* ministries and pastorates, then followed up with theological education in denominational accrediting situations in adult life. Their stories need to be heard to understand how significant biblical interpretation and message can be communicated or "caught." Would these tales be helped by the prophetic and priestly ministries of Old Testament Jeremiah and Ezekiel; Abraham, Isaac, Jacob, and Joseph; and Moses, Miriam, and the house of Aaron?

The historical-critical method in biblical interpretation grew out of the intellectual culture of the seventeenth and eighteenth centuries when the goal was to be free of imposed presuppositions and to examine with more "scientific objectivity." In Old Testament studies the point was to observe the characteristics in the first five books of the Bible that would lead to historical information about what "really happened" and what distinct sources in the text could be determined that produced that kind of information. The theories of progressive development and biological/Darwinian evolution, as well as fruitful discoveries that led to more complex and better human existence, were evident in many fields of endeavor. When Julius Wellhausen in 1878 presented his (first—but what came to be his only volume on the subject) *Prolegomena to the History of Israel* in German, he summarized and crystallized much previous scholarship. He began with the designation of four interwoven and separate historically dated sources by such easily observable features as the consistent use of particular Hebrew names for God in relatively long passages. And he continued with a learned and convincing analysis of the simpler faith of Abraham through the developments by Moses. This moved gracefully into the establishment of Israel's monarchy and nationhood. Then Wellhausen presented the Old Testament's apex as the moral and ethical preaching of the high prophets. The historically oriented analysis, by one within the grand tradition of Lutheran preachers, won a glorious day of elegant biblical research, dominated scholarship for at least three-quarters of a century, and is still present in various transmutations today. The Documentary Hypothesis, as the theory was termed, of the four main Pentateuchal (carefully posited) "documents"— J, E, D, and P—influenced a similar approach in New Testament scholarship.

To find the "real" or historical Jesus, critical research looked at the Gospels of Matthew, Mark, and Luke side by side to discern their most elementary constituent sources. The majority agreement came to be that Mark was the earliest of the three (and that this work was based on oral tradition to a great degree). Subsequently, Matthew and Luke used the completed Gospel of Mark, plus another hypothesized group of rather loosely collected "sayings," together designated "Q" for the German word *Quelle* (pronounced ke-vél-le) meaning "source." The "Two-Source Hypothesis" of Mark and Q, summarized in 1924 by B.H. Streeter, has been embellished with further analyses such as acknowledging special material only the writer of Matthew had (M) and similarly for Luke (L).

Another strand of the historical study of Jesus was influenced by the work of Old Testament scholar Hermann Gunkel, who published his work on Genesis in 1901 and on Psalms in 1933. His analysis compared the literary forms such as "psalm" and "historical legend" with new archaeological finds of similar material from ancient Babylonia, and with old German tales published in the 1830s by the Brothers Grimm, who were philology professors. For Gunkel the analysis of the "literary form" included historical research into determining the social setting in the life of people who produced it (the *Sitz im Leben*). When this kind of form criticism was used in service of the study of the Gospels, scholars asserted that more historical information could be found concerning the life and teachings of Jesus—the "real historical" person.

In the nineteenth century many books were written using the four Gospels as sources to piece together historical information about Jesus. Here the hope was to deal with the definitive, actual record of the life of Jesus. In these times many church people could *read the Bible* in their own vernacular language and had the benefit of publicly funded education, whose noble purpose beginning in New England with the Pilgrims had been to do exactly that. Many good citizens read the Bible learnedly and applied the resulting benefits to a new democratic society, the "city on the hill" for all the world to see, as Jesus taught. History, as Bible-reading folk were living it, was real and exciting, because they believed God's grace had bestowed on them the fulfilling desire to live in the footsteps of Jesus.

A major conclusion to the movement of writing a direct biography of Jesus by marshalling Gospel-and-other factual evidence came with the book (published in 1906 and still in print nearly a hundred years later) *The Quest of the Historical Jesus* by Albert Schweitzer. His powerfully influential conclusion was that the theological proclamation of eschatology in Jesus' own message was absolutely central. The final kingdom of God that would break in upon the world was the goal of Jesus' ministry. Yet sadly in the end his crucifixion meant that Jesus could not be a part of the fulfillment of his own words. The final kingdom was certainly not ushered in, argued *The Quest;* therefore, Jesus and his ministry *failed.* Such "dogmatic eschatology" did not have a message for the intellectual tenor of Schweitzer's times of scientific rationalism, Darwin's discoveries, and Hegel's harmonizing philosophical theories of optimistic progress. Christendom's historical quest had led to a less relevant and not significantly "real" Jesus. Still, Albert Schweitzer—biblical scholar, musician, and physician—served in Africa as a medical missionary and builder of hospitals for much of his life, which was dedicated to the precious ones of God.

Controversies raged in churches; more literal approaches to the Bible formed groups across mainline Protestant denominations; and congregations and even seminaries split, and professors were fired, as ecclesiastic bodies proliferated over the issues raised by historical-literary criticism, as represented in the works of Wellhausen, Gunkel, and Schweitzer. It is important to know about books like Schweitzer's and others to understand the dismal effects biblical scholarship can have on Bible-reading and Christian-oriented religious people and their delicate but sorely needed benevolent institutions. The phenomenon in American Protestant culture called "fundamentalism" rose at exactly this time and around these issues. (See the clear description of fundamentalism and some wise comments about it by Raymond E. Brown in his *Responses to 101 Questions on the Bible,* 43–48 and 137–42.) Is it any wonder that the Roman Catholic Church with its centralized leadership kept to a conservative theological path, and Jewish enclaves kept to a low profile during these decades, which also had two cataclysmic World Wars?!

Because of the controversies raised over eschatology, including the obsessive expectation of particular dates set for the end of the world by some disruptive and bizarre groups, mainline Protestant clergy were reticent about preaching on apocalyptic passages in the Bible and on that aspect of the ministry of Jesus. In this mix, nevertheless, came the lovely pietism of the brave Seventh Day Adventists, led by prophetic woman writer and giver of unpretentious biblical meditations, Ellen G. White (1827–1915) of New England, Illinois, and Michigan. Self-effacing Mrs. White managed to convoke a peaceful and gentle, but vast, foreign-mission movement; the establishment of church-related primary, secondary, and college-level private education; and a giant health reform with domestic and overseas hospitals, which led to the renowned Loma Linda medical school for research. All this Adventists did while sorting through a primarily eschatological message with the expectation of Jesus' Second Coming to be in God's own time, and celebrating every seventh-day Sabbath in rest and tranquility.

Mainline Protestantism met the bellicose times with the ministry of care for the needy as helpful momentary signs of the present-but-not-yet-earthly kingdom of the social Gospel. These churches urged participation in the labor movements on behalf of ravaged workers during the Gilded Age of the Robber Barons of American industry, and in the migrant slums of mill and mining towns and the teeming inner cities. Evangelists, especially in the Billy Graham campaigns, preached a simple biblical offer of personal salvation and forgiveness of sins to the war-torn service men, women, and families whose eyes had been thrust from the foxholes of battle toward the heavenly kingdom to come after death.

Then came the year 1947. The United Nations had gained enough prestige to put into tentative order an earthly state for one wounded multitude, by giving part of Palestine to Jewish refugees. Then the Dead Sea Scrolls were discovered in that sadly disputed territory. They were the most remarkable archaeological find ever to biblical studies, bringing to light what the Old Testament and Hebrew Scriptures "really" and literally said and what life must have been like in the Judaism of Jesus' time. And their main subject has turned out to be eschatology or the final kingdom of God.

The discovery of the Dead Sea Scrolls in 1947 ushered in a massive fascination with those areas where the Judeo-Christian faith tradition was present or tangentially influential throughout the entire world. The main tool was that first (Greek, *arché*) of ancient sciences—archaeology. Already biblical archaeology was handsomely honed by the British (e.g., Sir Flinders Petrie in Egypt and Palestine, and Dame Kathleen Kenyon at Jericho, Samaria, and Jerusalem) and by the burgeoning American "Albright school." The genius founder of the American school was the Holy Land archaeologist, linguist, and epigrapher Prof. William Foxwell Albright of Johns Hopkins University, whose early years were formed as the tender-eyed son of Christian missionaries (from eastern-Iowa farms) stationed in Chile. His Protestant, Catholic, and Jewish students rapidly came to hold a flock of chairs at major academic institutions, including Harvard, notably led by Profs. Frank Moore Cross and G. Ernest Wright. The first flurry of astonishing publications of the 1950s and '60s on the scrolls concerned the rule and lifestyle of a recognized monastic sect now dated to a hundred years or so earlier than, but indeed not later than, AD 68–69, when Vespasian's Tenth Roman Legion invaded the desert-cliff settlement.

This Qumran Community (from its modern Arab name for the long-evident ruins on the site), by its own 2,000-year-old handwritten manuscripts, was an apocalyptic society preparing in daily ritual for the end of history and the beginning of God's eschaton. Over and over the writings show that the group's convictions came from Hebrew Scriptures which were archived on the spot in the cave libraries. These aging manuscripts provide our times with the earliest extant copies of the Old Testament. The community's clearly written and translated interpretations tell firsthand about apocalyptic perspectives held by faithful believers during the life and ministry of Jesus, the mission of John the Baptist, and the founding years of Rabbinic Judaism, formative for modern Jews. If there has ever been a tool in 2,000 years of Christianity for contributing knowledge about the historical times of Jesus' ministry, the Dead Sea Scrolls are it! We might even have the actual leather scrolls Jesus held in his hands as he read the Bible. For example, Luke 4:16–21 shows him participating in worship at the Nazareth synagogue by reading and interpreting a passage from Isaiah.

Painstaking work on the Dead Sea Scrolls by scholars, who have been supported by some of the best professional facilities our global civilization can provide, has branched out into voluminous research projects, other archaeological enterprises, and entirely new fields of academic endeavor. And, importantly for studies of Jesus in the four Gospels, we are able with reasonable integrity to bring understandable background information to bear on passage after passage of our New Testament. Now we know more about such phenomena as groups who focused on eschatological hopes—who they were likely to be in their societies, under what kinds of governments (and even particularly named rulers) they lived, and why they probably felt so deeply about God. Their religious faith, even if it is not experienced sympathetically, shared, or even liked by a researcher, can be described, quoted from, and examined as cross-cultural data of history. Research on apocalyptic has been pioneered by F.M. Cross and his students Paul D. Hanson, John J. Collins, and A. Yarbro Collins, as well as many others.

Some of this kind of study is behind the work of N.T. Wright (*Jesus and the Victory of God,* 1996), as it has influenced the fine presentations of Paula Fredriksen, a Jewish scholar who interprets for our times that the key to Jesus' life and ministry is an eschatological one. We need to ask again today, "What is the eschatological message for us from the ministry of Jesus?" Recent advances in archaeology have stimulated and provided resources for a host of approaches and methods that had previously been underway in biblical interpretation. Tools to get at the "real Jesus" may have the goal of finding those elements that are satisfying to the spiritual needs of the persons who search. A primary set of tools comes from the form criticism scholarship of Prof. Rudolf Bultmann.

In the twentieth-century decades following Schweitzer's work on the historical Jesus and its message of the "eschatology that failed," the general trend of subsequent academic scholarship concentrated on separating out what might have been Palestinian and Jewish *during* the first century AD (closer to the time when Jesus lived) from what the church *after* Jesus' earthly ministry proclaimed about the risen Christ. Central to this enterprise was Rudolf Bultmann (1884–1976), who was interested in the small segments found in the Gospels that were discernable literary forms used for various purposes in the work of the early church. He lifted up as essential the faith in the resurrected Lord. He held the position that Christ in the New Testament is a supernatural figure in key ways influenced by Hellenistic mythology and Greek philosophical literature.

From Bultmann and certain of his heirs, we learn about the Hellenistic or Greek culture brought by Alexander the Great's empire as a primary contextual setting of the New Testament. After all, our Gospels were written in the language of ancient Greek for a Mediterranean area that proudly prized and continued to foster its Greek intellectual heritage. For many generations Holy Land pilgrimage tours have thrilled faithful travelers with visits to ever-standing Hellenistic cities, magnificent in their urban planning, with massive public-gathering plazas, theaters, basilicas, stadiums, and colonnaded boulevards. Not only Petra and Gerash in Transjordan, and the Roman cities of Galilee, but never before or again in its history was

Jerusalem more beautiful in architectural design than during the reigns of the Herods—the one superbly elegant backdrop for the New Testament.

Recently scholars have described the characteristics of wandering Hellenistic sages of the Cynic philosophy, who walked the roads between central cities and their supportive (and too often exploited) agricultural and pastoral food-producing settlements. They "traveled light" with their followers, teaching, discussing, and openly engaging varieties of folk in the wisdom of the ages about practical attitudes and common-sense approaches to human existence. Jesus was like this, they say, but with characteristic Jewish compassion for the socially outcast and peasant poor, who welcomed his touching of the sick and feeding of the rejected to bring the presence of an accepting and fulfilling community.

At this juncture we are ready to review the works from a sampling of excellent Roman Catholic commentators who bring a centrist approach and are carving out a strong avenue for growing tradition in biblical studies. Their roots are solidly within the church's heritage from ancient and medieval times, but their books on the four Gospels, *from the genre of adult education for the church comparable to what is presented here,* come mainly from the last two decades of the twentieth century under "the breath of the Spirit" of Vatican II.

CATHOLIC BIBLICAL SCHOLARSHIP:
A Selection from the 1980s and the 1990s Relating to the Four Gospels

Catholic biblical scholarship since the Second Vatican Council and *Dei Verbum,* 1965, has made outstanding contributions in biblical studies to the entire enterprise for Christendom. *An Introduction to the New Testament,* by Raymond E. Brown, S.S., received top evaluations and immediate acceptance as a balanced, exhaustive treatment of the present literature on New Testament issues. And *Reading the Old Testament: An Introduction,* by Lawrence Boadt, C.S.P., remains a classic for college, seminary, and adult education courses in the church. In light of the present study of Old Testament backgrounds for the four Gospels, there are a number of other books by Catholic scholars that will supplement and continue readers' interest and development in these subjects.

Another title of Father Brown's, *Responses to 101 Questions on the Bible,* treats an abundant number of topics in clear language without wading through bibliographies, scholarly nuances, and debates—a delight to read! The questions summarize in short paragraphs the contributions he has made in his many books of leading New Testament commentary. This is a good place to begin his thorough and more complex studies.

Considering Brown's masterworks on the Gospel according to John for points that relate to the present Bible study, for example, he reviews the literature on such issues as the identification of the author as the son of Zebedee prominently named John in the Synoptics. He also writes about the hypothesis that the "Beloved Disciple" is not a historical personage with a unique biography, but a symbolic model of the perfect follower. He mentions the theme of the "perfect disciple" being Mary, the mother of Jesus (in Luke). Brown himself prefers to see the "beloved one" in John as "a minor figure during the ministry of Jesus," who became important in the community's history, perhaps even a founding leader (see Brown 1996, 369). Brown would agree that this disciple became the ideal in John's portrait of Jesus. This disciple might even have been a primary source of the tradition for the follower or followers who made the final redaction of the completed work as it is now in the canon. The Beloved Disciple's contribution, then, "has been reflected upon over many years and expanded in the light of the Johannine community experience" (Brown 1996, 371). Brown posits complex and logical historical stages in the development of this community (Brown 1996, 374–76.)

The church congregation that grew up around the ministry of this Gospel in response to the Living Word, or revelation of the Holy Spirit, would be compelling evidence for the holiness of this portrayal of Jesus the Christ. Brown also writes that John's Jesus "used the language of his world to refer to the realities of the world from which he came" and in this "broader sense" is truly sacramental. Consequently we may see "specific symbolic references to baptism and Eucharist" in the Fourth Gospel. He comments that "the language of love" connects "believers to Jesus just as love binds the Son with the Father," and that discipleship "is a role that all can share." He also affirms that "for John there are no second-class citizens among true believers; all of them are God's children in Christ" (Brown 1996, 378).

For a classic annotated Bible with short notes for key passages as running commentary on each page, *The Catholic Study Bible: New American Bible,* by a relatively small group of contributors who together make an excellent presentation, comes highly recommended by church leaders. Especially helpful are the outstanding articles by Lawrence Boadt, C.S.P., on the Pentateuch; John J. Collins on the twelve prophets and apocalyptic Daniel; Daniel J. Harrington, S.J., on the "Bible in Catholic Life" (particularly excellent); Philip J. King on archaeology; Pheme Perkins on Luke, Acts, and John; Eileen M. Schuller on the design of the common/ecumenical lectionary's Scripture selections; and Donald Senior, C.P., main editor, the general introduction and New Testament commentary.

Eileen Schuller's article, "The Bible in the Lectionary" (NT 440–51), gives the general plan of the three-year lectionary for the reading of the Gospels in Ordinary Time: Year A Matthew, Year B Mark, and Year C Luke. John is read particularly during the high seasons of Advent-Christmas and Lent-Easter when "the focal point of the whole lectionary is Jesus Christ," especially "the paschal mystery of his blessed passion, resurrection from the dead and glorious ascension" (she is quoting from *The Constitution on the Sacred Liturgy,* 5). For the present Bible study it might be helpful to know that the term "paschal" comes into English by way of Latin and Greek from the Hebrew *pesach* meaning Passover.

The New Oxford Annotated Bible, senior editor Michael Coogan, has especially fine work by him on the nineteenth- to mid-twentieth-century history of biblical interpretation; Pheme Perkins on New Testament interpretation of the Jewish Scriptures; as well as running commentaries by John J. Collins, John S. Kselman, S.S., and associate editor Perkins herself.

Dr. Perkins, professor of theology at Boston College, has also written the well-received introduction *Reading the New Testament.* Combined with its companion volume by Father Boadt (listed above), the two make excellent basic textbooks for first-year seminary students, for lay-pastor schools, and for congregational adult education. These paperback volumes are inexpensive and thorough in coverage; they have clear formatting, charts, maps, line drawings, summary headings, questions on context, plus discussion issues at the end of each chapter. Both of these have been used as textbooks and continue to be central at the two associated schools of theology in Dubuque: Wartburg Theological Seminary (E.L.C.A. Lutheran) and the University of Dubuque Theological Seminary (in foundation the Presbyterian Church [U.S.A.]), but interdenominational in student body). The Old Testament work by Boadt was chosen for Dubuque's collaborative first-year Bible course with W.T.S. and U.D.T.S. in 1985, three years after an eleven-year similar course was held at Aquinas Institute of Theology in Dubuque. That association of schools of theology (seminaries for clergy) in the Mississippi River city of Iowa was planned in 1963–4 as an immediate result of the Second Vatican Council.

A fine commentary on the whole Bible in one (large) volume from the years immediately following Vatican II was *The Jerome Biblical Commentary.* One of the editors was John S. Kselman, S.S., an early colleague of Raymond E. Brown (the main editor) at St. Mary's Seminary in Baltimore. The JBC was revised in a new and completely updated edition, *The New Jerome Biblical Commentary,* again with Brown as the main editor.

A particularly well-expressed and brief introduction to Jesus in light of contemporary historical studies is a small paperback book by Anthony J. Tambasco, *In the Days of Jesus: the Jewish Background and Unique Teaching of Jesus* (out of print but well worth finding). The way this satisfying book exhibits the use of historical methodology as background for understanding Jesus' message is surely a prime example of the balanced scholarship Raymond Brown calls for in his "Evaluative Observations" of the historical Jesus' study

(Brown 1996, 827–829). For adult Bible study, Tambasco gives five chapters following the stages in Jesus' life from "Coming of Age in Galilee," through the crucifixion and empty-tomb passages. He has short reading assignments drawn from all four Gospels on a single page preceding each chapter. Tambasco does not look at each Gospel separately, as the study here does, but he is combining (conflating) them for his historical and religious purpose. His approach serves to make some sensitive observations (and provides bibliographies of similar treatments) and, indeed, does not differ greatly from the way introductory college textbooks have summary or concluding chapters on all four Gospels.

In other titles, Robert A. Spivey and D. Moody Smith (*Anatomy of the New Testament: A Guide to Its Structure and Meaning*) have separate chapters on each of the four Gospels and a final seventy-page summary on "Jesus the Messiah: A Portrait." Perkins (in RNT 1988) also treats each Gospel separately, after general studies of Paul. Toward the beginning of her book, she has four chapters, totaling sixty-two pages, of topics on Jesus' life, teachings, resurrection, and Christology.

Students who become deeply interested in the historical-literary critical methodology of New Testament studies, and who would particularly like to be trained in excellent teaching methods, would do well to work through (especially in a course on the subject of introducing the Bible) Vincent P. Branick's *Understanding the New Testament and Its Message: An Introduction*. Branick, professor of religious studies at the University of Dayton (Catholic), has presented a marvelous text whose exercises on mastering the issues presented in the chapters constitute a kind of "laboratory instruction" in New Testament methodological study. He opens with the chapter entitled "A Problematic Method" and lays before the reader church statements on Scripture as inspired Word of God from Catholic and mainline Protestant ecclesiastical bodies. Branick's explanations are clear and his humorous use of contemporary language idiom, effective. (See, for example, his summary comments on how people incorporate new information and experiences, that is, learn, by referring to comments based on misinformation.) He includes beautiful black-and-white photos with pertinent captions and well-designed outlines and charts. His work reflects vast reading maturely assimilated, and has traditional and centrist views simply stated but brought together creatively. These exciting ways of engaging students contribute to an outstanding textbook.

Branick also treats each of the four Gospels separately respecting their unique features, and puts forth reasons for the complex relationships of their materials. One of my favorite statements from the last pages of his treatment of the entire New Testament with all of its books is as follows:

> [The] larger horizon is theology, an attempt to get at the truth of the matter. We are no longer simply describing a historical faith. We are now trying to touch the reality of God and his gifts to us. The diversity encountered in the New Testament has forced us to do this—if we accept the need in principle for coherence, at least the need to search for it. By this search we join the writers of the New Testament in the very drive that moved them to write.
>
> …Spiritual and theological growth demands an *openness* to truth as the reality that lies within God's infinite horizon—even if we do not see that reality.
>
> The early Christians probably did not see how Mark's and John's views could fit together, but they knew that they could commit their lives to both views and their faith did not split apart. In holding on to both views, the early Christians felt moved toward some truth of Christ or salvation not described by either author.

...That compatibility, however, is not seen. It is only attested by the canon and the vitality of a church holding to that canon. (Branick 1998, 384–85)

Two books on the Paulist (Catholic) bookshelf deal with comparing just the four Gospels in New Testament studies, one by John F. O'Grady, *The Four Gospels and the Jesus Tradition,* and the other by Joseph A. Grassi, *Rediscovering the Jesus Story: A Participatory Guide.* Father O'Grady, a diocesan priest and professor of biblical theology at Barry University in Miami, Florida, writes for a college-level audience about the roots of the Jesus tradition as they came into the Scriptures from the earliest preaching and developed into the four Gospels. The first of the Gospels he treats is Mark with its theological emphasis on the passion and human suffering. After reviewing the general hypotheses for "Geographical Origin" of Mark's Gospel, he makes a sensible conclusion: "It matters little exactly where the gospel had its origin. We should recognize some of the circumstances in the gospel as depicting environmental conditions rather than try to discover the environment and use the environment to explain the gospel" (70–71).

Especially of note are O'Grady's comments on the search for the elusive author of Mark. After reviewing some of the recognized theories, based on Papias' and Eusebius' own views, plus various references in the New Testament, O'Grady writes: "As a fact, we know that Mark was one of the most common and popular names in the Roman empire. Who is to say that each reference to Mark referred to the same person? Would it not be more likely that it referred to different persons?" (69).

Thus, who wrote the Gospel of Mark is not as important as its contents. Essentially the emphasis is on "faith," particularly of the suffering Jesus, of the church of the author's time, and of all people who "perdure in a commitment in spite of failure and sin," in the hope that the future fulfillment will come to the covenant community (65, 76, and *passim*).

O'Grady treats the Gospel of John after Mark so that it will be possible for "the reader to experience the unusual approach of the author of John immediately after studying Mark" (2) and see readily the dramatic difference. This commentator has been a student of Raymond Brown, John Meier, and others, and can be expected to present his teachers' work on the Jesus tradition faithfully. In this perspective he aids in the cause of knowing traditional views on each distinctive Gospel (not a mixture into "the Gospel blur").

The topics are distinguished brightly for reference in the graphics with bold lettering and square bulleting, especially helpful in classroom discussion. For seminary students these topics could be accessed quickly for homily and sermon preparation in private study; the feature makes the volume appropriate for the pastor's library in order to review "traditional" approaches in brief summary form.

Joseph A. Grassi, a professor of Religious Studies at Santa Clara University, claims his writing is for a high-school group, but could also be for a "new-members" class in a church congregation. Summary (and well-digested) historical-critical information is given as background for the Gospels and acquaints the readers with words, phrases, and topics in bold from the actual text. Grassi suggests that the Gospel of Mark, for example, be read (even aloud) in its entirety in one or two sittings as dramatic narrative before starting the first chapter in his book (2). Nevertheless, his book goes verse by verse or paragraph by paragraph in the exact order of the biblical text. Suggestions are given for future study at the end of each Gospel unit, and journaling ideas draw in the student's own reflections. This is an effective format for close reading of each Gospel. He keeps each Gospel focused distinctly and makes homiletical statements to the reader.

As an example, here are Grassi's comments on the sentence quoted below in italics from Mark 16:5 about the young man dressed in a white robe in the empty tomb:

> To understand what happened, we must focus on Mark's story and not make comparisons to other gospels. The only one who could have rolled away the huge stone is the unlikely youth seated inside! Here is another audience surprise! The youth's description is similar to the youth in 14:50 who had followed Jesus faithfully and ran away naked after he was seized and arrested. The youth also represents the transformation of those who follow Jesus in the same way despite shame and embarrassment. They can also roll back the terrible stone barrier of death and teach others about Jesus' resurrection: *You are looking for Jesus of Nazareth, who was crucified. He has been raised; he is not here.* (Grassi 1995, 51)

Among the single-book commentaries on each of the four Gospels is one by Phillip J. Cunningham, C.S.P., entitled *Mark: The Good News Preached to the Romans.* His chapters are organized by general topics relative to the Gospel as a whole (e.g., all the miracles, all the teachings, all the possible members of Mark's congregation). There is a set of eight to sixteen study questions, mainly on content, at the end of each of the fourteen chapters. The selected two-page bibliography at the end has characteristic general readings for seminary students or more prepared adult students. Without question, the great value of Cunningham's work is his vivid portrayal of the historical setting in first-century Rome. His prologue begins with a fictitious (historical-novel) portrayal of a worship service. It is held in the commodious ground-floor residence of a large apartment house to which "Mark's Christians" come during the Mediterranean midday mealtime on a summer's day in AD 69. Here is a fascinating historical reconstruction of the middle-class church at Rome. It uses the archaeological data for the house churches under present-day Santa Prisca and San Clemente, ancient edifices extant in Italy's Eternal City. Cunningham realizes his conjecture goes against the following statement of Raymond Brown. "Studies [of Mark] do not allow us to reconstruct the profile of the community addressed by Mark....While we may be able to diagnose something of Matthew's and Luke's theology by seeing how they change a source known to us [Mark], we do not have Mark's sources" (Brown qtd. in Cunningham 1995, 6).

Cunningham believes (and the author agrees) that "others, with less formidable reputations, have more freedom" for "taking evidence to the limits of conjecture" and will have the happy result of enriching "our understanding of the first Gospel" (1995, 6). Those are welcome words for the readers of this study because of the view of Mark's community presented here. Still, for a theoretical alternative for an avid reader, Cunningham presents a fine case in the historical method of biblical interpretation. He makes me think that the *final redactor* of Mark's Gospel was indeed from Rome! Perhaps, too, the authentication of that church, which also played host to Paul and gave its name to the best of all his Epistles (Romans), so effectively promoted this first Gospel with the result that the *three others* rejoiced to accept it as their primary model in the Word of God about Jesus.

There is no doubt whatsoever that the similarity between Jerusalem on the eve of the Temple destruction and the throes of Rome in the last third of the first century are of a piece. If the Jerusalem Temple Mount was watching for the Parousia and the apocalyptic Son of Man, Rome came even more to be rocked by historical and political cataclysm as the capital of this world's greatest Empire. Cunningham says it beautifully on page 52 in his commentary on Jesus' rebuke of the Galilean storm in response to the anguished cry, "Teacher, do you not care that we are perishing?" (Mark 4:36–41).

Mark thus encourages his storm-tossed readers to trust in Jesus....Mark believes that there are even darker days ahead....Indeed, we might say that the underlying motive for the writing of the first Gospel was to inspire in Mark's Christians a trust that will sustain them as history itself comes to an end.

Among the many one-Gospel treatments on the library shelves are those in "commentary sets," which are sometimes placed as units with identically colored and printed bindings for all the New Testament books or for every book in the whole biblical canon. Teachers often find that some volumes are to be preferred over others, and so if funds are limited, it is prudent to check to see which ones are likely to be specially recommended. Among commentaries on the Gospels that emphasize Old Testament backgrounds, certainly the most outstanding for the purposes of continuing investigation after an introductory study such as the present one, is one by Daniel J. Harrington, S.J. It is *The Gospel of Matthew* and is the first volume in the Catholic series which Father Harrington edits, Sacra Pagina. The format is that of a standard commentary with important preparatory information and introductory material on the goals, viewpoints, and outline of the biblical book relative to the author's purposes. Then the main body of the work characteristically has a complete word-for-word translation, freshly the scholar's own, by delineated passages (chapter and verse). The commentary has notes on specific points involving the translation, and a brief interpretation of the passage's significance, with a short list of further readings. This kind of format enables the reader to look up commentary by the biblical chapters and verses consecutively, as needed over the years of regular preparation for preaching and teaching. There are many sets of these religious helps today, book by book from the Bible. Sometimes the sets are presented together in the noncirculating reference sections of academic libraries to be readily available for research.

Harrington's *Matthew* is particularly valuable because of its clear expression of a vast knowledge of biblical research in brief and appealing language, guided by sensitivity to religious meaning and strong personal faith. The rudder of *Dei Verbum* 24 in Catholic confessional theology carries Harrington's scholarship direction through the massive sea of literature in biblical research in both Hebrew Scriptures and Christian New Testament. His doctoral preparation in Old Testament and ancient Near Eastern studies at Harvard, his editorship since 1972 of *New Testament Abstracts* of books and articles as they are first published, his leadership in learned societies, his own writings in intertestamental literature and backgrounds, and his seminary teaching at Weston School of Theology in Cambridge, Massachusetts, are all evident in this maturely skilled presentation of studies in Matthew's Gospel.

Harrington's glorious and well-achieved purpose is to portray the Gospel of Matthew within its Jewish context of the first century so that today's readers have the opportunity to acknowledge themselves as part of that setting. The struggles of groups within Judaism of New Testament times can shed light on subsequent history when Christianity and Rabbinic Judaism developed their separate congregations. He writes: "I do not accuse Matthew of anti-Semitism, as some interpreters do. But I am aware of the anti-Semitic potential that some Matthean texts have, when taken out of their historical setting, and want to warn teachers and preachers about that" (Harrington 1991, 2). Under the guidance of the spirit of Vatican II, Christians and Jews have entered new dimensions of relationships. As biblical studies consider our points of common heritage, we grow together toward a better world.

Some of the highlights of this commentary on Matthew are the comments on this original language style of "semitic" Greek that closely translates the Hebrew of the Old Testament (p. 3) with short clauses connected by "and." He gives clear reasons why Old Testament quotations do not match up with the Septuagint texts known to us today, including the scribal practice of expanding or shaping, and using a common Christian anthology of quotations (*florilegium*) to express Jesus' theology. We do this often with passages from Isaiah that people take for granted are "Christian"—especially when singing Handel's *Messiah*. Harrington says that nevertheless, "the most important task facing the reader of Matthew is to attend to what the evangelist does with the biblical texts to express his convictions about Jesus" (39).

The historical setting of the writing of Matthew is in the tumultuous decades after the destruction of the Jerusalem Temple (AD 70). Some of the responses to that event were the early rabbinic, the apocalyptic, and the Christian that Matthew's audience represents (14–16). Harrington writes that the "stakes were high" for the survival of Judaism in the years around AD 90, and that the debates reflected in Matthew chapter 23 indicate the high tensions. Principally, Matthew's sincere intention was to present "a way of preserving and continuing the Jewish tradition" (16). His theology was one of fulfillment of the Hebrew Scriptures as he presents the Jesus message, and his key title for Jesus was the Messianic "son of God" (through Markan lenses), as well as Son of Man, Shepherd, Servant, etc. (17 and 18)—all rich in the Jewish heritage. But Jesus is "the authoritative interpreter of the Torah," that is, the Law (18). The disciples are examples of the Christian life through struggles and difficulties, but they "share in the power of the risen Lord and faithfully transmit the teaching of the earthly Jesus" (19).

Particularly in the narrative of the temptation in the wilderness, Jesus demonstrates his "solidarity with the Israel addressed by Moses" and takes upon himself faithfulness to the Exodus covenant; "far from replacing Israel, Jesus takes his identity from Israel" (69).

And finally, in summary, Harrington says,

> …the meaning of Jesus' death for the Matthean community [was that] it took place according to the Scriptures and…anticipated the general resurrection of the righteous…. These…emphases served to counter the charges…that Jesus died a criminal's death in shame….Matthew's answer is that what to some eyes was the execution of a rebel was in fact willed by God in accord with the Scriptures and that his death holds a central place in God's plan of salvation. (Harrington 1991, 403)

These fourteen books provide a handsome reference shelf, particularly in recent Catholic biblical scholarship, for the serious student of the four Gospels. They have been reviewed here in the following order:

Raymond E. Brown, S.S., *An Introduction to the New Testament* (New York: Doubleday, 1996).

Lawrence Boadt, C.S.P., *Reading the Old Testament: An Introduction* (New York/Mahwah, NJ: Paulist Press, 1984).

Raymond E. Brown, S.S., *101 Questions and Answers on the Bible* (New York/Mahwah, NJ: Paulist Press, 2003). This book originally was called *Responses to 101 Questions on the Bible*.

Donald Senior, C.P., et al., *The Catholic Study Bible: NAB* (New York: Oxford University Press, 1990).

Michael Coogan, et al., *The New Oxford Annotated Bible,* 3rd ed. NRSV (New York: Oxford University Press, 2001).

Pheme Perkins, *Reading the New Testament* (New York/Mahwah, NJ: Paulist Press, Revised Edition 1988).

Raymond E. Brown, S.S., et al., *The Jerome Biblical Commentary* (Englewood Cliffs, NJ: Prentice Hall, 1968).

Raymond E. Brown, S.S., et al., *The New Jerome Biblical Commentary* (Englewood Cliffs, NJ: Prentice Hall, 1990).

Anthony J. Tambasco, *In the Days of Jesus: The Jewish Background and Unique Teaching of Jesus* (New York/Ramsey, NJ: Paulist Press, 1983).

Vincent P. Branick, *Understanding the New Testament and Its Message: An Introduction* (New York/Mahwah, NJ: Paulist Press, 1998).

Joseph A. Grassi, *Rediscovering the Jesus Story: A Participatory Guide* (New York/Mahwah, NJ: Paulist Press, 1995).

Phillip J. Cunningham, C.S.P., *Mark: The Good News Preached to the Romans* (New York/Mahwah, NJ: Paulist Press, 1995).

Daniel J. Harrington, S.J., *The Gospel of Matthew,* vol. 1, Sacra Pagina (Collegeville, MN: The Liturgical Press, 1991).

EXEGESIS METHODOLOGIES

The portrayals of Jesus that have just been reviewed reflect recent serious scholarship within the academic realm of biblical studies. The *processes* by which passages from the Gospels are selected, analyzed literarily, and illuminated by archaeological/historical materials are basically held in common by most contemporary scholars, although the emphases, concerns, and conclusions may differ. These processes, called "exegesis methodologies," are used and taught especially in theological seminaries. "Exegesis" comes from a Greek term that means "to lead out" and refers to the process of interpretation when we seek to discover the leading-out meaning of biblical passages.

In the seminary, students are being trained to use a "tool kit," analogous to a physician's portable medical bag (mostly of bygone eras!), in order to bring the message of the Bible in appropriate application to various facets of church ministry—such as preaching, worship, liturgy, religious education, spiritual retreats, pastoral care and counseling, institutional administration, and so on. Because church life takes the Bible as its constitutive foundation and has done so for two thousand years (with a tradition whose roots go back at least two thousand years before that), being acquainted with and skilled in interpretative tools allows one to benefit from the abundant literature that has grown up around the Bible. In this sense exegesis or biblical interpretation has a number of resources, controls, new doorways, and formal correctives that contribute to the creativity and integrity of Bible study. Yet it must always be remembered that believers come to Scripture in God's grace by faith to hear the Word. It is neither a requirement nor a necessity to have access to the libraries upon libraries of studies *about* the Bible for believers to come to God in Christ. The key is our primary need to come together in church community. But it is an added blessing to know the written and expounded facets of the communal tradition of interpretation by many faithful believers, and especially leaders in this oldest of academic fields.

The "tool kit" methodologies of exegesis aid in analyzing and evaluating biblical materials. The study process encourages the student to develop a systematic approach to passages for interpretation and application. This "systematic approach" can take the form of an outline that the commentator makes to research a particular passage. The point is to choose methodologies that are appropriate both to the passage and to the occasion for which commentary will be used. The seven following methodologies offer a relatively thorough list for many exegesis outlines, and is the one that has been used here for this Bible study on the four Gospels. Whether preparing a Bible study, a sermon, a special liturgy for a worship service, a communal retreat, or any other congregational event, the art is to try to integrate the methodological tools into the final exegetical product so that the preparatory steps do not "show through" in obvious ways. Nevertheless, every single tool mentioned in the preparatory outline needs to be used—or we ask why the commentator did all the work and then not use the fruits of the research? The hearer, reader, or congregational member needs to have the benefit of the church's approach, tradition, and guidelines on Scripture, as worked through to a proclamation unique for "the hour," that moment in their life. A hasty presentation from "off the top of the head" is to be avoided at all costs; so is also, needless to say, a total appropriation of another times' message. The minister or leader is called to that moment just for this particular group of people with their own particular situations. The prayer is that Jesus be "made real" this day in the midst of his people through the proclamation and study of Scripture. On the inside of the pulpit or in the lector's notes are these words: "We would see Jesus!"

Because the chapters in this textbook presuppose the use of exegesis methodologies, there follows a brief description of the various types of "criticism." The terms "criticism," "critique," and "critic" in biblical studies come from a Greek root word that means to discern, analyze, question, and evaluate in order to come to an informed conclusion about an appropriate meaning. Although in everyday speech "to criticize" frequently means to say something negative, here the reference is more like the way we speak of movie and theater critics. Their job is to evaluate performances and pieces, using certain professional standards, as in the statement: "The *New York Times* movie *critic* gave top ratings and spectacular notices after the film's opening night."

1. Text criticism usually comes as the first step in analyzing the Bible. It deals with trying to ascertain the original wording of the selected passage. As yet there are not any "autographed" copies of biblical books by original authors, but we do have thousands of handwritten manuscripts and fragments that date from decades to centuries after the events they describe. In text-criticism studies, the goal is to get back to the very earliest wording possible, using original languages of Hebrew, Greek, and Aramaic (the language spoken in Palestine at the time of Jesus and at certain other times of the Old Testament) and then to make modern-language translations as correspondingly exact as possible. The Dead Sea Scrolls have given us our earliest copies of Old Testament manuscripts. In times before and after these manuscripts, scriptures were often given sacred burials (sometimes in congregational buildings) when the copies became too old to use. Ultimately, most used scriptures suffered decay and destruction; it is likely for this reason that ancient manuscripts are not available today. When original-language manuscripts preserved from medieval times (for example, those used for the 1611 King James Version, which became the Standard English Bible) are compared to the Dead Sea Scrolls, remarkably *there are very, very few significant differences.* How surprising that is when we think of all the centuries of hand copying and how easily *we* make mistakes in copying down everyday information! Manuscript study with the Dead Sea Scrolls can be important when working with Old Testament passages that relate to Gospel incidents, such as Jesus' reading of Isaiah in the Nazareth synagogue. But *the Dead Sea Scrolls have not changed our basic Bible: they have confirmed it.*

2. Grammatical criticism, the search for exact wording, can be linked to textual criticism, because it concentrates on the language of the text, the words themselves in their basic definitions and special uses in biblical themes and passages. Shades of meaning are expressed in the ways words are put with each other in sentences according to language customs and rules. Each of the four Gospels has preferred words and characteristic styles of grammar that appear to be chosen for impressions they make on the reader and for expressing the unique concerns of the writer. Mark's recurrent use of the word "immediately" is an obvious example. It conveys a sense of rapid movement, urgency, command, and the authority of a leader who can act to get things going, especially in times of emergency and crisis.

3. Form criticism has been in the last century a productive enterprise for discerning the kind of unit into which the words and sentences are placed—such as an announcement, a proverb or aphorism, a poem or song, a longer narrative, a parable ("an earthly story with a heavenly meaning"), plus many others. Form criticism asks as well, "What are the boundaries of the passage—with what verses or lines does it begin and end?" Then form criticism takes us to envisage the "setting in life" or ways that the society customarily used that kind of song or story or proverb. Did the faithful use that form at a pilgrimage festival, or to entertain impressively at a banquet, or to engage the interest of those in the neighborhood who had never before heard of such a thing?

4. Literary criticism is a general category that includes all other forms, then subsequently moves into a larger dimension of the written context as it served its oral use. How was it sensitive to mood and style in a culture where there was a very close relationship between what was written down and how it would be read aloud? The listeners addressed who were *not* reading it to themselves could be hearing it for the first time or repeatedly by choice or custom. How did it sound in worship then? As it does now? How are the climactic emphases indicated? Could Jesus' message in John 15, "I am the vine, you are the branches," have been designed to be rhetorically stunning in many beloved and sacred Last Supper services?

5. Historical criticism studies the passage's original setting in specific time and place. How does the vine-and-branches discourse disclose the mood and message of Jesus' last moments with his most intimate followers on the night of the arrest in the garden? What archeological information and historical resources from the ancient world give precise background for when the incident occurred, where it took place, who wrote it, or at least what were the circumstances that surrounded the writing down? Archaeology today has developed a massive number of supportive areas of endeavor, for example: in language and manuscript (epigraphical) study; in social anthropology, where living societies today are systematically compared with former ones; and in engineering, where technological and scientific achievements are charted in intermittent declines and advances. The wealth of relevant information has enabled our times to know more about the Bible and its cultural presuppositions than people in the Bible knew about each other's!

6. Tradition criticism traces many stages in the development of the text to see what literary materials (and component oral collections, community recitations, documenting reports, poetic meditations, etc.) are discernable in our present passages. For example, there is strong agreement among many scholars that in the Gospels, Mark's life of Jesus came first, and that Matthew, Luke, and John used Mark's basic formulation of "religious biography-with-a-message" as foundation. The theory of "the priority of Mark" demonstrated by H. J. Holtzmann (1832–1910) pioneered the way to account for similarities in Matthew, Mark, and Luke. Holtzmann notably hypothesized about another source common to Matthew and Luke that Mark did not have. That common block of Jesus information is called "Q" from the German word *Quelle,* meaning "source." Then Matthew had additional information, like the visit of the Magi and certain sayings in the Sermon on the Mount, that Luke evidently did not have. And Luke had special sources about the births of John the Baptist and Jesus, for example, that Matthew did not have. These are now designated respectively "M" and "L." This theory of an early state in the interrelationship of the Synoptic Gospels is referred to as the "Two Document Hypothesis," meaning Mark and Q.

An alternative theory holds that Matthew came first, and Luke, using Matthew as a basis, edited out parts so that the remainder emphasized the concerns of a Gentile audience. Then Mark used first Luke's order and then Matthew's material to harmonize seeming contradictions. A main proponent of this Two *Gospel* Hypothesis today is William Farmer, who finds further political reasons for the predominance of scholarship about the priority of Mark in the German Second Reich. He seeks to emphasize atonement Christology in the early composition of the Gospels, beginning with the priority of Matthew (William R. Farmer, *The Gospel of Jesus: The Pastoral Relevance of the Synoptic Problem* [Louisville, KY: Westminster/John Knox Press, 1994]).

The processes of study here are those of separating out and bringing together, of looking at a small part in great detail, then seeing it in its context of a larger whole. This is a pie cut at first into flat pieces (like pizza) that fit into some kind of a circle; subsequently, cuts are made in another direction and it comes to have distinct layers like a cake. Or, to change the metaphor, we can think of an archaeological mound of many cities that is cut downward in small areas to find strata of civilizations. Imbedded columns in one house have been salvaged from an earlier temple in a city below. Each layer is examined and hypothetically reconstructed to see the relationships to other layers and then to larger entities, districts, nations, and societies as "wholes."

7. *Redaction criticism* has been *the focus of the present book.* "Redactor" means "editor," and redaction criticism does presuppose the study and contributions of all the approaches above. But since the others, especially form criticism and tradition criticism, can become intensely concerned with very small pieces and subunits of biblical text and their possible former contexts, redaction criticism wants to see the finished whole as it is now before us in our own hands. New Testament studies have the striking opportunity to view the wholeness of each Gospel and to contemplate how the recorded incidents in Jesus' life are selected and developed to present four distinct portraits.

When the same event is presented in all four Gospels, we can see amazingly clearly four different interpretive themes operating; when there are four sets of similar materials on various subjects, we can pursue specialized interests with remarkable results. We can study a particular episode, such as the feeding of a multitude, the dinner when a woman ministered to Jesus' feet, the trial before Pilate, the words from the cross, or the discovery of the empty tomb. We can compare all accounts in their distinctive contexts and draw from them what *each Gospel* writer is helping us to understand about one key event or one kind of event concerning Jesus. The Bible does not give us one definitive narrative of the "right" life and message of Jesus; to our knowledge Jesus did not write down his own book, but we have four distinctive vantage points of who Jesus was and is. All four Gospels are finished, complete canonized works that in their entireties and together as a family are the lenses through which the church is called to see the living Lord. Christianity impoverishes itself when it presents to the world one pasted together and mixed-up Jesus. It denies the breadth and depth of the sparkling variety of God's greatest revelation yet given to humanity when it amalgamates and "harmonizes" into someone's so-called "media masterpiece" something that overlooks what is in the Bible. At times it is helpful to focus on the treasures of a microscopic dot, especially when it may be macrocosmic in value, but to ignore, deny, block out, or cut away major portions of the Christian Scriptures can lead to disasters worse than provincialism, heresies, and religious wars. Wonders of interpretive freedom and tolerance can come from receiving the variety of the colors of God's brilliant grace shining through the four Gospel portraits. What God meant for us to know about the historical Jesus who journeyed on the roads of Roman Palestine can be found by letting the four Gospels guide us, as it has the church, into the revelation of the real and living Lord.

INDEX

This Index is for important terminology not listed in the Table of Contents. It indicates both terms and the beginning places or instances where main contexts are discussed. It may be helpful to keep in mind that, in general, topics about Matthew's Gospel occur on pages 39–75; Mark's, 76–15; Luke's, 116–43; and John's, 144–75.

Because the Appendix topics are not listed in the Table of Contents, they are indexed here; however, the Appendix entries do not include a number of instances where the topics also occur in the Bible study.

Index Key

Roman numerals (e.g., xiv)—indicates a page number in the Preface
ff—means "and the pages following" the index entry

⚠ Always soak the plank before using. A soaked plank produces maximum smoke and is less likely to burn. Submerge it in water at least an hour. Weigh it down with a can.

⚠ Food that touches the wood takes on more flavor, so arrange it on the wooden plank in a single layer.

⚠ A rotisserie slowly rotates food impaled on a spit over a heat source. This process allows heat to circulate evenly around meat or poultry while it self-bastes with its own juices. Most rotisseries are motorized. Extra-large rotisseries accommodate whole carcasses as shown above. Smaller rotisseries are made to fit family-size grills.

Braggin' Rights

As long as there's been a South, we've loved barbecue—the one food that defines us most as a region. From the nation's capital, south to Florida, across the Gulf states, to the Oklahoma plains, barbecue scents nearly all Southern breezes.

"There are four barbecue meccas," says Carolyn Wells, executive director of the Kansas City Barbeque Society. "The Carolinas form the cradle of American barbecue. Memphis is the undisputed pork barbecue capital of the world. The entire state of Texas considers itself a capital. Kansas City is the melting pot, where all regional styles come together."

The definition of **SOUTH CAROLINA** barbecue is as hard to nail down as hickory smoke. Folks along the coast and up toward Columbia prefer the state's trademark mustard sauce, while the people of the Pee Dee region are passionate about **vinegar-and-pepper sauce.** Upstate, they favor **red sauce.** In some establishments, you'll find all three flavors on the table; in others, serving them together is an act of heresy. And then, depending on to whom you're talking, the

geographic boundaries of these preferences can vary widely. Though a few restaurants outside the state may serve **mustard sauce,** its true home is mid- to lower-South Carolina.

In **NORTH CAROLINA,** barbecue means pork—cooked slowly, finely chopped, and seasoned with controversy. A culinary rift (some say battle line) cleaves the state into two deeply held barbecue traditions. These two traditions are **Eastern-style and Lexington-style** sometimes called Piedmont-style. Each elevates pork into a distinctively delicious offering that is aromatic, tender, and succulent. The fuss is part pride, part preference. **EASTERN-STYLE** barbecue is **prepared from the whole hog;** the cooked meat is finely chopped and seasoned with a sauce of **vinegar, salt, black pepper, and red pepper. LEXINGTON-STYLE** barbecue cooks only **pork shoulders,** which are chopped (also sliced) and seasoned with **ketchup, brown or white sugar, salt, pepper,** and other seasonings that impart a sweet flavor. Each tradition offers preferred sides and sweet tea, but coleslaw—**barbecue slaw**—reinforces the regional schism. Made from finely shredded or coarsely chopped cabbage, it's never creamy and comes in three colors: white, yellow, or red. **Eastern slaw** is dressed with

Pit Stops

From pig stands and rib shacks to smokehouses and smoke pits, here's a listing of joints we visited on our search for the best Southern barbecue.

Alabama
■ **Archibald's BBQ**
1211 Martin Luther King Blvd.
Northport, AL 35476
(205) 345-6861
other locations in Alabama

■ **Big Bob Gibson Bar-B-Q**
1715 Sixth Avenue SE
Decatur, AL 35601
(256) 350-6969
www.bigbobgibsonbbq.com
other locations in Decatur

■ **Bob Sykes BarB-Q**
1724 Ninth Avenue North
Bessemer, AL 35020
(205) 426-1400
ordering info: 1-800-447-9537
www.bobsykes.com

■ **Chuck's Bar-B-Que**
905 Short Avenue
Opelika, AL 36801
(334) 749-4043

■ **Dreamland Bar-B-Que**
5535 15th Avenue East
Tuscaloosa, AL 35405
(205) 758-8135
ordering info: 1-800-752-0544
www.dreamlandbbq.com
other locations in Alabama
and in Atlanta

■ **Whitt's Barbecue**
1397 East Elm Street
Athens, AL 35611
(256) 232-7928

Arkansas
■ **McClard's Bar-B-Q**
505 Albert Pike
Hot Springs, AR 71901
(501) 623-9665 or toll free
1-866-622-5273
www.mcclards.com

■ **Sim's Bar-B-Que**
716 West 33rd Street
Little Rock, AR 72206
(501) 372-6868
other locations in
Little Rock

Delaware
■ **Where Pigs Fly**
617 East Lockerman Street
Dover, DE 19901
(302) 678-0586
www.wherepigsflyrestaurant.com

Florida
■ **B.C.'s General Store**
8730 County Road 48
Yalaha, FL 34797
(352) 324-3730

■ **Brodus' Bar-B-Que**
103 Taylor Avenue
Groveland, FL 34736
(352) 429-4707

■ **Bubbalou's Bodacious Bar-B-Que**
12100 Challenger Parkway
Orlando, FL 32826
(407) 423-1212
www.bubbalous.com
other locations in Florida

■ **Choctaw Willy's**
214 West Broad Street
Groveland, FL 34736
(352) 429-4188
other locations in Florida

■ **Jack's Barbeque**
100 South U.S. 27
Minneola, FL 34711
(352) 394-2673

■ **King's Taste Barbecue**
503 Palmetto Street
Eustis, FL 32726
(352) 589-0404

mayonnaise (white) or mustard (yellow) and sweetened with sugar and even chopped sweet pickles, giving a mellow taste. **Lexington slaw** is red because it is dressed with vinegar, sugar, and barbecue dip—a sweet-flavored vinegar-based sauce—or ketchup, giving a sweet-tart, peppy flavor. Slaw is indispensable, whether served alongside or on the sandwich.

For some purists, the border of the barbecue belt goes no further than North Carolina's state line. But if you are 'cue hopping across the **DELMARVA PENINSULA,** you're in for a surprise. Here, you'll find plates piled with meat from **pulled pork to chicken** and sauces that range from **Texas-style to South Carolina mustard-based.**

In **DELAWARE AND MARYLAND,** where broilers, roosters, and hens outnumber people, **slow-roasted chicken halves and quarters** are the barbecue of choice. In **VIRGINIA,** there's a barbecue joint every few miles, and, not surprisingly, **pork is king.** Still, the sauces vary from South Carolina mustard-style to Memphis-style reds, depending on who started the restaurant. **Red sauce** tends to rule in central Virginia. **Vinegar-style** eastern North Carolina barbecue is found in southernmost spots.

The heart of barbecue beats in **MEMPHIS,** a city of 1.1 million people, where more than one hundred restaurants specialize in **pork and ribs** traditionally slow-cooked over coals. A Memphis native and amateur cook who competes in the Memphis in May World Championship Barbecue Cooking Contest says it best when asked where good barbecue is prepared elsewhere in Tennessee. "Nowhere," he states. "Our worst is better than the best anywhere else."

In **TEXAS,** African-Americans, Anglos, Germans, and Mexicans have tossed their flavors onto the grills and pits. **German smoked sausages** (often in hot links) and **Mexican** *cabrito* (goat) join **chicken, pork ribs, slaw, beans, and potato salad** on plates. **Beef brisket** stars, however, with a sweet, hot sauce (properly served on the side) in a color between Texas burnt orange and Aggie maroon.

more **Pit Stops**

Georgia
■ **Colonel Poole's Bar-B-Q**
164 Craig Street
East Ellijay, GA 30539
(706) 635-4100
www.poolesbarbq.com
■ **Fresh Air Barbecue**
1164 Highway 42 South
Jackson, GA 30233
(770) 775-3182
www.freshairbarbecue.com
other locations in Georgia
■ **Johnny Harris Restaurant & Lounge**
1651 East Victory Drive
Savannah, GA 31404
(912) 354-7810
ordering info: 1-888-547-2823
www.johnnyharris.com
■ **Old Clinton Barbecue House**
4214 Gray Highway
Gray, GA 31032
(478) 986-3225
■ **Pink Pig**
824 Cherrylog Street
Cherrylog, GA 30522
(706) 276-3311
■ **Sprayberry's Barbecue**
229 Jackson Street
Newnan, GA 30263
(770) 253-4421
www.sprayberrysbbq.com

Kentucky
■ **Carr's Barn**
216 West Broadway Street
Mayfield, KY 42066
(270) 247-8959
■ **George's Bar-B-Q**
1362 East Fourth Street
Owensboro, KY 42303
(270) 926-9276
■ **Hill's Bar-B-Que**
1002 Cuba Road
Mayfield, KY 42066
(270) 247-9121
■ **Moonlite Bar-B-Q Inn**
2840 West Parrish Avenue
Owensboro, KY 42301
(270) 684-8143 or
1-800-322-8989
www.moonlite.com
■ **Old Hickory Pit Bar-B-Que**
338 Washington Avenue
Owensboro, KY 42301
(270) 926-9000
■ **Ole South BBQ**
3523 State 54 East
Owensboro, KY 42303
(270) 926-6464

■ **Shady Rest Barbecue Inn**
3955 East Fourth Street
Owensboro, KY 42303
(270) 926-8234
■ **Starnes Bar-B-Q**
1008 Joe Clifton Drive
Paducah, KY 42001
(270) 444-9555

Louisiana
■ **Grayson's Barbeque**
5849 State 71
Clarence, LA 71414
(318) 357-0166
■ **Pig Stand Restaurant**
318 East Main Street
Ville Platte, LA 70586
(337) 363-2883

Maryland
■ **Em-Ing's**
9811 Whaleyville Road
Bishopville, MD 21813
(410) 352-5711 or toll free
1-888-458-7436
www.em-ings.com
other locations in Delaware

Mississippi
■ **Goldie's Trail Bar-B-Q**
4127 Washington Street
Vicksburg, MS 39180
(601) 636-9839
■ **Leatha's Bar-B-Que Inn**
6374 U.S. 98 West
Hattiesburg, MS 39402
(601) 271-6003
www.leathas.com
■ **Westside Bar-B-Que**
Highway 30 West
New Albany, MS 38652
(662) 534-7276

Missouri
■ **Arthur Bryant's BBQ**
1727 Brooklyn Avenue
Kansas City, MO 64127
(816) 231-1123
www.arthurbryantsbbq.com
other locations in Kansas City
■ **Danny Edwards Famous Kansas City Barbecue**
1227 Grand Blvd.
Kansas City, MO 64106
(816) 283-0880
■ **Fiorella's Jack Stack Barbecue**
101 West 22nd Street
Suite 300
Kansas City, MO 64108
(816) 472-7427
www.jackstackbbq.com
other locations in Missouri
and Kansas
■ **Gates Bar-B-Q**
1325 East Emmanuel Cleaver Blvd.
Kansas City, MO 64110
(816) 531-7522
www.gatesbbq.com
other locations in Missouri
and Kansas

States west of the Mississippi and east of the Red River blend Eastern and Texas traditions with their own unique styles. **ARKANSAS** feels the tug of Southeast and Southwest. It's a state divided between **beef and pork** and colored with **clear, yellow, and dark red sauces**. **OKLAHOMA** welcomes barbecued **bologna** to the plate. It accompanies beef and pork, and also forms one layer of a sandwich, the "Badwich," which is served in **TULSA** piled high with sausage, beef, ham, and chopped pork.

KANSAS CITY is no place for a vegetarian. If it runs, flies, walks, swims, or crawls, chances are it's smoked on a barbecue pit somewhere in Kansas City. In this town, nearly everyone is a "barbecutioner." October's American Royal Barbecue competition draws around 400 teams, while residents can dine at some 85 restaurants in the metropolitan area. The aromas of roasting pork and beef waft under many a visitor's nose before he or she steps off the plane at Kansas City International. Stroll into a local grocery store, and you'll find 75-plus brands of barbecue sauce sitting on the shelves. College professors debate the finer points of **tomato- versus vinegar-based sauces,** and on certain windless days, Kansas City seems to linger under a smoky haze. While the rest of the South squabbles over how and what to barbecue, Kansas City has simply adopted every conceivable style. **Hot sauces vie with sweet. Pork rubs up against brisket. Turkey, ham, and chicken share plates with spareribs, lamb ribs, baby back ribs, and beef ribs.** Kansas City sauces tend not to be as vinegary as in Memphis or as spicy as in Texas.

In **KENTUCKY,** a once-plentiful but now-vanished local resource—**sheep**—has given **OWENSBORO** a special place in the world of barbecue. Why mutton? Simple: It was available. In the late 1800s, Dutch settlers raised lots of sheep in Daviess County. When it came time to contribute to the church picnic, local farmers would often butcher a sheep that was past its prime as a breeder or wool producer. The meat of mature sheep can be tough, so the slow, tenderizing process of barbecuing became the cooking method of choice. Today, most of the mutton comes from the sheep belt running from Texas into Canada, but the folks in Owensboro still favor mutton's distinctive taste.

Drive 50 miles in any direction in **GEORGIA,** and you'll find barbecue **pulled here, chopped there, and soaked in sauces of all kinds.** While much of Georgia runs red with ketchup, **COLUMBUS** favors mustard. As one restaurant owner surmises, "It goes back to the African-American cooks here. All the old barbecue places used mustard."

BARBECUE RESTAURANT, JOINT, OR DIVE?

In the upside-down world of barbecue, many think the food is better if it's served in a joint or in a dive. Here's a handy field guide of definitions.

■ **Restaurant:** Matching furniture, taped music, printed menus. Accepts credit cards. Member of the chamber of commerce.

■ **Joint:** Screened door, jukebox, beer, chalkboard menu. The cook is nicknamed Bubba. Cash only.

■ **Dive:** Torn screened door, tattoos, beer, whiskey, flies. No menu. The cook's real name is Bubba, and she has a prison record. You don't tell your mama you go there.

more Pit Stops

■ **Earl's Rib Palace**
6816 North Western Avenue
Oklahoma City, OK 73116
(405) 843-9922
www.earlsribpalace.com
other locations in Oklahoma City

■ **Elmer's B.B.Q.**
4130 South Peoria Avenue
Tulsa, OK 74105
(918) 742-6702
www.elmersbbq.net

North Carolina

■ **Allen & Son Pit-Cooked Bar-B-Q**
6203 Millhouse Road
Chapel Hill, NC 27516
(919) 942-7576
other locations in North Carolina

■ **Barbecue Center**
900 North Main Street
Lexington, NC 27292
(336) 248-4633
www.barbecuecenter.com

■ **Bill's Barbecue & Chicken**
3007 Downing Street SW
Wilson, NC 27893
(252) 237-4372 or
1-800-682-4557
www.bills-bbq.com

■ **Jimmy's BBQ**
1703 Cotton Grove Road
Lexington, NC 27292
(336) 357-2311

■ **Lexington Barbecue**
10 U.S. 29/70 South
Lexington, NC 27295
(336) 249-9814

■ **Rick and Tina Sauls' Café**
8627 Caratoke Highway
Harbinger, NC 27941
(252) 491-5000

■ **Skylight Inn**
4617 Lee Street
Ayden, NC 28513
(252) 746-4113

■ **Speedy's Barbecue**
1317 Winston Road
Lexington, NC 27292
(336) 248-2410

■ **Stamey's Barbecue**
2206 High Point Road
Greensboro, NC 27403
(336) 299-9888
www.stameys.com
other locations in Greensboro

■ **Whitley's Barbecue**
Route 11 South
Murfreesboro, NC 27855
(252) 398-4884

■ **Wilber's Barbecue**
4172 U.S. 70 East
Goldsboro, NC 27534
(919) 778-5218 or
1-888-778-0838
other locations in Goldsboro

Oklahoma

■ **Bad Brad's Bar-B-Q**
1215 West Main Street
Pawhuska, OK 74056
(918) 287-1212
www.badbrads.com

South Carolina

■ **Bessinger's Bar-B-Que House**
1602 Savannah Highway
Charleston, SC 29407
(843) 556-1354
www.bessingersbbq.com

■ **Big T Barbecue**
7535-C Garners Ferry Road
Columbia, SC 29209
(803) 776-7132
other locations in South Carolina

■ **Bryan's The Pink Pig Bar-B-Que**
Highway 170-A
Hardeeville, SC 29927
(843) 784-3635

■ **Dukes Bar-B-Que**
789 Chestnut Street
Orangeburg, SC 29115
(803) 534-9418
other locations in South Carolina

■ **Jackie Hite's Barbecue**
Highway 23
Leesville, SC 29070
(803) 532-3354

■ **McCabe's BBQ**
480 North Brooks Street
Manning, SC 29102
(803) 435-2833

■ **Shuler's Bar-B-Que**
419 Highway 38 West
Latta, SC 29565
(843) 752-4700

Tennessee

■ **Bar-B-Q Shop**
1782 Madison Avenue
Memphis, TN 38104
(901) 272-1277
www.dancingpigs.com

■ **Buddy's Bar-B-Q**
5806 Kingston Pike
Knoxville, TN 37919
(865) 588-0051
www.buddysbarbq.com
other locations in Tennessee

■ **Corky's Ribs & BBQ**
5259 Poplar Avenue
Memphis, TN 38119
(901) 685-9744 or
1-800-926-7597
www.corkysbbq.com
other locations in the U.S.

■ **Hog Heaven**
115 27th Avenue North
Nashville, TN 37203
(615) 329-1234
www.hogheavenbbq.com
other locations in Tennessee

In **ALABAMA,** sauces coat meat in many colors. A **light vinegar** soaks the chopped pork in **ATHENS.** In **DECATUR,** a **tangy mayonnaise sauce** flavors chicken, but diners may also select a **mild red sauce or a fiery vinegar** and then douse the flames with cool cream pies. As one *Southern Living* editor explains, "Sometimes the pie is as important as the pig."

Smoking is a popular method of outdoor cooking in **FLORIDA.** Just about any meat, foul, or fish that can be smoked is smoked, including mullet, snapper, shellfish, game, pork, beef, and turkey. From the tip of the Keys to the top of the Panhandle, Floridians savor barbecue today just as they have done through the ages. Each bite taken here has been seasoned by natives, immigrants, retirees, and folks just passing through.

In the gumbo and jambalaya provinces of **LOUISIANA,** what is considered traditional Southern barbecue often takes a backseat to the pot dishes of New Orleans and Cajun Country. However, contrary to popular opinion, for those bent on barbecue, all is not lost. In **VILLE PLATTE,** on the northern cusp of Cajun Country, locals dote on turtle stew and tasso and, yes, **smoked pork ribs** smothered in an **onion-and-garlic barbecue sauce.** Then there's **NATCHITOCHES,** the first European settlement in what is now the state of Louisiana. In this Central Louisiana town, you can see that French influences endure. Order a barbecue sandwich in nearby **CLARENCE,** and you have your choice of smoked ham or beef served on homemade French bread, or **"frog bun"** as some locals—in a jab at the French—sometimes call it.

Not surprisingly, barbecue tastes develop close to home. Despite the regional preferences, most Southerners agree that barbecue is the food of home that feeds the heart.

Tennessee *(continued)*

■ **Jim Neely's Interstate Bar-B-Que**
2265 South Third Street
Memphis, TN 38109
(901) 775-2304
www.jimneelysinterstate
barbecue.com

■ **Neely's Bar-B-Que**
670 Jefferson Avenue
Memphis, TN 38103
(901) 521-9798 or
1-888-780-7427
other locations in Tennessee

■ **Rib & Loin**
5946 Brainerd Road
Chattanooga, TN 37421
(423) 499-6465
other location in Tennessee

■ **Shuford's Smokehouse**
924 Signal Mountain Road
Chattanooga, TN 37405
(423) 267-0080

■ **The Rendezvous**
52 South Second Street
Memphis, TN 38103
(901) 523-2746

Texas

■ **Black's BBQ**
215 North Main Street
Lockhart, TX 78644
(512) 398-2712
www.blacksbbq.com

■ **Cooper's Old Time Pit Bar-B-Que**
505 West Dallas
Llano, Texas 78643
(325) 247-5713
www.coopersbbq.com

■ **Country Tavern**
Highway 31, west of Kilgore
Kilgore, TX 75663
(903) 984-9954

■ **Kreuz Market**
619 North Colorado Street
Lockhart, TX 78644
(512) 398-2361
www.kreuzmarket.com

■ **Lone Star BBQ**
2010 South Bridge Street
Brady, TX 76825
(915) 597-1936

■ **Louie Mueller BBQ**
206 West Second Street
Taylor, TX 76574
(512) 352-6206

■ **Meyer's Elgin Smokehouse**
188 Highway 290
Elgin, TX 78621
(512) 281-3331
www.meyerselginsausage.com

■ **The Salt Lick**
18001 FM 1826
Driftwood, TX 78619
(512) 894-3117
www.saltlickbbq.net

■ **Stubb's Bar-B-Q**
801 Red River
Austin, TX 78701
(512) 480-8341
www.stubbsbbq.com

Virginia

■ **Allman's Bar-B-Que**
1299 Jeff Davis Highway
Fredericksburg, VA 22401
(540) 373-9881

■ **King's Barbecue No.1**
3221 West Washington Street
Petersburg, VA 23803
(804) 732-5861

■ **Olde Virginia Barbecue**
35 Meadow View Avenue
Rocky Mount, VA 24151
(540) 489-1788

■ **Pierce's Pitt Bar-B-Que**
447 East Rochambeau Drive
Williamsburg, VA 23185
(757) 565-2955

■ **Short Sugar's**
2215 Riverside Drive
Danville, VA 24540
(434) 793-4800

■ **The Smokey Pig**
212 South Washington Hwy.
Ashland, VA 23005
(804) 798-4590

Washington, D.C.

■ **Capital Q**
707 H Street NW
Washington, DC 20001
(202) 347-8396

■ **Old Glory All-American Bar-B-Que**
3139 M Street NW
Washington, DC 20007
(202) 337-3406
www.oldglorybbq.com

■ **Rocklands Barbeque and Grilling Company**
2418 Wisconsin Avenue NW
Washington, DC 20007
(202) 333-2558
www.rocklands.com

West Virginia

■ **Big Frank's Bar-B-Que**
1629 West Virginia Avenue
Clarksburg, WV 26301
(304) 623-1009

■ **Dirty Ernie's Rib Pit**
310 Keller Avenue
Fayetteville, WV 25840
(304) 574-4822
www.dirtyernies.com

■ **The Teays House Family Restaurant**
120 Carl's Lane
Scott Depot, WV 25560
(304) 757-5265

■ **Three Little Pigs, Inc.**
HC 37 Box 220
Lewisburg, WV 24901
(304) 645-3270

Barbecue
Cook-offs
and
Festivals

These barbecue cook-offs and festivals, held
from Memorial Day weekend to Labor Day weekend,
are sanctioned by the International Barbeque
Cookers Association, Kansas City Barbeque
Society, and Memphis in May.

International Barbeque Cookers Association

■ Colorado County Fair BBQ Cook-off, Columbus, TX
Contact Fausta Kaiser at (979) 732-5030, or e-mail coloradocountybbq@yahoo.com

■ Annual American Legion Barbeque Cook-off, Clifton, TX
Contact American Legion at (254) 675-8782.

■ Annual Itasca Chamber of Commerce BBQ Cook-off, Itasca, TX
Contact Bob Wilson at (254) 687-2331, or e-mail bwilson@hilcozap.net

Kansas City Barbeque Society

■ American Royal Barbecue Contest, Kansas City, MO
Contact Sharon Brown at (816) 569-4030, or email BBQ@americanroyal.com

■ Annual Blue Ridge BBQ Festival, Tryon, NC
Contact Peggy Bolen at (828) 859-7427, e-mail bobbolen@alltel.net, or visit www.blueridgebbqfestival.com

■ Platte City Barbecue Fest Missouri State Championship, Platte City, MO
Contact Karen Wagoner at (816) 858-5270, or e-mail karenwagoner@earthlink.net

■ Wild Turkey Bourbon & Lawrenceburg Kiwanis Club Tennessee State Championship BBQ Cook-off, Lawrenceburg, TN
Contact Carl Counce at (931) 762-3399, or e-mail ccounce@bellsouth.net

■ Annual Pawnee Bill Smoke-off, Pawnee, OK
Contact Sandy Beaudoin at (918) 762-3205, or e-mail pawneetrader@sbcglobal.net

■ Tennessee Amazin' Blazin BBQ Cook-off, Lebanon, TN
Contact Kristina McKee or Wanda Bates at (615) 444-5730, or e-mail tnamazinblazin@aol.com

■ Whistle Stop Festival & Rocket City BBQ Cook-off, Huntsville, AL
Contact Dorothy Havens at (256) 564-8116, e-mail dorothy.havens@hsvcity.com, or visit www.rocketcitybbq.com

■ Florence Labor Day BBQ Cook-off, Florence, KS
Contact Les Allison at (620) 878-4310, or e-mail lesallison@kans.com

■ Benton County Fair & BBQ Cook-off, Ashland, MS
Contact Cathy McMullen at (662) 224-6330, or e-mail cathym@ext.msstate.edu

■ Smoke on the Water BBQ & Music Festival, Pine Bluff, AR
Contact Ron Cates at (870) 537-8175, or e-mail ronnie@catesandcompany.com

Memphis in May

■ Safeway's National Capital Barbecue Battle, Pennsylvania Avenue, Washington, D.C.
Contact Allen Tubis at (301) 860-0630, e-mail barbecue1@aol.com, or visit www.bbq-usa.com

■ Memphis in May World Championship Barbecue Cooking Contest, Memphis, TN
Contact www.memphisinmay.org

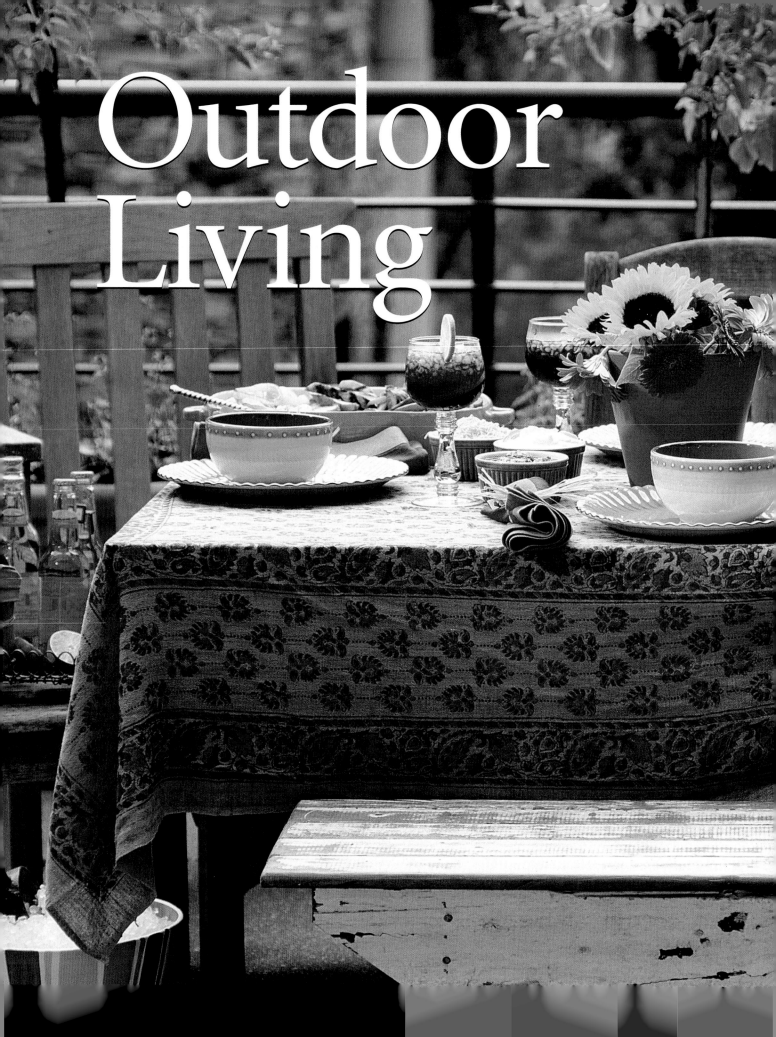

Outdoor Living

Setting the Scene

A little ingenuity ensures that your outdoor dining experience is comfortable, relaxed, and stylish.

A Handy Sideboard

A simple deck bench is the inspiration for this multiuse outdoor table.

■ To create a buffet from a standard bench design, double the height of the bench from 18 to 36 inches.

■ Include a shelf underneath to store such items as an ice chest, which is especially useful when entertaining.

■ Craft a skirt from outdoor fabric, and attach it to the buffet with a tension rod. It hides the storage shelf and gives the buffet indoor style.

■ For entertaining at night, add lamps to the table.

Table to Go

If you don't have an outdoor dining table, create one on the spot.

- Start with a 7-foot-long folding table.
- To accommodate eight guests, place three 40- x 30-inch plywood rectangles over the top of the table to form one extended 40- x 90-inch top. Using three sections instead of one makes the top more convenient to transport and store.
- Install latch hooks and eyes underneath each corner to lock the pieces together when placed side by side. Fit small wooden pegs into adjacent drilled holes for a tight fit.
- When the party is over, lift off the plywood, stack the pieces, and fold up the table. The parts can be stored easily under a bed, in a closet, or in a garage.

Gather the Goods

Having everything you need on hand in advance of the party means a more relaxed prep time.

■ Stock up on baskets. They're great for serving breads, chips, and cookies.

■ Before a party, bring some of your indoor pillows outside and place them on chairs to add color and comfort.

■ If you're short on outdoor furniture, carry ottomans outside for extra seating, use a tea cart as a bar, and clean up a potting bench to serve as a buffet.

■ String white Christmas lights on deck rails for sparkle.

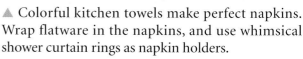

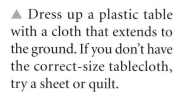

▲ Colorful kitchen towels make perfect napkins. Wrap flatware in the napkins, and use whimsical shower curtain rings as napkin holders.

▲ Dress up a plastic table with a cloth that extends to the ground. If you don't have the correct-size tablecloth, try a sheet or quilt.

▶ Paint the inside of terra-cotta pot saucers with acrylic paint to coordinate with your table setting. When the paint dries, the saucers serve as colorful coasters. Stack additional sets of coasters and tie with ribbon to give as party favors to guests.

CASUAL CARD HOLDERS

Terra-cotta pot feet (normally used to elevate planters) make perfect place-card holders at a barbecue. Use them as easels to hold cards in place.

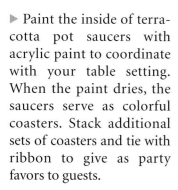

Tips for the Table

A few decorative touches at the table make your barbecue seem even more special.

■ Lay out serving pieces and utensils ahead so they'll be handy when the food comes off the grill.

■ Pair patterned dishes with solid-colored napkins and vice versa. Mix and match different-colored napkins, and then embellish each place setting with a fresh flower or herb sprig.

■ Turn place mats vertically for a creative twist and to make room for more guests at the table.

■ When guests bring food to the barbecue, use a sticky note or tape to label each dish on the underside with the name of the person who brought it.

■ For candlelight, use votive holders, lanterns, or glass vases to avoid open flames.

▼ For colorful accents, fill vases with aquarium sand; set pillar candles securely in the sand.

▲ Use a multi-plant stand to organize condiments and tableware. Toy bugs are a fun addition to the table decorations.

Add Flair
with Flowers

Flowers needn't be fussy. Keep a few key containers on hand for a head start on quick-and-easy arrangements. Here's advice for freshening the scene with blooms.

■ Don't hesitate to use items not traditionally used for floral arranging. If a container won't hold water or is too large, place a jar or cup inside to hold the flowers.

■ Pick up fresh flowers the day before your cookout. Prepare them by stripping the leaves, cutting each stem at an angle under cool running water, and then soaking the stems overnight in a cool place.

■ Arrange the tallest stems first so they set an outline for the bouquet. Insert taller flowers in the center, and fill in with flowers that become progressively shorter as you near the edges of the container.

■ Feel free to supplement garden flowers with blooms purchased from the florist for variety.

■ To keep an arrangement from wilting, place it away from direct sunlight.

■ Keep centerpieces at a height that allows good eye contact among guests.

■ For a long table, use several small arrangements, placing a few blooms in small vases spaced along the length of the table.

▼ Arrange on a coordinating dinner plate small bud vases filled with flowers for an instant centerpiece.

◀ Simple vases, bottles, and canning jars are suitable containers for instant flower arranging. Use a platter to corral a few bedding plants from a garden shop.

▲ Search your kitchen cabinets for an eclectic mix of teapots to compose an interesting—and easy—centerpiece. To arrange long-stemmed flowers, fit a block of water-soaked florist foam in the teapot opening. Insert the flower stems at slight angles to create the appearance of a lush bouquet.

A HINT OF FRAGRANCE

Garnish stemmed glasses with fresh sprigs of rosemary woven around the base. The day before, run cut sprigs under cool water; wrap sprigs in damp paper towels and store in the refrigerator until you're ready to decorate.

Secrets to Great Get-Togethers

Planning ahead is the key to a relaxing party. Here are ways to make the day fun for everyone—even the host and hostess!

Family Reunions

Warm weather and sizzling barbecue signal the season of family gatherings. Follow these suggestions for a carefree event.

Invitations

Clever invitations set the mood for a great party and convey all the essential information so everyone knows "what, when, and where." Here are some pointers.

- Add a personal touch with handwritten invitations. Use standard wording, or show your poetic side with a rhyming verse. Keep the tone and design casual to match the barbecue mood.
- Include the necessary facts—who, what, when, where, why—and the how-tos: how to respond, how to get there, and perhaps how to help (what to bring).
- Use unexpected materials in creative ways. For example, for an outdoor barbecue write party facts on paper fans using a paint pen or permanent marker.
- Include "RSVP" or "please reply" instead of "regrets only." You need to know how many people will be attending.
- "Save-the-date" notices are popular for family reunions and other large parties, where people will be traveling to attend. Make these compatible with the invitations to follow.
- Package your invitations to make a statement. The appearance, the handwriting, and the stamps all factor in having your envelopes grab attention. Visit your post office, or go to www.usps.com to order designer stamps online.

REUNION SURVIVAL TIPS

A good time had by all is the goal of every reunion. Here are a few considerations that can make things run smoothly.

- Simplify bookkeeping by choosing one person to pay deposits in advance for any rentals—location, cooking equipment, seating—and the balances upon arrival.
- Spread the fun around: Ask each family to prepare a meal and bring a snack and dessert to share.
- Find out about special events in the area, consider having a family talent show or sing-along to help pass the time, and don't forget to bring the equipment for outdoor games.
- A group that arrives early can call others to request last-minute or forgotten items.

Tips for Take-Alongs

Transporting food and other amenities to an outdoor event takes planning. These suggestions make organizing easy.

■ Shop for lightweight, sealable serving containers. Shallow containers provide more surface area to keep food cold and make packing easier.

■ Arrange heavier items on the bottom of your basket and lighter, more fragile items on top. Begin by packing items that you'll need last, ending with the tablecloth.

■ Pack a cooler for perishable food. Use frozen gel packs or ice sealed in zip-top freezer bags to avoid soggy food. Also, freeze water or fruit juice in plastic bottles to help keep food cold; you can have the drinks later with your meal.

■ Know your perishables. Milk products, eggs, poultry, meats, fish, shellfish, cream pies, custards, and creamy salads should be kept at 40° or below. Chill the food before placing it in the cooler.

■ Use a thermos designed to keep hot foods hot.

Don't forget to rinse the thermos with boiling water just before filling it, and heat the food to a high temperature before pouring it into the thermos.

■ On warm days, don't leave food out for more than an hour. Be safe: When in doubt, throw it out.

■ Take along folding chairs for extra seating.

■ Plan entertainment, such as games, and bring a portable CD player and a beach ball, soccer ball, or Frisbee. Add a telescope for stargazing.

■ Tuck in disposable cameras and a small journal to record the memories.

■ For evening gatherings, pack breezeproof torches, hurricane lanterns, or citronella candles, which provide light and repel bugs. To create luminarias, fill paper bags with sand and place a votive holder and candle inside each bag.

■ Bring bug spray, and keep insects away from food with mesh domes.

■ Prepare for cleanup by bringing wet wipes and paper towels. Include two garbage bags: one for trash and one for dirty dishes.

Backyard Buffets

Buffets are a blessing. You can invite more friends than you have seating and set up ahead so guests can dine at their leisure. Consider these ways to make buffet entertaining a breeze.

Strategy

■ Let guests eat with plates on their laps at large, casual parties, but be sure to serve food that doesn't require a knife. (It's awkward, if not dangerous, to cut while balancing a plate on two knees.)

■ When dining alfresco, consider setting up the buffet table inside to keep bugs at bay. Use citronella candles to keep bugs away outdoors.

■ Have a separate table for desserts. Also, put out extra forks and napkins, as guests may not have kept their first set after the main course.

Hardware

■ Use separate dinner, salad, and dessert plates for small seated gatherings. At large barbecues, guests should be able to put all their food on one plate.

■ Use a metal bucket or wall pocket to organize bundles of napkins and flatware.

■ Help traffic flow by placing beverage glasses on a separate table. Offer a variety of sizes, but reserve the largest ones for water. (A 16-ounce cup for wine is just as awkward as a 4-ounce glass for water.)

■ Designate a tray for dirty plates and glasses, and frequently move dirty dishware out of sight.

Table

■ Go with the flow. For large parties, set out a double-sided buffet to avoid bottlenecks. Circular tables are fine for small parties. Ask a friend to be first in line in case other guests are hesitant to begin.

■ Set up the buffet table in logical order. Keep flatware and napkins together at the end for guests to pick up after getting their food.

■ Use varying heights for visual appeal. Place food on pedestals or over sturdy cloth-covered containers. Fill vertical space with flowers or breadsticks.

■ Have additional trays of food ready so that you can replenish by exchanging a full tray for an empty one.

■ Fill serving bowls at least three-fourths full for a sumptuous spread. Bread and buns can spill over to give the look of abundance. Use simple garnishes.

Drink Details

■ A gracious host offers each guest upon arrival something to drink: iced tea, soft drink, wine, or spirited beverage. However, an elaborate bar setup is not necessary. Place the bar out of the main traffic flow to give room for guests to mingle while getting their drinks.

RAISE THE BAR

Before the crowd gathers, check your supply of bar equipment. Here's a list to get you started.

■ Bar glasses
■ Jiggers
■ Blender (Purchase an extra canister to handle a large party.)
■ Mixing/serving pitcher
■ Ice bucket and scoop
■ Corkscrews
■ Bottle opener, stoppers
■ Sharp knife and small cutting board
■ Party tub
■ Cocktail napkins

■ For a small barbecue, offer a limited selection of beverages, such as wine or beer, lemonade, and one special mixed drink. For a large party, offer a wider variety of mixed drinks.

■ Have a supply of sparkling and mineral waters, fruit juices, and nonalcoholic beer on hand.

■ To make the bar area look inviting, set beverage supplies on an attractive cart, tray, table, or counter.

■ A wheelbarrow makes a handy ice chest for beverages. If your wheelbarrow is used, line it with a plastic tablecloth.

Do the Math

Plan on approximately two drinks per hour per guest. To help in planning, count on these figures:

■ There are four 6-ounce servings in each 750-milliliter bottle of wine.

■ There are about 17 drinks per 750-milliliter bottle of liquor when 1½ ounces are used per drink.

■ One 10-ounce bottle of mixer per person is usually sufficient.

■ For large parties, consider a keg of beer. It makes for easy serving and serves 30 to 40 guests.

Barbecue Bounty

Blackberry Iced Tea,
page 50

Thirst Quenchers and Nibbles

It sure gets hot on long summer days—especially when the smoker's fired up. Cool off with refreshing tea, fresh-squeezed lemonade, or a spirited beverage. Keep cravings satisfied with a smorgasbord of snacks.

Party Cheese Ball

Party Cheese Ball
Prep: 10 min., Other: 1 hr.

1 (2¼-oz.) jar dried beef, finely chopped, or
   1 (2½-oz.) package thinly sliced ham, chopped
1 (8-oz.) package cream cheese, softened
1 cup finely chopped mixed vegetables of your choice
   (such as green onions, pimiento, and ripe olives)
¼ tsp. garlic powder
¼ tsp. hot sauce
¾ cup chopped pecans or walnuts, toasted
Garnish: fresh parsley sprigs

Combine first 5 ingredients; stir well. Cover and chill at least 1 hour.
Shape cheese mixture into a ball; roll in pecans. Wrap cheese ball in heavy-duty plastic wrap; refrigerate up to 3 days. Garnish, if desired. Serve with unsalted crackers. **Makes** 10 appetizer servings.

Pecan Cheese Ball
Prep: 10 min., Other: 30 min.

2 (8-oz.) packages cream cheese, softened
1 (8-oz.) can crushed pineapple, drained
¼ cup chopped green bell pepper
2 Tbsp. finely chopped onion
1 Tbsp. seasoned salt
2 cups chopped pecans, toasted and divided
Garnishes: pineapple slices, maraschino cherries,
   fresh parsley sprigs

Combine first 5 ingredients; stir in 1 cup pecans. Cover and chill 30 minutes or until firm.
Shape mixture into a ball; roll in remaining 1 cup chopped pecans.
Place cheese ball on a serving platter; garnish, if desired. Serve with crackers, green bell pepper squares, and celery sticks. **Makes** 10 appetizer servings.

Roasted Corn and Avocado Dip
Prep: 10 min., Cook: 15 min., Other: 8 hrs.

If your guests like maximum heat from their jalapeños, chop the peppers—seeds and all.

1 cup frozen whole kernel corn, thawed
2 tsp. olive oil
1 ripe avocado, peeled and mashed
1 ripe avocado, peeled and chopped
¾ cup seeded, diced tomato
3 Tbsp. lime juice
3 Tbsp. chopped fresh cilantro
2 Tbsp. minced onion
2 small canned jalapeño peppers, seeded and diced
2 garlic cloves, minced
½ tsp. salt
¼ tsp. ground cumin

Combine corn and oil in a shallow pan. Bake at 400° for 15 minutes or until corn is lightly browned, stirring occasionally. Cool.
Combine corn, mashed avocado, chopped avocado, and remaining ingredients, stirring well. Cover and chill at least 8 hours before serving. Serve with tortilla chips. **Makes** 2¾ cups.

Guacamole
Prep: 10 min.

5 ripe avocados
½ to ¾ cup reduced-fat sour cream
¼ cup chopped fresh cilantro
3 Tbsp. fresh lime juice
2 Tbsp. Italian dressing
½ tsp. garlic salt
¼ tsp. hot sauce (we tested with Cholula Hot Sauce)

Cut avocados in half. Scoop pulp into a bowl; mash with a potato masher or fork just until slightly chunky. Stir in sour cream and next 5 ingredients. Serve with tortilla chips. **Makes** 4 cups.

Tomato-Basil Dip
Prep: 10 min., Other: 1 hr.

1 cup mayonnaise
½ cup sour cream
½ cup chopped fresh basil
1 Tbsp. tomato paste
1 Tbsp. grated lemon rind

Stir together all ingredients. Cover and chill at least 1 hour or up to 2 days. Serve with fresh vegetables. **Makes** 1½ cups.

Roasted Poblano Guacamole with Garlic and Parsley
Prep: 5 min., Cook: 12 min., Other: 10 min.

Roasted poblanos add spark to the creamy, almost nutty flavor of avocados, especially when bolstered with a little roasted tomato and flat-leaf parsley.

2 poblano chile peppers (about 6 oz.)
2 plum tomatoes (about 6 oz.)
2 garlic cloves, unpeeled
1⅓ cups ripe peeled avocado, seeded and coarsely mashed (about 3 avocados)
3 Tbsp. chopped fresh flat-leaf parsley
2 Tbsp. fresh lime juice
¼ tsp. salt
2 Tbsp. grated queso añejo or Parmesan cheese
2 Tbsp. sliced radishes

Cut poblanos in half lengthwise, and discard seeds and membranes. Place poblano halves, skin sides up, tomatoes, and garlic on an aluminum foil-lined baking sheet.
Broil for 12 minutes or until poblanos are blackened, turning tomatoes once. Place poblanos in a zip-top freezer bag, and seal. Let stand 10 minutes. Peel poblanos, tomatoes, and garlic.
Place poblanos and garlic cloves in a food processor, and pulse until coarsely chopped. Combine poblano mixture, tomato, avocado, parsley, juice, and salt in a bowl. Sprinkle with cheese and radishes. Serve with tortilla chips. **Makes** 2 cups.

Tomato-Basil Dip

Creamy Chipotle-Black Bean Dip
Prep: 5 min.

½ cup sour cream
½ cup prepared black bean dip
1 tsp. minced canned chipotle peppers in adobo sauce
1 tsp. adobo sauce from can
¼ tsp. salt

Stir together all ingredients. Cover and chill until ready to serve. Serve with tortilla chips. **Makes** 1 cup.

White Bean Hummus
Prep: 20 min., Other: 1 hr.

2 garlic cloves
1 tsp. chopped fresh rosemary
2 (15.5-oz.) cans great Northern beans, rinsed and drained
3 Tbsp. lemon juice
3 Tbsp. tahini
¾ tsp. salt
¼ tsp. ground red pepper
¼ cup olive oil
Garnish: paprika

Pulse garlic and rosemary in a food processor 3 or 4 times or until minced.
Add beans and next 4 ingredients; process until smooth, stopping to scrape down sides.
Pour olive oil gradually through food chute with processor running; process until mixture is smooth. Cover and chill 1 hour. Garnish, if desired. Serve with crackers, sliced cucumber, pimiento-stuffed olives, and pitted kalamata olives. **Makes** 3 cups.

Florentine Artichoke Dip
Prep: 5 min., Cook: 25 min.

1 (10-oz.) package frozen chopped spinach, thawed
2 (6-oz.) jars marinated artichoke hearts
3 garlic cloves, minced
½ cup mayonnaise
1½ (8-oz.) packages cream cheese, softened
2 Tbsp. lemon juice
1 cup grated Parmesan cheese
1½ cups fine, dry breadcrumbs

Drain spinach; press between layers of paper towels. Drain and chop artichoke hearts.
Combine spinach, artichoke hearts, garlic, and next 4 ingredients, stirring well. Spoon into a lightly greased 11- x 7-inch baking dish; sprinkle with breadcrumbs.
Bake at 375° for 25 minutes, and serve with crackers or breadsticks. **Makes** 4 cups.

Layered Nacho Dip
Prep: 12 min.

1 (16-oz.) can refried beans
½ (1.25-oz.) package taco seasoning mix (2 Tbsp.)
1 (6-oz.) carton avocado dip or 1 cup guacamole
1 (8-oz.) container sour cream
1 (4½-oz.) can chopped black olives, drained
2 tomatoes, diced
1 small onion, finely chopped
1 (4.5-oz.) can chopped green chiles, undrained
1½ cups (6 oz.) shredded Monterey Jack or Cheddar Jack cheese

Combine beans and seasoning mix; spread in an 11- x 7-inch dish, a 9- or 10-inch deep-dish pieplate, or a cast-iron skillet. Layer avocado dip and remaining ingredients in order listed. Serve with corn or tortilla chips. **Makes** 8 cups.

Blue Cheese-Bacon Dip

Prep: 15 min., Cook: 15 min.

7 bacon slices, chopped
2 garlic cloves, minced
2 (8-oz.) packages cream cheese, softened
⅓ cup half-and-half
4 oz. crumbled blue cheese
2 Tbsp. chopped fresh chives
3 Tbsp. chopped walnuts, toasted

Cook chopped bacon in a skillet over medium-high heat 10 minutes or until crisp. Drain bacon; set aside. Add minced garlic to skillet, and sauté 1 minute.
Beat cream cheese at medium speed with an electric mixer until smooth. Add half-and-half, beating until combined. Stir in bacon, garlic, blue cheese, and chives. Spoon mixture evenly into 4 (1-cup) individual baking dishes.
Bake at 350° for 15 minutes or until golden and bubbly. Sprinkle evenly with chopped walnuts; serve with grape clusters and flatbread or assorted crackers. **Makes** 12 to 15 appetizer servings.

Crab-Stuffed Mushrooms
Prep: 20 min., Cook: 20 min.

1½ lb. very large fresh mushrooms (about 18 mushrooms)
3 Tbsp. butter or margarine
½ cup chopped onion
1 garlic clove, minced
½ cup soft breadcrumbs
¼ cup chopped fresh parsley
2 Tbsp. dry sherry
½ tsp. Worcestershire sauce
½ tsp. salt
¼ tsp. ground red pepper
¼ cup mayonnaise
2 to 3 Tbsp. grated Parmesan cheese
8 oz. fresh lump crabmeat, drained
2 Tbsp. butter or margarine, melted

Remove and chop mushroom stems; set mushroom caps aside.
Melt 3 Tbsp. butter in a large skillet. Add chopped mushroom stems, onion, and garlic; sauté 3 to 5 minutes or until tender. Stir in breadcrumbs and next 7 ingredients until well blended; gently stir in crabmeat.
Spoon crabmeat mixture evenly into mushroom caps, and place on a rack in a broiler pan. Drizzle with 2 Tbsp. melted butter.
Bake at 350° for 20 minutes. **Makes** about 1½ dozen.

Grilled Zucchini-Wrapped Shrimp
Prep: 20 min., Cook: 6 min., Other: 15 min.

1 lb. unpeeled, large fresh shrimp
½ cup fresh lime juice
8 Tbsp. vegetable oil, divided
2 garlic cloves, pressed
¾ tsp. salt
½ tsp. ground red pepper
2 large zucchini

Peel shrimp; devein, if desired.
Combine lime juice, 3 Tbsp. vegetable oil, and next 3 ingredients in a zip-top freezer bag, gently squeezing to blend; add shrimp. Seal and chill 15 minutes.
Remove shrimp from marinade, reserving marinade.
Bring reserved marinade to a boil in a small saucepan; remove from heat.

Cut zucchini lengthwise into thin slices with a vegetable peeler. Wrap each shrimp with a zucchini slice, and secure with a wooden pick. Brush rolls with remaining 5 Tbsp. vegetable oil.
Grill rolls, without grill lid, over medium-high heat (350° to 400°) about 4 minutes.
Brush with reserved marinade; turn and brush again. Grill 2 more minutes or just until shrimp turn pink. Serve shrimp hot or at room temperature. **Makes** 6 appetizer servings.

Coconut Shrimp with Mustard Sauce
Prep: 30 min., Cook: 2 min. per batch

1½ lb. unpeeled, jumbo fresh shrimp
2 cups all-purpose baking mix, divided
1 cup beer
½ tsp. salt
⅛ to ¼ tsp. ground red pepper
3 cups sweetened flaked coconut
Vegetable oil
Mustard Sauce

Peel shrimp, leaving tails intact; devein, if desired. Set aside. Stir together 1 cup baking mix and 1 cup beer until smooth. Stir together remaining 1 cup baking mix, salt, and ground red pepper.
Dredge shrimp in dry mixture, and dip in beer mixture, allowing excess coating to drip.
Gently roll shrimp in flaked coconut.
Pour vegetable oil to a depth of 3 inches into a Dutch oven or heavy saucepan, and heat to 350°. Cook shrimp, in batches, 1 to 2 minutes or until golden; remove shrimp, and drain on paper towels. Serve immediately with Mustard Sauce. **Makes** 10 to 12 appetizer servings.

Mustard Sauce
Prep: 5 min.

½ cup Dijon mustard
2 Tbsp. light brown sugar
2 Tbsp. beer
⅛ to ¼ tsp. ground red pepper

Stir together all ingredients. **Makes** ⅔ cup.

Tabb's Barbecue
Pork, page 110

Great Outdoor Cooking

Get ready to wow family and friends

with restaurant-style barbecue

from your own backyard!

Barbecued and slow-smoked

briskets, ribs, pork shoulders,

chicken, and more have endless

possibilities when firing up the pit.

Barbecue Beef Brisket

Prep: 10 min.; Cook: 4 hrs., 30 min.; Other: 1 hr., 10 min.

The slow cooking of the meat makes this barbecue melt in your mouth—we gave it our best rating.

1 (5- to 6-lb.) boneless beef brisket, trimmed
2 tsp. paprika
½ tsp. pepper
1 (11- x 9-inch) disposable aluminum roasting pan
1 cup water
Hickory chunks
Smoky Barbecue Sauce

Sprinkle brisket with paprika and pepper; rub over surface of roast. Place roast in disposable pan; add 1 cup water, and cover with aluminum foil.
Soak hickory chunks in water to cover 1 hour; drain. Wrap chunks in heavy-duty aluminum foil, and make several holes in foil. Light gas grill on one side; place foil-wrapped chunks directly on hot coals. Let grill preheat 10 to 15 minutes. Place pan with brisket on grate opposite hot coals; cover and grill 3½ to 4 hours or until tender. Turn brisket every hour, adding water as needed. Remove brisket from pan, reserving 1 cup pan drippings for sauce.
Coat food grate with cooking spray; place grate over hot coals. Place brisket on grate; cover and grill 10 to 15 minutes on each side. Let stand 10 minutes before slicing. Slice against grain into thin slices. Serve with Smoky Barbecue Sauce. **Makes** 12 servings.

Smoky Barbecue Sauce
Prep: 5 min., Cook: 18 min.

1 small onion, finely chopped
1 Tbsp. butter or margarine, melted
1 cup reserved pan drippings
½ tsp. pepper
1½ cups ketchup
1 Tbsp. lemon juice
1 Tbsp. Worcestershire sauce
1 tsp. hot sauce

Sauté onion in butter in a large skillet over medium-high heat until tender. Stir in drippings and remaining ingredients. Bring to a boil; reduce heat, and simmer 15 minutes, stirring occasionally. **Makes** 3 cups.

Texas-Smoked Beer-Marinated Brisket

Prep: 10 min.; Cook: 8 hrs.; Other: 8 hrs., 10 min.

1 (8-lb.) boneless beef brisket, untrimmed
1 garlic bulb, peeled
1 Tbsp. salt
1 Tbsp. pepper
2 (12-oz.) cans dark beer
1 (8-oz.) bottle Italian dressing
Mesquite chunks
6 bacon slices

Cut 1-inch-deep slits into brisket with a paring knife; insert garlic cloves into each slit. Rub brisket with salt and pepper, and place in a shallow dish or large zip-top freezer bag. Pour beer and dressing over brisket. Cover or seal, and chill, turning occasionally, 8 hours.
Soak wood chunks in water at least 1 hour.
Remove brisket from marinade, discarding marinade.
Prepare charcoal fire in smoker; let burn 15 to 20 minutes.
Drain chunks, and place on coals. Place water pan in smoker; add water to depth of fill line.
Place brisket on lower food grate; arrange bacon on top of brisket, and close smoker.
Smoke 4 hours; remove bacon, and cook 4 more hours or until a meat thermometer registers 155°. Let stand 10 minutes before slicing. **Makes** 8 servings.

> 66 Texas likes to bill itself as 'a whole other country.' So is its barbecue—smoky blends of beef and pork from the Anglo and African-American traditions by way of the Deep South and seasoned with accents from Mexico and Germany. 99

—Gary D. Ford, *Southern Living* Staff

Traditional Red-Sauced Brisket

Prep: 40 min.; Cook: 7 hrs.; Other: 9 hrs., 30 min.

1 (5¾-lb.) boneless beef brisket, trimmed
Brisket Rub
Hickory chunks
Brisket Mopping Sauce
Mop
Brisket Red Sauce (optional)

Sprinkle each side of beef with ¼ cup Brisket Rub; rub thoroughly into meat. Wrap brisket in plastic wrap, and chill 8 hours.

Soak hickory chunks in water for 8 hours. Drain.

Prepare smoker according to manufacturer's directions, regulating temperature with a thermometer to 225°; allow it to maintain that temperature for 1 hour before adding beef.

Remove beef from refrigerator, and let stand 30 minutes.

Place brisket, fat side up, on food grate. Insert heat-proof thermometer horizontally into thickest portion of beef. Maintain smoker temperature between 225° and 250°.

Add a handful (about ¼ cup) of hickory chunks about every hour.

Brush beef liberally with Brisket Mopping Sauce when beef starts to look dry (internal temperature will be about 156°). Mop top of brisket every hour. When internal temperature reaches 170°, place brisket on a sheet of heavy-duty aluminum foil; mop liberally with Brisket Mopping Sauce. Wrap tightly, and return to smoker.

Remove brisket from smoker when internal temperature reaches 190° with an instant-read thermometer. Let stand 1 hour. Cut into very thin (⅛- to ¼-inch thick) slices. Serve with Brisket Red Sauce, if desired. **Makes** 8 servings.

Brisket Rub

Prep: 5 min.

¼ cup kosher salt
¼ cup sugar
¼ cup black pepper
¾ cup paprika
2 Tbsp. garlic powder
2 Tbsp. garlic salt
2 Tbsp. onion powder
2 Tbsp. chili powder
2 tsp. ground red pepper

Combine all ingredients. Store in an airtight container up to 6 months. **Makes** 2 cups.

Brisket Mopping Sauce

Prep: 10 min.

This makes enough sauce for about two briskets, so make half the recipe if you're preparing just one brisket.

1 (12-oz.) bottle beer
1 cup apple cider vinegar
1 onion, minced
4 garlic cloves, minced
½ cup water
½ cup Worcestershire sauce
¼ cup vegetable oil
2 Tbsp. Brisket Rub

Stir together all ingredients until blended. **Makes** 4 cups.

Brisket Red Sauce

Prep: 10 min.

1½ cups cider vinegar
1 cup ketchup
½ tsp. ground red pepper
¼ cup Worcestershire sauce
1 tsp. salt
½ tsp. black pepper
½ tsp. onion powder
½ Tbsp. garlic powder
½ Tbsp. ground cumin
2 Tbsp. unsalted butter, melted
½ cup firmly packed brown sugar

Stir together all ingredients until blended. Serve sauce heated or at room temperature. **Makes** 3½ cups.

Smoked Brisket Sandwiches

Prep: 5 min.; Cook: 3 hrs., 30 min.; Other: 1 hr.

Hickory chunks
2 Tbsp. dried rosemary
2 Tbsp. paprika
2 Tbsp. pepper
2 Tbsp. dried garlic flakes
1 tsp. salt
1 (7-lb.) boneless beef brisket, untrimmed
Favorite barbecue sauce
Hamburger buns
Pickles
Garnish: fresh rosemary sprigs

Soak wood chunks in water for at least 1 hour.
Prepare charcoal fire in smoker; let burn 15 to 20 minutes.
Combine rosemary and next 4 ingredients; rub on brisket.
Drain wood chunks, and place on coals. Place water pan in smoker; add water to depth of fill line. Place brisket on lower food grate; cover with smoker lid.
Smoke 3½ hours or until meat thermometer inserted into thickest portion registers 155°. Slice and serve with barbecue sauce, buns, and pickles. Garnish, if desired. **Makes** 8 servings.

GRILLING TIPS

■ Keep a spray bottle full of water handy to extinguish flare-ups that can char food.
■ When turning meats, use a pair of tongs rather than a meat fork, which pierces food and allows valuable juices to escape.
■ Always place grilled food on a clean platter or cutting board.

Smoked Garlic Prime Rib

Prep: 5 min.; Cook: 6 hrs.; Other: 8 hrs., 10 min.

1 (10-lb.) beef rib roast
2 Tbsp. kosher salt
3 Tbsp. freshly ground pepper
6 garlic cloves, minced
Hickory chunks

Rub rib roast with salt, pepper, and garlic; cover and chill at least 8 hours.
Soak wood chunks in water 1 hour.
Prepare charcoal fire in smoker; let burn 15 to 20 minutes.
Drain chunks, and place on coals. Place water pan in smoker; add water to depth of fill line.
Place rib roast in center on the lower food grate, and cover with smoker lid.
Smoke, covered, 6 hours or until a meat thermometer inserted into thickest portion of roast registers 145° (medium-rare), refilling water pan and adding charcoal and wood chunks as needed. Let stand 10 minutes before slicing. **Makes** 12 servings.

Smoked Herbed Prime Rib

Prep: 10 min.; Cook: 5 hrs.; Other: 1 hr., 10 min.

Red wine bathes the roast and drips into the water pan, infusing the smoke with fruity essence.

Hickory chunks
4 garlic cloves, minced
1 Tbsp. salt
2 Tbsp. coarsely ground pepper
1 Tbsp. dried rosemary
1 tsp. dried thyme
1 (6-lb.) beef rib roast
1½ cups dry red wine
1½ cups red wine vinegar
½ cup olive oil

Soak wood chunks in water 1 hour.
Combine minced garlic and next 4 ingredients, and rub garlic mixture evenly over rib roast.
Stir together wine, vinegar, and olive oil; set wine mixture aside.
Prepare charcoal fire in smoker; let burn 15 to 20 minutes.
Drain wood chunks, and place on coals. Place water pan in smoker, and add water to just below fill line.
Place rib roast in center on lower food grate. Gradually pour wine mixture over rib roast.
Smoke roast, covered, 5 hours or until a meat thermometer inserted into thickest portion of roast registers 145° (medium-rare), refilling water pan and adding charcoal and wood chunks as needed. Let stand 10 minutes before slicing. **Makes** 8 to 10 servings.

66Two things fundamental to great barbecue are the right temperature and smoke. Long, slow cooking allows the meat to tenderize, while the smoke gives the meat flavor.99

—Troy Black, *Southern Living* Contributor

Smoked Marinated Eye of Round

Prep: 6 min.; Cook: 6 hrs.; Other: 12 hrs., 10 min.

½ cup Worcestershire sauce
½ cup teriyaki sauce
⅓ cup lemon juice
¼ cup white wine vinegar
2 Tbsp. seasoned salt
1 (4- to 5-lb.) eye of round roast
Hickory or mesquite chunks

Combine first 5 ingredients; stir well. Place roast in a zip-top freezer bag or large shallow dish; pour marinade over roast. Seal or cover, and marinate in refrigerator 12 to 24 hours, turning occasionally.
Remove roast from marinade, discarding marinade.
Soak wood chunks in water 1 hour.
Prepare charcoal fire in smoker, and let burn 15 to 20 minutes. Drain chunks and place on hot coals. Place water pan in smoker, and fill with water.
Place roast on lower food grate; cover with smoker lid.
Cook, covered, 5 to 6 hours or until tender, refilling water pan and adding charcoal and wood chunks as needed.
Let stand 10 minutes. Slice roast thinly to serve.
Makes 12 servings.

THE LOWDOWN ON SMOKING

■ The amount of charcoal or logs you start out with when smoking depends on the size of your smoker, its heat retention, and the weather.
■ Remember, you'll need to add charcoal and/or logs regularly during smoking to maintain the right temperature (generally between 225° and 250°—any hotter and you're grilling).
■ Your smoker should have a built-in thermometer that gives you an exact temperature reading. If it doesn't, purchase a heatproof one.

Smoked Strip Steaks

Prep: 10 min.; Cook: 1 hr., 18 min.; Other: 1 hr., 5 min.

Strip steaks offer a lot of surface area relative to their total size, which allows them to absorb a maximum amount of smoke. Serve thin slices of the steak over rice pilaf.

2 cups hickory or mesquite chunks
2 tsp. freshly ground pepper
1 tsp. garlic powder
½ tsp. salt
¼ tsp. dry mustard
2 (12-oz.) New York strip or sirloin strip steaks, trimmed
2 tsp. Worcestershire sauce

Soak wood chunks in water 1 hour; drain.
Combine pepper, garlic powder, salt, and mustard, and rub evenly over both sides of steaks. Place coated steaks in a large zip-top freezer bag; add Worcestershire sauce. Seal and shake to coat. Marinate in refrigerator 30 minutes.
Prepare grill for indirect grilling, heating one side to low and leaving one side with no heat. Maintain temperature at 200° to 225°.
Heat a large, heavy skillet over high heat. Remove steaks from bag, and discard marinade. Coat pan with cooking spray. Add steaks to pan; cook 1½ minutes on each side or until browned. Remove from pan.
Place wood chunks on hot coals. Place a disposable aluminum foil pan on unheated side of grill. Pour 2 cups water in pan. Coat the food grate with cooking spray, and place on grill.
Place steaks on food grate over aluminum foil pan on unheated side. Close lid; smoke 1 hour and 15 minutes or until a thermometer inserted into steak registers 145° (medium-rare) or until desired degree of doneness. Let stand 5 minutes. Cut steaks across grain into thin slices. **Makes** 4 to 6 servings.

Beef Fajitas with Pico de Gallo

Prep: 5 min.; Cook: 13 min.; Other: 8 hrs., 5 min.

1 (8-oz.) bottle zesty Italian dressing
3 Tbsp. fajita seasoning
2 (1-lb.) flank steaks
12 (6-inch) flour tortillas, warmed
Shredded Cheddar cheese
Pico de Gallo
Garnishes: lime wedges, fresh cilantro sprigs

Combine Italian dressing and fajita seasoning in a shallow dish or zip-top freezer bag; add steak. Cover or seal, and chill 8 hours, turning occasionally. Remove steak from marinade, discarding marinade.
Grill steaks, covered with grill lid, over medium-high heat (350° to 400°) for 8 minutes. Turn and grill 5 more minutes or to desired degree of doneness. Let stand 5 minutes before slicing.
Cut steaks diagonally across the grain into very thin slices, and serve with tortillas, cheese, and Pico de Gallo. Garnish, if desired. **Makes** 6 servings.

Pico de Gallo

Prep: 25 min., Other: 1 hr.

1 pt. grape tomatoes, chopped*
1 green bell pepper, chopped
1 red bell pepper, chopped
1 avocado, peeled and chopped
½ medium-size red onion, chopped
½ cup chopped fresh cilantro
1 garlic clove, pressed
¾ tsp. salt
½ tsp. ground cumin
½ tsp. grated lime rind
¼ cup fresh lime juice

Stir together all ingredients; cover and chill 1 hour.
Makes about 3 cups.

*Substitute 2 large tomatoes, chopped, if desired.

Beef-and-Chicken Fajitas
with Peppers and Onions

Beef-and-Chicken Fajitas with Peppers and Onions
Prep: 30 min., Cook: 16 min., Other: 4 hrs.

¼ cup olive oil
1 tsp. grated lime rind
2½ Tbsp. fresh lime juice
2 Tbsp. Worcestershire sauce
1½ tsp. ground cumin
1 tsp. salt
½ tsp. dried oregano
½ tsp. coarsely ground pepper
2 garlic cloves, minced
1 (14-oz.) can beef broth
1 (1-lb.) flank steak
1 lb. skinned and boned chicken breasts
2 red bell peppers, each cut into 12 wedges
2 green bell peppers, each cut into 12 wedges
1 large Vidalia or other sweet onion, cut into
    16 wedges
16 (6-inch) flour tortillas
1 cup bottled salsa
¼ cup sour cream
½ cup chopped fresh cilantro
Garnish: fresh cilantro sprigs

Combine first 10 ingredients in a large bowl; set marinade aside.
Trim fat from steak. Score a diamond pattern on both sides of the steak using a sharp knife. Combine 1½ cups marinade, steak, and chicken in a large zip-top freezer bag. Seal and marinate in refrigerator 4 hours or overnight, turning occasionally. Combine remaining marinade, bell peppers, and onion in a large zip-top freezer bag. Seal and marinate in refrigerator for 4 hours or overnight, turning occasionally.
Remove steak and chicken from bag; discard marinade. Remove vegetables from bag; reserve marinade. Place reserved marinade in a small saucepan; set aside. Place steak, chicken, and vegetables on food grate coated with cooking spray; grill 8 minutes on each side or until desired degree of doneness.
Wrap tortillas tightly in foil; place tortilla packet on food grate during the last 2 minutes of grilling time. Bring reserved marinade to a boil. Cut steak and chicken diagonally across grain into thin slices. Place steak, chicken, and vegetables on a serving platter; drizzle with reserved marinade. Serve with tortillas, salsa, sour cream, and cilantro. Garnish, if desired. Serve immediately. **Makes** 8 servings.

Java Fajitas
Prep: 10 min., Cook: 27 min., Other: 8 hrs.

⅓ cup tomato paste
1¼ cups strong brewed coffee
½ cup Worcestershire sauce
1 Tbsp. sugar
2 tsp. ground red pepper
1 tsp. ground black pepper
3 Tbsp. fresh lime juice
1 Tbsp. vegetable oil
2 (1½-lb.) flank steaks
24 (10-inch) flour tortillas
Pico de Gallo (page 103)
Garnishes: fresh cilantro, lime wedges, avocado slices

Combine tomato paste and next 7 ingredients in a shallow dish or large zip-top freezer bag; add steaks. Cover or seal; chill 8 hours. Turn steaks occasionally.
Remove steaks from marinade, reserving marinade.
Grill steaks, covered with grill lid, over high heat (400° to 500°) about 6 minutes on each side or to desired degree of doneness.
Cut steaks diagonally across grain into thin slices; keep warm. Bring reserved marinade to a boil in a skillet; boil 10 to 15 minutes or until reduced to 1 cup.
Serve steak with tortillas, reduced marinade, and Pico de Gallo. Garnish, if desired. **Makes** 12 servings.

Barbecue Chopped Steaks
Prep: 9 min., Cook: 10 min.

1 lb. ground round
¼ cup barbecue sauce, divided
2 Tbsp. Italian-seasoned breadcrumbs
2 Tbsp. minced onion
¼ tsp. freshly ground pepper
1 egg white, lightly beaten

Combine ground round, 2 Tbsp. barbecue sauce, and remaining 4 ingredients, stirring well. Shape into 4 (¾-inch-thick) oval patties.
Coat food grate with cooking spray; place on grill over medium-high heat (350° to 400°). Place patties on grate; grill, covered, 5 minutes. Turn patties, and brush with remaining 2 Tbsp. barbecue sauce. Grill, covered, 5 more minutes or until juices run clear. **Makes** 4 servings.

North Carolina Smoked
Pork Shoulder

North Carolina Smoked Pork Shoulder

Prep: 30 min.; Cook: 5 hrs., 30 min.; Other: 1 hr.

Pair this Carolina favorite with Cider Vinegar Barbecue Sauce (page 186) or Peppery Barbecue Sauce (page 185).

Hickory chunks
1 (5- to 6-lb.) bone-in pork shoulder or Boston butt
    pork roast
2 tsp. salt
10 lb. hardwood charcoal, divided
Cider Vinegar Barbecue Sauce (page 186) or Peppery
    Barbecue Sauce (page 185)

Soak hickory chunks in water 1 hour. Drain well.
Sprinkle pork with salt; cover and chill 30 minutes.
Prepare charcoal fire with half of charcoal in grill; let burn 15 to 20 minutes or until covered with gray ash. Push coals evenly into piles on both sides of grill. Carefully place 2 hickory chunks on top of each pile, and place food grate on grill.
Place pork, meaty side down, on grate directly in center of grill. Cover with lid, leaving ventilation holes completely open.
Prepare an additional charcoal fire with 12 briquettes in an auxiliary grill or fire bucket; let burn 30 minutes or until covered with gray ash. Carefully add 6 briquettes to each pile in smoker; place 2 more hickory chunks on each pile. Repeat procedure every 30 minutes.
Smoke, covered, 5½ hours or until meat thermometer inserted into thickest portion registers at least 165°, turning once during the last 2 hours. (Cooking the pork to 165° makes the meat easier to remove from bone.)
Remove pork; cool slightly. Chop and serve with Cider Vinegar Barbecue Sauce or Peppery Vinegar Sauce. **Makes** 6 servings.

Smoked Teriyaki-Marinated Boston Butt

Prep: 15 min.; Cook: 6 hrs.; Other: 8 hrs., 10 min.

1 (10-oz.) bottle teriyaki sauce
1 cup honey
½ cup cider vinegar
2 Tbsp. black pepper
2 Tbsp. garlic powder
1 tsp. dried crushed red pepper
1 (6-lb.) Boston butt pork roast
 Hickory chunks

Combine first 6 ingredients in a shallow dish or large zip-top freezer bag. Cut deep slits in roast using a paring knife; add roast to marinade. Cover or seal, and chill 8 hours, turning occasionally.
Soak wood chunks in water 1 hour.
Prepare charcoal fire in smoker; let burn 15 to 20 minutes.
Drain wood chunks, and place on coals. Place water pan in smoker; add water to depth of fill line. Drain roast, discarding marinade. Place roast in center of lower food grate.
Smoke, covered, 6 hours or until a meat thermometer inserted into thickest portion registers 165°, adding additional water, if necessary. Let stand 10 minutes. Chop or shred; serve with barbecue sauce, if desired. **Makes** 6 to 8 servings.

> ❝Eastern North Carolina goes whole hog for vinegar sauce, while western North Carolina shoulders the demand for a little ketchup.❞

—Glenn Morris, *Southern Living* Contributor

Smoked Mustard-Sauced Pork
Prep: 10 min.; Cook: 6 hrs.; Other: 1 hr., 10 min.

Hickory chunks
2 cups prepared mustard
1½ cups ketchup
¾ cup cider vinegar
2 Tbsp. sugar
2 Tbsp. Worcestershire sauce
1 Tbsp. hot sauce
2 Tbsp. butter or margarine
1 (5- to 6-lb.) Boston butt pork roast
5 garlic cloves, chopped
2 Tbsp. salt
1 Tbsp. pepper

Soak hickory chunks in water 1 hour.

Cook mustard and next 6 ingredients in a saucepan over low heat, stirring often, 20 minutes; set aside.

Cut deep slits in roast using a paring knife. Stir together garlic, salt, and pepper; rub on all sides of roast.

Prepare charcoal fire in smoker; let burn 15 to 20 minutes.

Drain wood chunks, and place on coals. Place water pan in smoker; add water to depth of fill line.

Place roast on lower food grate, and top with 1 cup mustard mixture.

Smoke, covered, 5 to 6 hours or until a meat thermometer inserted into thickest portion registers 165°. Let stand 10 minutes; chop and serve with remaining mustard sauce. **Makes** 8 to 10 servings.

Mesquite-Smoked Pork with Texas Caviar
Prep: 20 min.; Cook: 2 hrs., 5 min.; Other: 2 hrs., 15 min.

Texas Caviar is a mixture of black-eyed peas, fresh vegetables, and seasonings.

1 cup frozen black-eyed peas
1 cup water
⅓ cup seeded, chopped tomato
¼ cup chopped yellow bell pepper
¼ cup chopped green bell pepper
¼ cup chopped onion
¼ cup oil-free Italian dressing
1 Tbsp. chopped fresh parsley
2 tsp. seeded, minced jalapeño pepper
¼ tsp. minced garlic
⅛ tsp. black pepper
⅛ tsp. ground cumin
Mesquite chunks
1 (8-rib) center rib pork roast (about 4 lb.)
8 garlic cloves, minced
½ tsp. salt
½ tsp. coarsely ground pepper

Combine peas and 1 cup water. Bring to a boil. Cover, reduce heat, and simmer 35 minutes or until tender. Drain; cool.

Combine peas, tomato, and next 9 ingredients in a medium bowl, stirring well. Cover; chill at least 2 hours.

Soak mesquite chunks in water at least 1 hour; drain. Wrap chunks in heavy-duty aluminum foil, and make several holes in foil.

Light gas grill on one side; place foil-wrapped chunks directly on hot lava rocks. Coat food grate on opposite side of grill with cooking spray. Place grate over cool lava rocks; preheat grill to medium-high (350° to 400°) 10 to 15 minutes.

Trim fat from roast. Mash 8 minced garlic cloves, salt, and ½ tsp. pepper to a paste. Rub surface of roast with garlic paste. Coat roast with cooking spray. Insert meat thermometer into thickest part of roast, making sure it does not touch the bone. Place roast on grate opposite hot lava rocks.

Smoke, covered, 1½ hours or until meat thermometer registers 150°. Remove roast from grill. Cover with aluminum foil; let stand 15 minutes or until thermometer registers 160°.

Carve roast into 8 chops, and serve with black-eyed pea mixture. **Makes** 8 servings.

Three-Alarm BBQ
Prep: 10 min.; Cook: 5 hrs., 5 min.; Other: 8 hrs., 10 min.

Choose your own fate of 1, 2, or 3 tsp. of hot sauce in this barbecue with a kick.

2 to 4 cups hickory chunks
1 (2½-lb.) lean, bone-in pork loin roast
1 cup cider vinegar
2 Tbsp. grated fresh onion
2 Tbsp. ketchup
1 tsp. salt
1 tsp. black pepper
1 to 3 tsp. hot sauce
2 tsp. Worcestershire sauce
½ tsp. ground red pepper
4 garlic cloves, minced
12 white bread slices
12 hamburger dill pickle slices
Garnish: red onion slices

Soak hickory chunks in water 1 to 24 hours. Drain well.

Trim fat from roast. Combine vinegar and next 8 ingredients in a large zip-top freezer bag. Add roast; seal bag. Marinate in refrigerator 8 hours, turning bag occasionally.

Remove roast from bag, reserving marinade. Place reserved marinade in refrigerator.

Prepare charcoal fire in smoker; let burn 20 minutes or until coals are gray. Place hickory chunks on top of coals. Place water pan in smoker; add hot water to fill pan.

Coat food grate with cooking spray, and place in smoker. Place roast on grate; cover with lid.

Smoke 5 hours or until meat thermometer inserted into thickest part of roast registers 160°. Refill pan with water, and add charcoal and hickory chunks to fire as needed.

Remove roast from smoker; let stand 10 minutes. Cut roast from bone. Separate into bite-size pieces using 2 forks. Place in a bowl; set aside, and keep warm.

Bring reserved marinade to a boil over medium heat; cook 1 minute. Pour over roast; toss well. Serve with bread and pickles. Garnish, if desired. **Makes** 6 servings.

Note: If you prefer your barbecue with only one alarm, use 1 tsp. hot sauce and decrease the ground red pepper to ¼ tsp.

kids love it
Barbecue Pork Shoulder
Prep: 15 min.; Cook: 7 hrs.; Other: 1 hr., 10 min.

1 (2-lb.) package hickory chunks, divided
2 qt. white vinegar
½ cup ground red pepper, divided
5 oranges, quartered and divided
5 lemons, quartered and divided
½ cup firmly packed brown sugar
¼ cup ground black pepper
2 Tbsp. lemon juice
¼ cup liquid smoke
1 (7- to 8-lb.) bone-in pork shoulder roast (Boston butt)

Soak 1 lb. of wood chunks in water 1 hour.

Bring vinegar, ¼ cup ground red pepper, 3 oranges, and 3 lemons to a boil in a Dutch oven over medium heat; cook 10 minutes. Remove vinegar mixture from heat, and cool.

Combine remaining ¼ cup ground red pepper, brown sugar, and next 3 ingredients. Rub evenly over pork. Drizzle 1 cup vinegar mixture over pork; set aside 2 cups vinegar mixture for basting, and reserve remaining mixture to fill the water pan.

Prepare charcoal fire in smoker; let burn 15 to 20 minutes.

Drain wood chunks, and place on coals. Place water pan in smoker; add vinegar mixture and remaining 2 oranges and 2 lemons to depth of fill line. Place pork on lower food grate; cover with smoker lid.

Smoke pork roast 6 to 7 hours or until a meat thermometer inserted into the thickest part of roast registers 170°. Baste with reserved 2 cups vinegar mixture every hour after pork roast has cooked 3 hours. Add more charcoal, remaining 1 lb. wood chunks, and vinegar mixture to smoker as needed. Let stand 10 minutes before slicing. **Makes** 10 servings.

kids love it

Slow-Smoked Pork with Ranch-Barbecue Sauce

Prep: 15 min.; Cook: 4 hrs., 30 min.; Other: 8 hrs., 40 min.

A Creole sauce injected into the pork tenderizes and flavors the roast.

1 (5-lb.) bone-in pork shoulder roast (Boston butt)
1 (1-oz.) envelope Ranch dressing mix
½ (16-oz.) bottle Creole butter injector sauce (with injector) (we tested with Cajun Injector Creole Butter Injectable Marinade)
Ranch-Barbecue Sauce (page 188)
Garnish: bread-and-butter pickle slices

Rub roast with dressing mix. Inject butter sauce evenly into roast. Wrap tightly with plastic wrap, and place in a shallow dish or large zip-top freezer bag; cover or seal, and chill 8 hours. Let stand at room temperature 30 minutes before grilling. Remove plastic wrap.

Light one side of grill, heating to high heat (400° to 500°); leave other side unlit. Place roast, fat side up, over unlit side of grill.

Smoke, covered with grill lid, 3½ to 4½ hours or until meat thermometer inserted into thickest portion registers 185°. (Meat will easily pull away from bone.) Let stand 10 minutes. Coarsely chop, and serve with Ranch-Barbecue Sauce. Garnish, if desired. **Makes** 6 servings.

Tabb's Barbecue Pork

Prep: 5 min.; Cook: 8 hrs.; Other: 9 hrs., 10 min.

The sweet, not-too-spicy rub on Tabb's Barbecue Pork is the perfect complement to the lip-smacking tanginess of Honey-Mustard Barbecue Sauce (page 187).

1 (6-lb.) bone-in pork shoulder roast (Boston butt)
1 cup Sweet 'n' Spicy Barbecue Rub (page 192)
Hickory chunks
Apple juice

Trim fat on pork shoulder roast to about ⅛ inch thick.

Sprinkle pork evenly with Sweet 'n' Spicy Barbecue Rub; rub thoroughly into meat. Wrap pork tightly with plastic wrap, and chill 8 hours.

Discard plastic wrap. Let pork stand at room temperature 1 hour.

Soak hickory chunks in water 1 hour.

Prepare smoker according to manufacturer's instructions, bringing internal temperature to 225° to 250°; maintain temperature for 15 to 20 minutes.

Drain wood chunks, and place on coals. Place pork, fat side up, on lower food grate.

Spritz pork with apple juice each time charcoal or wood chunks are added to the smoker.

Smoke pork roast, maintaining the temperature inside smoker between 225° and 250°, for 6 hours or until a meat thermometer inserted horizontally into thickest portion of pork registers 170°.

Remove pork from smoker, and place on a sheet of heavy-duty aluminum foil; spritz with apple juice. Wrap tightly, and return to smoker; smoke 2 hours or until thermometer inserted horizontally into the thickest portion of pork registers 190°. Let stand 10 minutes. Remove bone, and chop pork. **Makes** 8 servings.

Pork Tenderloin with Molasses Barbecue Sauce and Mango Salsa
Prep: 10 min.; Cook: 2 hrs., 30 min.; Other: 3 hrs., 10 min.

1 small onion, finely chopped
1 jalapeño pepper, seeded and minced
1 garlic clove, minced
2 tsp. olive oil
½ cup molasses
½ cup cider vinegar
¼ cup Dijon mustard
1 Tbsp. soy sauce
1 (1½-lb.) package pork tenderloin
Hickory chunks
Fresh Mango Salsa (page 207)

Cook first 3 ingredients in olive oil in a saucepan over medium-high heat, stirring constantly, until tender. Stir in molasses and next 3 ingredients. Bring to a boil; reduce heat, and simmer, uncovered, 5 minutes, stirring occasionally. Cool.

Place tenderloins in a large zip-top freezer bag. Pour marinade over tenderloins. Seal bag; marinate in refrigerator 3 hours, turning occasionally.

Soak hickory chunks in water to cover at least 1 hour.

Prepare charcoal fire in smoker; let burn 15 to 20 minutes. Place hickory chunks on coals. Remove tenderloins from marinade, reserving marinade. Place water pan in smoker; add reserved marinade and water to pan to fill line. Coat food grate with cooking spray. Place grate in smoker. Place tenderloins on food grate; cover with smoker lid.

Smoke 2½ hours or until meat thermometer inserted in thickest portion of tenderloin registers 160° (medium). (Add additional charcoal and wood chunks to maintain an internal smoker temperature of 200° to 225°.) Let stand 10 minutes before serving. Serve with Fresh Mango Salsa. **Makes** 6 servings.

Fiery-Barbecued Pork Tenderloin
Prep: 10 min., Cook: 59 min., Other: 10 min.

3 cups apple cider vinegar
¼ cup ketchup
1 Tbsp. dried crushed red pepper
1 Tbsp. hot sauce (we tested with Texas Pete Hot Sauce)
1 Tbsp. Worcestershire sauce
¼ tsp. black pepper
2 (2-lb.) packages pork tenderloin

Bring first 6 ingredients to a boil in large saucepan over medium-high heat. Reduce heat to low, and simmer 30 minutes. Reserve 1 cup mixture.

Grill pork, without grill lid, over medium-high heat (350° to 400°) 10 to 12 minutes on each side or until a meat thermometer inserted in thickest portion of tenderloin registers 155°, basting often with remaining vinegar mixture. Remove from grill, and let stand 10 minutes or until temperature registers 160°. Serve with reserved 1 cup vinegar mixture. **Makes** 12 servings.

Pork Chops with Tangy Barbecue Sauce
Prep: 5 min., Cook: 14 min.

8 (4-oz.) boneless pork loin chops (½ inch thick)
Sweet-and-Tangy Barbecue Sauce (page 183)

Grill pork chops, covered with grill lid, over medium-high heat (350° to 400°) 7 minutes on each side, basting often with 1 cup Sweet-and-Tangy Barbecue Sauce. Serve with remaining 1 cup sauce. **Makes** 8 servings.

❝In North Carolina, barbecue means pork—cooked slowly, finely chopped, and seasoned with controversy.❞

—Glenn Morris, *Southern Living* Contributor

Smoky Chipotle Baby Back Ribs

Prep: 10 min.; Cook: 2 hrs., 30 min.; Other: 8 hrs., 40 min.

3 slabs baby back pork ribs (about 5½ lb.)
2 oranges, halved
Chipotle Rub (page 192)
Chipotle Barbecue Sauce (page 186)

Rinse and pat ribs dry. If desired, remove thin membrane from back of ribs by slicing into it with a knife and then pulling it off (this makes ribs more tender).
Rub meat with cut sides of oranges, squeezing as you rub. Massage Chipotle Rub into meat, covering all sides. Wrap tightly with plastic wrap, and place in a zip-top freezer bag or 13- x 9-inch baking dish; chill 8 hours. Let ribs stand at room temperature 30 minutes before grilling. Remove plastic wrap.

Prepare hot fire by piling charcoal on one side of grill, leaving the other side empty. If using a gas grill, light only one side. Place food grate on grill; position rib rack on grate over unlit side. Place slabs in rack.
Grill, covered with grill lid, over medium-high heat (350° to 400°) 1 hour. Reposition rib slabs, placing the one closest to the heat source away from heat, moving other slabs closer.
Grill 1 more hour or until meat is tender. Grill 30 more minutes over medium heat (300° to 350°), basting with half of Chipotle Barbecue Sauce. Remove ribs from grill, and let stand 10 minutes. Cut ribs, slicing between bones. Serve with remaining sauce.
Makes 6 servings.

BARBECUE SMOKY CHIPOTLE BABY BACK RIBS LIKE A PRO

Follow these easy steps to get the most flavor out of your rib-smoking experience.

1. Don't skip rubbing the ribs with citrus fruit halves; the juice adds a perky zip to the flavor. You'll find the canned chipotle peppers at the grocery store alongside other ethnic ingredients. Remove the thin membrane on the back, or bone side, of each rib rack if you want the meat to almost fall off the bone; leave it on if you like a crispy texture.

2. For best flavor, wrap seasoned ribs in plastic wrap to hold rub mixture close to the meat. Place each slab in a separate 2-gal. zip-top freezer bag, and refrigerate overnight. Slide ribs into rib rack as you remove them from the bag; then discard bag.

3. When the meat is tender and done, bones should wiggle easily when moved, and the meat will be shrunk down from the bones. Slow the fire by partially or fully closing vents before basting. Pour sauce over ribs, guiding it to cover with a grill brush.

Sweet-and-Sour Baby Back Ribs

Prep: 10 min.; Cook: 2 hrs., 30 min.; Other: 8 hrs., 40 min.

3 slabs baby back pork ribs (about 5½ lb.)
2 limes, halved
Ginger Rub
Sweet-and-Sour 'Cue Sauce

Rinse and pat ribs dry. If desired, remove thin membrane from back of ribs by slicing into it with a knife and then pulling it off (this makes ribs more tender). **Rub** meat with cut sides of limes, squeezing as you rub. Massage Ginger Rub into meat, covering all sides. Wrap tightly with plastic wrap, and place in a zip-top freezer bag or 13- x 9-inch baking dish; chill 8 hours. Let ribs stand at room temperature 30 minutes before grilling. Remove plastic wrap.
Prepare hot fire by piling charcoal on one side of grill, leaving the other side empty. If using a gas grill, light only one side. Place food grate on grill; position rib rack on grate over unlit side. Place slabs in rack.
Grill, covered with grill lid, over medium-high heat (350° to 400°) 1 hour. Reposition rib slabs, placing the one closest to the heat source away from heat, moving other slabs closer.
Grill 1 more hour or until meat is tender.
Grill 30 more minutes over medium heat (300° to 350°); baste with half of Sweet-and-Sour 'Cue Sauce.
Remove ribs from grill, and let stand 10 minutes.

Cut ribs, slicing between bones. Serve with remaining sauce. **Makes** 6 servings.

Ginger Rub
Prep: 5 min.

2 Tbsp. ground ginger
½ tsp. dried crushed red pepper
1 tsp. salt
1 tsp. black pepper

Combine all ingredients. **Makes** about 3 Tbsp.

Sweet-and-Sour 'Cue Sauce
Prep: 5 min., Cook: 35 min.

2 (10-oz.) bottles sweet-and-sour sauce (we tested with Ty Ling Sweet & Sour Sauce)
2 cups ketchup
½ cup cider vinegar
½ tsp. ground ginger
2 tsp. hot sauce

Stir together all ingredients. Bring to a boil over medium-high heat. Reduce heat; simmer 30 minutes. **Makes** 3½ cups.

Beer-Smoked Baby Back Ribs

Prep: 30 min., Cook: 5 hrs., Other: 1 hr.

3 slabs baby back pork ribs (about 6 lb.)
¼ cup lemon juice
¼ cup olive oil
6 Tbsp. Pork Ribs Rub
Hickory chunks
4 to 6 (12-oz.) bottles dark beer
2 cups Sweet Jalapeño Barbecue Sauce (page 125)

Rinse and pat ribs dry. If desired, remove thin membrane from back of ribs by slicing into it with a knife and then pulling it off (this makes ribs more tender).
Place lemon juice in a small bowl; add oil in a slow, steady stream, whisking constantly. Coat ribs evenly with lemon juice mixture. Sprinkle meat evenly with Pork Ribs Rub, and rub into meat. Let stand at room temperature 30 minutes.
Soak wood chunks in water for at least 1 hour.
Prepare smoker according to manufacturer's directions, substituting beer for water in water pan. Bring internal temperature to 225° to 250°, and maintain temperature for 15 to 20 minutes.
Drain wood chunks, and place on coals. Place rib slabs in a rib rack on upper food grate; cover with smoker lid.
Smoke ribs, maintaining the temperature inside smoker between 225° and 250°, for 4½ hours. Remove lid, baste with half of Sweet Jalapeño Barbecue Sauce, and, if necessary, add more beer to water pan. Cover with smoker lid, and smoke 30 more minutes. Cut meat into 3-rib sections, slicing between bones, and serve with remaining half of Sweet Jalapeño Barbecue Sauce. **Makes** 6 servings.

Pork Ribs Rub

Prep: 5 min.

1 cup Greek seasoning (we tested with Cavender's
    All-Purpose Greek Seasoning)
¼ cup garlic powder
¼ cup paprika
¼ cup firmly packed brown sugar

Combine all ingredients. Store in an airtight container. **Makes** about 1¾ cups.

Barbecued Country-Style Ribs

Prep: 10 min.; Cook: 2 hrs., 30 min.

1 small onion
1 cup finely chopped celery
1½ Tbsp. bacon drippings
1 (15-oz.) can tomato sauce
¾ cup honey
½ cup water
¼ cup dry red wine
2 Tbsp. lemon juice
2 Tbsp. Worcestershire sauce
1 tsp. salt
½ tsp. pepper
¼ tsp. garlic powder
1 cup water
2 Tbsp. white vinegar
4 lb. bone-in or boneless country-style ribs, cut apart

Sauté onion and celery in hot bacon drippings in a saucepan over medium-high heat until tender. Add tomato sauce and next 8 ingredients. Bring to a boil. Reduce heat; simmer, stirring occasionally, 1 hour. Remove from heat.
Combine 1 cup water and vinegar in a spray bottle.
Grill ribs, covered with grill lid, over medium heat (300° to 350°) 1 to 1½ hours, spraying with vinegar solution, turning ribs occasionally, and basting with 1 cup tomato sauce mixture every 30 minutes. Serve with remaining tomato sauce mixture. **Makes** 8 servings.

> **"**Having been swept up in a few rib-induced feeding frenzies over the years, there have been times when I thought I could never eat the stuff again. But I always rally and recover.**"**
>
> ——Richard Banks, *Southern Living* Staff

Maple Spareribs

Prep: 45 min.; Cook: 1 hr., 30 min.

3 to 4 lb. pork spareribs
1 cup maple syrup
⅓ cup soy sauce
1 Tbsp. garlic powder
3 Tbsp. sweet rice wine (we tested with Kikkoman
  Aji-Mirin Sweet Cooking Rice Wine)
2 tsp. salt
½ tsp. sugar

Bring ribs and water to cover to a boil in a large Dutch oven; reduce heat, and simmer 30 minutes. Drain. Place ribs in a lightly greased 13- x 9-inch pan.
Stir together maple syrup and remaining 5 ingredients; pour half of marinade over ribs, reserving other half of marinade for basting.
Prepare a hot fire by piling charcoal on 1 side of grill, leaving other side empty. Coat rack with cooking spray, and place on grill. Arrange ribs over unlit side, and grill, covered with grill lid, 1½ hours, basting occasionally with reserved marinade. **Makes** 2 to 3 servings.

Peach-Glazed Barbecue Pork Chops and Peaches

Prep: 20 min., Cook: 40 min., Other: 35 min.

The cooking time for your peaches varies depending on their ripeness. This glaze also works well on chicken.

3 cups chopped peeled peaches (about 1½ lb.)
1 cup dry white wine
¼ cup sugar
1 tsp. salt, divided
¼ tsp. black pepper, divided
2 Tbsp. white wine vinegar
2 Tbsp. molasses
1 tsp. chili powder
½ tsp. paprika
¼ tsp. ground red pepper
6 (6-oz.) bone-in center-cut pork chops
   (about ½ inch thick), trimmed
6 peaches, halved and pitted

Combine first 3 ingredients in a small saucepan; bring to a boil. Cover, reduce heat, and simmer 25 minutes. Uncover and simmer 5 minutes. Place peach mixture in a food processor; process until smooth. Add ¾ tsp. salt, ⅛ tsp. black pepper, vinegar, and next 4 ingredients; pulse to combine. Let stand 5 minutes. Place half of peach mixture in a large zip-top freezer bag; reserve other half for basting. Add chops to bag; seal bag and refrigerate 30 minutes to 4 hours.

Remove pork from bag; discard marinade. Sprinkle pork with remaining ¼ tsp. salt and remaining ⅛ tsp. black pepper. Place pork and peach halves on food grate coated with cooking spray.

Grill pork, without grill lid, over medium-high heat (350° to 400°) 10 minutes or until pork is done and peaches are tender, turning once. Baste pork and peach halves with reserved peach mixture every 2 minutes during first 6 minutes of cooking. **Makes** 6 servings.

Barbecue Pork Chops with Grilled Corn Salsa

Prep: 5 min., Cook: 8 min., Other: 8 hrs.

Pork needs to cook to an internal temperature of 160° and to be still slightly pink in the center. An instant-read thermometer is perfect for quickly testing for doneness.

½ cup ketchup
⅓ cup cola soft drink
1 Tbsp. minced fresh onion
½ tsp. dry mustard
½ tsp. garlic powder
¼ tsp. ground red pepper
4 (4-oz.) lean, boneless center-cut loin pork chops
　(about ½ inch thick)
Grilled Corn Salsa

Stir together first 6 ingredients in a small bowl. Combine one half marinade and chops in a large zip-top freezer bag; seal bag, and marinate in refrigerator 8 hours, turning bag occasionally. Reserve remaining one-half marinade for basting.
Remove chops from bag; discard marinade. Place chops on food grate coated with cooking spray; grill 4 minutes on each side or until chops are done, basting frequently with reserved marinade. Serve with Grilled Corn Salsa. **Makes** 4 servings.

Grilled Corn Salsa

Prep: 20 min., Cook: 10 min., Other: 2 hrs.

3 ears fresh corn
1 large sweet onion, cut into ½-inch-thick slices
1 red bell pepper, halved
2 large tomatoes, seeded and chopped
2 jalapeño peppers, seeded and minced
2 garlic cloves, minced
¼ cup chopped fresh cilantro
½ tsp. salt
¼ tsp. ground cumin
1 Tbsp. olive oil
1 Tbsp. lime juice

Grill first 3 ingredients, covered with grill lid, over medium-high heat (350° to 400°) 8 to 10 minutes or until tender, turning occasionally.
Cut corn kernels from cobs. Coarsely chop onion and red bell pepper halves. Combine grilled vegetables, tomato, and next 7 ingredients in a large bowl; cover and chill 2 hours or up to 2 days. **Makes** 5 cups.

Sage-Smoked Maple Quail

Prep: 1 hr., Cook: 2 hrs., Other: 1 hr.

The combination of ingredients that are stuffed in, wrapped around, and brushed on these quail is flavor blending at its best.

4 Golden Delicious apples, diced
½ cup chopped pecans
½ tsp. salt
1 (0.4-oz.) jar dried sage, divided
12 quail, dressed
12 pepper-cured bacon slices
Hickory chunks
1 qt. apple cider
⅓ cup pure maple syrup

Combine apple, pecans, salt, and 2 tsp. sage; stuff each quail with apple mixture, and wrap a bacon slice around each quail, securing ends with a wooden pick. Cover and chill 30 minutes.
Soak chunks in water 1 hour; moisten remaining sage with water.
Prepare charcoal fire in smoker; let burn 15 to 20 minutes. Drain chunks; place chunks and one-third of remaining sage on hot coals. Place water pan in smoker; add 1 qt. cider.
Place quail, breast sides up, on food grate; brush quail with maple syrup.
Smoke, covered with smoker lid, 2 hours or until done, adding remaining sage at 30-minute intervals.
Makes 6 servings.

66During hunting season, game hunters thrive in the South. And when the prize reaches the table, it's time for the hunter's feast.99

—Julie Gunter, *Southern Living* Books

Asian Grilled Quail

Asian Grilled Quail

Prep: 20 min., Cook: 30 min., Other: 30 min.

¼ cup hoisin sauce
2 Tbsp. sesame seeds
3 Tbsp. garlic-chili sauce
3 Tbsp. dark sesame oil
3 Tbsp. honey
1 tsp. ground ginger
8 quail, dressed
1 (14-oz.) can chicken broth
2 tsp. cornstarch
Garnish: sliced green onions or green onion curls

Combine first 6 ingredients in a shallow dish or large zip-top freezer bag, gently squeezing to blend; add quail. Cover or seal, and chill 30 minutes, turning occasionally.

Remove quail from marinade, reserving marinade. Prepare fire by piling charcoal or lava rocks on one side of grill, leaving the other side empty. Place food grate on grill. Arrange quail over empty side; grill, covered with grill lid, 30 minutes or until done.

Pour reserved marinade into a small saucepan. Reserve ¼ cup chicken broth, and add remaining chicken broth to marinade. Bring mixture to a boil over medium-high heat; boil, stirring occasionally, 5 minutes.

Whisk together cornstarch and reserved ¼ cup chicken broth until smooth. Whisk into marinade mixture; boil, whisking constantly, 1 minute. Serve with quail. Garnish, if desired. **Makes** 4 servings.

Asian Grilled Cornish Hens: Substitute 4 (1- to 1½-lb.) Cornish hens for quail. Grill as directed 45 to 50 minutes or until done.

editor's favorite
Mesquite-Grilled Quail

Prep: 20 min., Cook: 25 min., Other: 30 min.

Jalapeño peppers are a simple but not-so-subtle seasoning for this quail. For a tamer flavor, cut off stem ends of the peppers and remove the seeds with a grapefruit knife.

8 bacon slices
8 quail, dressed
8 jalapeño peppers
Mesquite chips

Place bacon on a food grate in a 13- x 9-inch baking dish; cover with paper towels.

Microwave at HIGH 3 to 4 minutes or until bacon is partially cooked. Drain bacon; set aside.

Rinse quail thoroughly with cold water; pat dry with paper towels. Place a jalapeño pepper into body cavity of each quail; tie ends of legs together with string. Wrap 1 bacon slice around each quail, and secure with wooden picks.

Soak mesquite chips in water 30 minutes; drain. Wrap chips in heavy-duty aluminum foil, and make several holes in foil. Light gas grill on one side; place foil-wrapped chips directly on hot coals. Coat food grate on opposite side with cooking spray. Place grate over cool lava rocks; let grill preheat 10 to 15 minutes or until chips smoke. Arrange quail on grate opposite hot coals; cover and grill 25 minutes or until done. **Makes** 4 servings.

QUAIL 101

■ Quail are lean game birds—the most commonly eaten in the United States. Domestic quail are mildly flavored, but the wild variety have a subtle gamey taste.

■ When serving quail as an entrée, allow two birds per person. Look for domestic quail in the frozen meats section at the supermarket or special-order them from your grocer.

■ Quail are really too small to check for doneness using a thermometer. Whether slow-smoked for a long period of time or grilled more quickly, you'll know they're done when you can easily wiggle the legs in their joints and no pink juices remain.

BBQ Grilled Salmon

Prep: 5 min., Cook: 14 min., Other: 45 min.

Mesquite or hickory chips
4 (6-oz.) salmon fillets
2 Tbsp. Sweet 'n' Spicy Barbecue Rub (page 192)

Soak wood chips in water to cover at least 30 minutes; drain well. Wrap chips in heavy-duty aluminum foil; pierce several holes in foil.
Coat salmon with Sweet 'n' Spicy Barbecue Rub; cover and chill 30 minutes.
Place foil-wrapped chips on left side of food grate over medium-high heat (350° to 400°); cover with grill lid, and heat 10 to 15 minutes or until chips begin to smoke. Coat right side of food grate with cooking spray. Place salmon on grate. Grill, covered with grill lid, 5 to 7 minutes on each side or until fish flakes easily with a fork. **Makes** 4 servings.

Smoked Salmon with Sweet-Hot Mustard and Dill

Prep: 20 min., Cook: 35 min., Other: 30 min.

Rich, meaty salmon fillets are seasoned with a paste that offers more flavor than a marinade.

2 cups wood chips
1 Tbsp. minced fresh dill
1 Tbsp. fresh lemon juice
3 Tbsp. sweet-hot mustard (we tested with Inglehoffer)
½ tsp. salt
1 (1½-lb.) salmon fillet

Soak wood chips in water 30 minutes; drain.
Combine dill, juice, mustard, and salt, stirring well. Place salmon, skin side down, in a shallow baking dish; brush mustard mixture over salmon. Cover and refrigerate 20 minutes.
Prepare grill for indirect grilling, heating one side to low and leaving one side with no heat. Maintain temperature at 200° to 225°. Place wood chips on hot coals. Place a disposable aluminum foil pan on unheated side of grill. Pour 2 cups water in pan. Coat food grate with cooking spray; place on grill. Place salmon, skin side down, on grate over foil pan on unheated side. Close lid; smoke 35 minutes or until fish flakes easily when tested with a fork. **Makes** 4 servings.

editor's favorite
Smoked Dilled Salmon

Prep: 10 min., Cook: 25 min., Other: 2 hrs.

The fish in this recipe is extra-moist because it soaks in a brine (salt-water solution). Start soaking the wood chunks while the salmon brines.

3½ cups water
½ cup kosher salt (we tested with Diamond Crystal)
¼ cup sugar
2 Tbsp. dried dill
2 Tbsp. low-sodium soy sauce
1 cup ice cubes
1 (1½-lb.) salmon fillet (about 1 inch thick)
Hickory chips
Freshly cracked black pepper
Garnish: fresh dill sprigs

Combine water, salt, sugar, dill, and soy sauce in a large bowl, stirring until salt and sugar dissolve. Pour salt mixture into a large zip-top freezer bag. Add ice and salmon; seal. Refrigerate 2 hours, turning bag occasionally.
Soak the wood chips in water for 30 minutes. Drain well.
Prepare the grill for indirect grilling, heating one side to medium and leaving one side with no heat.
Place half of wood chips on hot coals. Remove salmon from bag, and discard brine. Pat salmon dry with paper towels. Place salmon on food grate coated with cooking spray over unheated side. Close lid; smoke 10 minutes. Place remaining wood chips on hot coals; close lid, and smoke 15 more minutes or until fish flakes easily when tested with a fork. Sprinkle with black pepper; garnish, if desired. **Makes** 4 servings.

> ❝Versatile shrimp and fish swimmingly take on the bold flavors of barbecue and slow smoking.❞

—Joy Zacharia, *Southern Living* Contributor

Smoked Rosemary-Scented Salmon

Prep: 10 min., Cook: 50 min., Other: 3 hrs.

Hickory or alder chunks
1 (3-lb.) salmon fillet, halved crosswise
¾ cup fresh lime juice
3 Tbsp. minced fresh rosemary
2 Tbsp. olive oil
1½ tsp. prepared horseradish
1½ tsp. cracked pepper
¾ tsp. salt
Garnishes: fresh rosemary sprig, lime wedges

Soak wood chunks in water to cover 1 to 24 hours. Drain well.

Place fish in a large zip-top freezer bag. Combine lime juice and next 3 ingredients. Pour over fish; seal bag, and shake gently until fish is well coated. Marinate in refrigerator 3 hours, turning bag occasionally. Remove fish from bag, reserving marinade. Sprinkle fish with pepper and salt; set aside.

Prepare charcoal fire in smoker; let burn 15 to 20 minutes. Place soaked wood chunks on top of coals. Place water pan in smoker; add reserved marinade. Add hot tap water to fill pan.

Coat food grate with cooking spray; place grate in smoker. Arrange fish, skin side down, on grate, allowing enough room between fish pieces for air to circulate. Cover with smoker lid, and smoke 50 minutes or until fish flakes easily when tested with a fork. Garnish, if desired. **Makes** 12 servings.

Smoked King Crab Legs and Lobster Tails

Prep: 30 min.; Cook: 1 hr., 20 min.; Other: 1 hr.

Apple or alder wood chunks
1 cup butter or margarine, melted
¼ cup fresh lemon juice
1 Tbsp. minced fresh parsley
½ tsp. grated lemon rind
Pinch of salt
5 lb. frozen king crab legs, thawed
4 frozen lobster tails, thawed (about 2 lb.)

Soak wood chunks in water to cover at least 1 hour.

Prepare charcoal fire in smoker; let burn 15 to 20 minutes.

Drain chunks, and place on coals. Place water pan in smoker; add water to fill line.

Stir together butter and next 4 ingredients. Divide lemon-butter mixture in half. Crack crab legs, and split lobster tails. Brush lobster and crab with half of mixture; set aside remaining mixture.

Coat food grate with cooking spray; place in smoker. Arrange crab legs and lobster tails on grate; cover with grill lid. Smoke crab about 20 minutes and lobster about 45 minutes to 1 hour or until flesh is white and firm.

Serve with reserved lemon-butter mixture. **Makes** 4 servings.

editor's favorite

Smoked Sea Scallops

Prep: 20 min., Cook: 20 min., Other: 2 hrs.

Mesquite chips
6 cups water
⅓ cup kosher salt
¼ cup sugar
36 sea scallops
⅔ lb. thinly sliced prosciutto
6 green onions, sliced

Soak wood chips in water to cover at least 30 minutes.

Combine 6 cups water, salt, and sugar in a bowl, stirring to dissolve. Rinse scallops, and stir into brine. Cover and chill 1 hour; drain.

Arrange scallops in a single layer on a wire rack; chill 1 hour.

Prepare charcoal fire in smoker; let burn 15 to 20 minutes. Drain chips, and place on coals. Place water pan in smoker; add water to fill line.

Wrap strips of prosciutto around scallops, securing with wooden picks. Place scallops on upper food grate. Place grate in smoker. Sprinkle green onions over scallops (most will drop into water); cover with smoker lid. Smoke 20 minutes or until done. **Makes** 6 servings.

Grilled Corn with Jalapeño-Lime Butter

Prep: 25 min., Cook: 15 min., Other: 1 hr.
(pictured on page 139)

To make the butter a bit more kid-friendly, make a second batch and omit the jalapeño peppers.

¾ cup butter, softened
2 large jalapeño peppers, seeded and minced
2 Tbsp. grated lime rind
1 tsp. fresh lime juice
10 ears fresh corn, husks removed
2 Tbsp. olive oil
1 Tbsp. kosher salt
1 tsp. freshly ground pepper

Combine first 4 ingredients, and shape into a 6-inch log; wrap in wax paper or plastic wrap, and chill 1 hour.
Rub corn with olive oil; sprinkle evenly with salt and pepper.
Grill, covered with grill lid, over high heat (400° to 500°), turning often, 10 to 15 minutes or until tender. Serve with flavored butter. **Makes** 10 servings.

quick & easy
Grilled Corn with Creamy Chipotle Sauce

Prep: 15 min., Cook: 15 min.

Instead of using butter, try this smoky, spicy sauce—it's a savory complement to the sweet corn. Though the corn needs to be grilled at the last minute, the sauce can be prepared a day ahead. To remove the silks from an ear of corn, rub with a damp paper towel or a damp soft-bristled toothbrush.

¼ tsp. salt
1 drained canned chipotle pepper, seeded
1 garlic clove
½ cup 2% reduced-fat cottage cheese
2 Tbsp. light mayonnaise
2 Tbsp. plain fat-free yogurt
6 ears fresh corn, husks removed

Place first 3 ingredients in a food processor; process until minced. Add cottage cheese; process until smooth, scraping sides of bowl occasionally. Add mayonnaise and yogurt; process until blended. Spoon sauce into a bowl; cover and chill.
Place corn on food grate coated with cooking spray. Grill, covered with grill lid, over high heat (400° to 500°), turning often, 10 to 15 minutes or until tender. Serve corn with sauce. **Makes** 6 servings.

Sage-Grilled Eggplant

Prep: 10 min., Cook: 15 min., Other: 1 hr.

1 large eggplant, unpeeled
1½ tsp. salt
⅓ cup Sage Butter
¼ tsp. pepper

Cut eggplant crosswise into ½-inch slices; sprinkle cut sides with salt. Place in a single layer on paper towels; let stand 1 hour.
Rinse eggplant with water, and pat dry. Arrange in a single layer in a lightly greased grill basket.
Melt Sage Butter in a small saucepan over low heat; stir in pepper. Brush on eggplant.
Grill, covered with grill lid, over medium-high heat (350° to 400°) 12 to 15 minutes or until lightly browned, turning and brushing with melted butter mixture. **Makes** 4 servings.

Sage Butter

Prep: 10 min.

Try this butter on grilled chicken or fish, or toss with steamed vegetables.

½ cup fresh sage leaves, loosely packed
1 large shallot
½ cup butter, softened
1 tsp. grated lemon rind
½ tsp. fresh lemon juice
¼ tsp. freshly ground pepper

Process sage and shallot in a food processor until chopped.
Add butter and remaining ingredients; process until mixture is thoroughly blended, stopping occasionally to scrape down sides. **Makes** ½ cup.

Grilled Red Onions

Prep: 20 min., Cook: 10 min., Other: 8 hrs.

If you've tried to grill onions only to have the rings separate and end up in the fire, then we have a solution. Insert a skewer through an onion slice to hold the rings together.

12 (8-inch) wooden skewers
3 medium-size red or sweet onions
1½ cups dry white wine
2 to 4 Tbsp. butter or margarine, melted
1 tsp. chopped fresh thyme
⅛ tsp. pepper

Insert 4 wooden skewers (1 at a time) through each onion about ½-inch apart to create horizontal segments. Cut onions into slices between skewers. (Leave skewers in place to hold onion slices together during marinating and cooking.)
Place slices in a shallow container; add wine. Cover and chill 8 hours, turning occasionally. Drain.
Melt butter in small saucepan; stir in thyme and pepper. Brush onion slices with butter mixture, reserving some for basting.
Grill onions, covered with grill lid, over medium-high heat (350° to 400°) 6 to 10 minutes, turning and basting often with reserved butter mixture. **Makes** 6 servings.

Grilled Yellow Squash Halves

Prep: 2 min., Cook: 2 min., Other: 20 min.

This is the best two-ingredient side dish you can make. It's easy, delicious, and healthy.

6 yellow squash
½ cup Italian dressing

Cut yellow squash in half lengthwise. Place squash in a large zip-top freezer bag; add dressing. Seal and chill 20 minutes. Remove squash from marinade, discarding marinade.
Grill, cut sides down, covered with grill lid, over medium-high heat (350° to 400°) 2 minutes or until tender. **Makes** 6 servings.

Grilled Summer Squash

Prep: 10 min., Cook: 10 min., Other: 15 min.

¼ cup fresh lemon juice
¼ cup plain fat-free yogurt
1 Tbsp. olive oil
2 tsp. chopped fresh rosemary
½ tsp. freshly ground pepper
2 garlic cloves, minced
¾ tsp. salt, divided
3 small yellow squash, halved lengthwise (about 1 lb.)
3 small zucchini, halved lengthwise (about 1 lb.)

Combine first 6 ingredients in a 13- x 9-inch baking dish. Add ½ tsp. salt. Make 3 diagonal cuts, ¼-inch deep, across cut side of each squash and zucchini half. Place squash and zucchini halves, cut sides down, in baking dish. Marinate squash and zucchini at room temperature 15 minutes.
Remove squash and zucchini from marinade, and discard marinade. Place squash and zucchini on food grate coated with cooking spray. Grill over medium-high heat (350° to 400°) 5 minutes on each side or until tender. Sprinkle evenly with remaining ¼ tsp. salt. **Makes** 6 servings.

Grilled Asparagus

Prep: 10 min., Cook: 4 min.

This grilling time is for pencil-thin asparagus; increase the time for thicker spears.

1 lb. fresh asparagus
1 Tbsp. olive oil
1 tsp. balsamic vinegar
¼ tsp. salt
¼ tsp. pepper
1 tsp. grated lemon rind

Snap off and discard tough ends of asparagus.
Combine olive oil, balsamic vinegar, salt, and pepper in a shallow dish or large zip-top freezer bag; add asparagus, turning to coat.
Remove asparagus from oil mixture. Grill asparagus, covered with grill lid, over medium-high heat (350° to 400°) 2 to 4 minutes or until tender, turning once. Remove asparagus, and sprinkle evenly with grated lemon rind; serve immediately. **Makes** 4 servings.

Grilled Tomatoes
Prep: 5 min., Cook: 4 min.

Serve these savory tomatoes with your favorite burgers, Grilled Corn with Jalapeño-Lime Butter (page 137), and dill pickle spears.

2 garlic cloves, minced
2 Tbsp. olive oil
5 large tomatoes, cut in half crosswise
½ tsp. salt
½ tsp. pepper
½ cup chopped fresh basil

Stir together garlic and oil. Brush cut sides of tomato halves evenly with garlic mixture; sprinkle evenly with salt and pepper.

Grill tomato halves, covered with grill lid, over medium-high heat (350° to 400°) about 2 minutes on each side. Sprinkle evenly with basil. **Makes** 10 servings.

Grilled Vegetables
with Cilantro Butter

Grilled Vegetables with Cilantro Butter

Prep: 10 min., Cook: 25 min., Other: 1 hr.

4 ears fresh corn with husks
Cilantro Butter
4 medium tomatoes, halved
4 medium zucchini, cut into 1-inch-thick slices
½ tsp. salt
½ tsp. freshly ground pepper
Garnish: fresh cilantro sprigs

Soak corn in water to cover 1 hour. Peel back corn husks, leaving husks attached. Remove silks.
Spread Cilantro Butter evenly over corn, tomato, and zucchini; sprinkle with salt and pepper. Pull husks over corn, and twist ends tightly. Place corn on food grate. Place tomato and zucchini in a grill basket.
Grill vegetables, covered, over medium-high heat (350° to 400°) 10 to 15 minutes or until zucchini and tomato are tender, turning corn often. Grill corn 5 to 10 more minutes or until tender. (Husks will blacken.) Remove husks, or pull them back and knot ends to make a "handle" for corn. Serve with beef fajitas. Garnish, if desired. **Makes** 4 servings.

Cilantro Butter

Prep: 5 min.

½ cup butter or margarine, softened
¼ cup minced fresh cilantro
4 garlic cloves, pressed

Stir together all ingredients. **Makes** ½ cup.

Grilled Sweet Potatoes with Orange-Chipotle Glaze

Prep: 10 min., Cook: 13 min.

4 large sweet potatoes (about 2 lb.)
1 (7-oz.) can chipotle peppers in adobo sauce
2 Tbsp. butter or margarine, melted
1 Tbsp. chopped fresh cilantro
½ tsp. salt
1 (6-oz.) can orange juice concentrate, thawed and undiluted

Cut potatoes in half lengthwise. Cook potato halves in boiling water 5 minutes or until crisp-tender; drain. Rinse with cold water; drain well.
Meanwhile, remove 3 Tbsp. adobo sauce from canned chiles. Place remaining sauce and chiles in a zip-top freezer bag; freeze for another use.
Combine 3 Tbsp. adobo sauce, butter, cilantro, salt, and juice in a small bowl.
Place potatoes on food grate coated with cooking spray; grill over medium-high heat (350° to 400°) 4 minutes on each side or until potatoes are done, basting frequently with juice mixture. **Makes** 8 servings.

Grilled Portobello Mushrooms and Asparagus

Prep: 5 min., Cook: 14 min.

For a hearty veggie burger, place whole mushrooms caps on buns after grilling, add condiments, and serve asparagus on the side.

4 portobello mushroom caps
2 Tbsp. Rosemary Oil
1 lb. fresh asparagus

Remove brown gills from undersides of portobello mushroom caps using a spoon, discarding gills. Brush mushrooms with 1 Tbsp. Rosemary Oil. Snap off tough ends of asparagus; brush asparagus with remaining 1 Tbsp. Rosemary Oil.
Grill mushrooms, covered with grill lid, over high heat (400° to 500°) 5 minutes on each side. Cut mushrooms into strips. Grill asparagus, covered with grill lid, over high heat 2 minutes on each side. **Makes** 6 servings.

Rosemary Oil

Prep: 5 min., Cook: 3 min.

⅓ cup olive oil
2 fresh rosemary sprigs
1 tsp. pepper

Bring all ingredients to a boil over high heat, and cook, stirring occasionally, 3 minutes. Remove from heat; cool. Discard rosemary sprigs. **Makes** ⅓ cup.

Grilled Balsamic-Glazed Peaches

Prep: 10 min., Cook: 15 min., Other: 10 min.

Serve these tangy peaches with barbecue entrées or scoop homemade ice cream on top of a half peach for a luscious hot-and-cold dessert

½ cup balsamic vinegar
3 Tbsp. brown sugar
1 tsp. cracked pepper
⅛ tsp. salt
6 firm, ripe peaches, halved
¼ cup vegetable oil

Combine first 4 ingredients in a saucepan. Bring to a boil; reduce heat, and simmer 2 to 3 minutes.

Place peaches in a shallow dish. Pour vinegar mixture over peaches, tossing gently to coat. Let stand 10 minutes.

Remove peaches from vinegar mixture, reserving 2 Tbsp. mixture. Set aside remaining vinegar mixture.

Whisk together reserved 2 Tbsp. vinegar mixture and oil, blending well. Set vinaigrette aside.

Place peach halves, cut sides down, on a lightly greased food grate. Grill, covered with grill lid, over medium heat (300° to 350°) 5 minutes on each side or until firm and golden, basting with remaining vinegar mixture. Serve peaches with vinaigrette. **Makes** 6 servings.

Goat Cheese-and-Grilled Pepper Pizza

Prep: 10 min., Cook: 20 min. per pizza

Any combination of bell peppers can be used for this dynamic veggie pizza.

2 tsp. olive oil
¼ tsp. salt
¼ tsp. pepper
1 cup yellow bell pepper rings
1 cup green bell pepper rings
1 cup red bell pepper rings
1 cup sliced red onion, separated into rings
2 (10-inch) Quick-and-Easy Pizza Crusts (page 143)
½ cup crumbled herbed goat cheese, at room
 temperature

Combine first 3 ingredients in a small bowl; set aside.

Prepare grill. Place bell peppers and onion on food grate coated with cooking spray; grill 10 to 12 minutes or until tender. Set aside.

Place 1 crust on food grate coated with cooking spray; grill 3 minutes or until puffy and golden. Turn crust, grill mark side up; brush with half of oil mixture. Top with half of grilled vegetables and half of goat cheese. Grill, covered, over medium heat (300° to 350°) 4 to 5 minutes or until cheese melts and crust is lightly browned. Repeat with remaining crust and toppings. **Makes** 6 servings.

PIZZA GRILLING 101

■ A little preparation goes a long way. Be sure you have all of your topping ingredients ready and nearby before you start to grill the pizza dough.

■ To give your pizza a more pronounced smoky flavor, soak a couple of handfuls of aromatic wood chips in water for about 30 minutes. Sprinkle them over the hot coals, and close the grill lid. Wait a few minutes before you place the pizza crust on the food grate.

■ Always remember to coat the pizza dough or food grate with cooking spray unless the recipe calls to do otherwise.

■ Don't fret when your crust has irregular, puffy circles and grill marks—they're part of the rustic attraction.

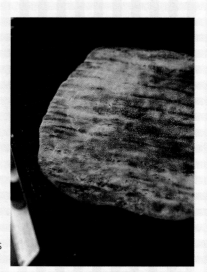

Quick-and-Easy Pizza Crusts

Prep: 30 min.; Other: 1 hr., 5 min.

We call for bread flour because it's higher in protein than all-purpose flour and makes a firmer, denser crust. You can, however, substitute all-purpose flour.

2 cups bread flour
½ tsp. salt
½ tsp. sugar
1 (¼-oz.) envelope rapid-rise yeast
¾ cup warm water (120° to 130°)
1 Tbsp. olive oil
2 Tbsp. cornmeal

Combine first 4 ingredients in a large bowl; make a well in center of mixture. Combine water and oil; add to flour mixture. Stir until mixture forms a ball. Turn dough out onto a lightly floured surface; knead until smooth and elastic (about 10 minutes).

Place the dough in a large bowl coated with cooking spray, turning to coat top. Cover and let rise in a warm place (85°), free from drafts, 45 minutes or until doubled in bulk. Punch dough down; divide in half. Cover and let dough rest 10 minutes.

Working with 1 portion at a time (cover remaining dough to keep from drying), roll each portion into a 10-inch circle on a lightly floured surface. Place dough on 2 baking sheets, each sprinkled with 1 Tbsp. cornmeal. **Makes** 2 (10-inch) pizza crusts.

Food Processor Variation: Place the first 4 ingredients in a food processor, and pulse 2 times or until well blended. With processor on, slowly add water and oil through food chute; process until dough forms a ball. Process 1 more minute. Turn out onto a lightly floured counter; knead 9 to 10 times. Proceed with recipe as directed.

Bread Machine Variation: Follow manufacturer's instructions for placing all ingredients except cornmeal into bread pan. Select dough cycle; start bread machine. Remove dough from machine. (Do not bake.) Proceed with recipe as directed.

quick & easy
Grilled Vegetable Pizza with Feta and Spinach

Prep: 10 min., Cook: 11 min. per pizza

Any flavor of feta cheese works on this pizza. The tangy, fresh spinach mixture is a nice contrast to the grilled veggies and cheese.

3 Tbsp. balsamic vinegar
1 garlic clove, crushed
1 (1¼-lb.) eggplant, cut crosswise into ¼-inch-thick slices
½ tsp. pepper
¼ tsp. salt
2 (10-inch) Quick-and-Easy Pizza Crusts (at left)
2 tsp. olive oil, divided
2 cups chopped plum tomato (about 8 tomatoes)
1 cup crumbled feta cheese with basil and tomato
2 Tbsp. chopped fresh or 1 tsp. dried oregano
2 cups thinly sliced spinach leaves
2 Tbsp. balsamic vinegar

Combine 3 Tbsp. vinegar and garlic in a small bowl; brush over both sides of eggplant slices. Sprinkle both sides of eggplant with pepper and salt. Place eggplant on food grate coated with cooking spray; grill 2 minutes on each side or until tender. Remove from grill; set aside.

Place 1 crust on food grate coated with cooking spray; grill, covered, over medium heat (300° to 350°) 3 minutes or until puffy and golden.

Turn crust, grill mark side up; brush with 1 tsp. oil. Arrange half of eggplant slices over crust, overlapping slightly. Top with half of tomato, cheese, and oregano. Cover and grill 3 to 4 minutes or until thoroughly heated; remove from heat.

Combine spinach and 2 Tbsp. vinegar in a small bowl. Top pizza with half of spinach mixture. Repeat with remaining crust and toppings. **Makes** 6 servings.

Grilled Pizza with Smoked Tofu and Roasted Red Peppers

Prep: 35 min.; Cook: 19 min.; Other: 1 hr., 35 min.

With its firm texture, smoked tofu shreds easily and replaces some of the cheese that traditionally tops pizza.

1 tsp. sugar
1 (¼-oz.) envelope active dry yeast
1 cup warm water (100° to 110°)
2¾ cups all-purpose flour, divided
2 Tbsp. olive oil, divided
1¼ tsp. salt, divided
1 garlic clove, minced
1 (28-oz.) can plum tomatoes, undrained and chopped
¼ tsp. pepper
2 red bell peppers
2 cups shredded smoked tofu (about 6 oz.)
1½ cups (6 oz.) shredded fresh mozzarella cheese

Dissolve sugar and yeast in warm water in a large bowl; let stand 5 minutes. Lightly spoon flour into dry measuring cups; level with a knife.

Add 2½ cups flour, 1 Tbsp. oil, and 1 tsp. salt; stir well to form a stiff dough. Turn dough out onto a lightly floured surface. Knead until smooth and elastic (about 10 minutes); add enough of remaining flour, 1 Tbsp. at a time, to prevent dough from sticking to hands. (The dough will feel tacky.)

Place dough in a large bowl coated with cooking spray, turning to coat top.

Cover and let rise in a warm place (85°), free from drafts, 45 minutes or until dough is doubled in size. (Gently press two fingers into dough. If indentation remains, the dough has risen enough.)

Heat remaining 1 Tbsp. olive oil in a medium non-stick skillet over medium-high heat. Add garlic, and sauté 1 minute. Add tomatoes; bring to a boil. Reduce heat; simmer 30 minutes or until sauce is thick. Stir in remaining ¼ tsp. salt and ¼ tsp. black pepper.

Punch the dough down. Cover and let rest 5 minutes. Divide dough into 6 equal portions; working with 1 portion at a time, shape each into a ball. (Cover remaining dough to prevent drying.)

Roll each ball into a 6-inch circle. Place on baking sheets coated with cooking spray. Lightly coat dough with cooking spray; cover with plastic wrap. Let rest 15 minutes.

Cut bell peppers in half lengthwise; discard seeds and membranes. Place pepper halves, skin sides down, on food grate coated with cooking spray; grill 15 minutes or until blackened. Place in a zip-top freezer bag; seal. Let stand 15 minutes. Peel and cut into strips.

Place dough rounds on food grate coated with cooking spray; grill, covered, over medium heat (300° to 350°) 2 minutes or until lightly browned. Turn dough over.

Spread ⅓ cup tomato sauce over each dough round, leaving a ½-inch border. Sprinkle ⅓ cup tofu and ¼ cup cheese evenly over each pizza. Divide pepper strips evenly among pizzas.

Close grill lid; grill 2 minutes or until cheese melts. Serve immediately. **Makes** 6 servings.

quick & easy
Grilled Onion Pizzas

Prep: 5 min., Cook: 19 min.

Grilling caramelizes the natural sugars in onions; the flavor is unbeatable.

2 large red onions
3 Tbsp. olive oil, divided
1½ Tbsp. minced fresh rosemary
½ tsp. ground cinnamon
¼ tsp. salt
¼ tsp. ground red pepper
4 (6-inch) Italian bread shells
1 (4-oz.) package crumbled blue cheese
½ cup chopped walnuts, toasted

Cut each onion into 4 (½-inch-thick) slices. Combine 2 Tbsp. oil, rosemary, and next 3 ingredients; brush over both sides of onion slices.

Cook onion, covered with grill lid, 4 to 5 minutes on each side or until browned and tender.

Brush tops of bread shells with remaining 1 Tbsp. oil; cook, without grill lid, 1 to 2 minutes. Sprinkle with crumbled cheese; top with onion, and sprinkle with chopped walnuts.

Grill, covered with grill lid, over medium heat (300° to 350°) 5 to 7 minutes or until cheese melts and bread shells are golden. Cut into wedges, and serve immediately. **Makes** 4 servings.

Grilled Veggie Pizzas

Prep: 20 min.; Cook: 21 min.; Other: 1 hr., 20 min.

Homemade pizza on the grill tastes like wood-fired restaurant pizza. Personalize the recipe by using your favorite vegetable or cheese combinations. Mushrooms, asparagus, squash, or eggplant also works well for the following vegetable toppings.

1 (¼-oz.) envelope active dry yeast
1½ cups warm water (100° to 110°)
2 Tbsp. extra-virgin olive oil
4 cups all-purpose flour, divided
½ tsp. salt
2 large zucchini, cut lengthwise into ¼-inch strips
2 red bell peppers, cut into ¼-inch rings
1 large onion, halved and cut into ½-inch slices
1 Tbsp. extra-virgin olive oil
¼ tsp. freshly ground pepper
2 garlic cloves, minced
6 Tbsp. (about 1½ oz.) shredded part-skim mozzarella
6 Tbsp. (about 1½ oz.) shredded Gruyère cheese

Dissolve yeast in warm water in a large bowl. Stir in 2 Tbsp. oil, and let stand 5 minutes.

Lightly spoon all-purpose flour into dry measuring cups; level with a knife. Add 3½ cups flour and salt to yeast mixture; stir until a dough forms.

Turn dough out onto a lightly floured surface. Knead until smooth and elastic (about 10 minutes); add enough of remaining flour, 1 Tbsp. at a time, to prevent dough from sticking to hands.

Place dough in a large bowl coated with cooking spray, turning to coat top. Cover and let rise in a warm place (85°), free from drafts, 1 hour or until doubled in size. (Gently press two fingers into dough. If indentation remains, dough has risen enough.) Punch dough down; cover and let rest 5 minutes.

Place zucchini, bell pepper, and onion in a large bowl; stir in 1 Tbsp. oil and pepper, tossing well. Place on food grate coated with cooking spray; grill 5 minutes on each side or until tender. Remove from grill; stir in garlic.

Divide dough into 6 equal portions, pressing each portion into a 7-inch round. Coat both sides of dough rounds with cooking spray. Place 3 dough rounds on food grate. Grill, covered, over medium heat (300° to 350°) 4 minutes or until puffed and golden. Remove from grill.

Turn rounds over; top each round with 1 Tbsp. mozzarella, about one-sixth of vegetables, and 1 Tbsp. Gruyère cheese. Place topped rounds on grill.

Cover and cook 1½ minutes or until bottoms are browned. Repeat procedure with remaining 3 dough rounds, vegetables, and cheeses. **Makes** 6 servings.

Grilled Andouille Grits

Prep: 5 min., Cook: 23 min., Other: 8 hrs.

Once chilled, these sturdy wedges of grits hold their shape; just make sure the grill is good and hot to keep them from sticking. These are especially tasty with smoked pork.

½ large Vidalia onion, chopped
½ cup chopped andouille or spicy smoked sausage
2 Tbsp. vegetable oil
1 (14-oz.) can chicken broth
¾ cup half-and-half
1 cup quick-cooking grits, uncooked
½ tsp. salt
2 Tbsp. butter or margarine, melted

Sauté onion and sausage in hot oil in a 3-qt. saucepan over medium-high heat until tender. Add chicken broth and half-and-half; bring to a boil. Gradually stir in grits and salt. Cover, reduce heat, and simmer, stirring occasionally, 10 minutes or until thickened.

Pour grits onto a lightly greased baking sheet into a 10½-inch circle (should be about ⅓-inch thick); cover and chill 8 hours.

Invert grits circle onto a flat surface; cut into 8 wedges. Brush top and bottom of each wedge with melted butter.

Grill, uncovered, over medium heat (300° to 350°) 3 to 4 minutes on each side. Remove and keep warm. **Makes** 6 servings.

Note: Grits may be broiled, if desired. Prepare as directed, and arrange buttered wedges on baking sheet. Broil 6 inches from heat 2 minutes on each side or until golden.

Barbecue Meat Loaf
Sandwiches, page 157

Rainy-Day Barbecue Options

Never mind the grill if it's
rainy or cold outside.
You can slow-simmer tender
and tasty 'cue indoors on the
cooktop, in the oven, or in the
slow cooker. Those familiar flavors
come through just the same—the
secret's in the sauce.

Barbecue
Beefwiches

Barbecue Beefwiches

Prep: 20 min., Cook: 4 hrs.

1 (3-lb.) lean beef rump roast
1½ cups ketchup
¼ cup plus 2 Tbsp. red wine vinegar
⅓ cup firmly packed dark brown sugar
1 Tbsp. dried onion flakes
1 tsp. liquid smoke
½ tsp. salt
½ tsp. pepper
⅛ tsp. garlic powder
2½ cups finely shredded cabbage
½ cup finely shredded carrot
2 Tbsp. white vinegar
2 Tbsp. minced sweet pickle
1½ Tbsp. sugar
1½ tsp. vegetable oil
⅛ tsp. celery seeds
12 hamburger buns, split and toasted

Trim fat from roast. Coat a Dutch oven with cooking spray; place over medium heat until hot. Add roast; cook until browned on all sides, turning frequently. Remove roast from pan; wipe drippings from pan with a paper towel.

Combine ketchup and next 7 ingredients, stirring well. Return roast to pan, and pour ketchup mixture over roast. Bring to a boil. Cover, reduce heat, and simmer 4 hours or until meat is tender. Remove roast from pan, reserving sauce in pan. Cool slightly. Shred meat with 2 forks, and return to pan. Cover and cook over medium heat until thoroughly heated, stirring occasionally.

Combine cabbage and carrot. Combine vinegar and next 4 ingredients in a saucepan; bring to a boil, stirring occasionally. Boil 1 minute. Pour over cabbage mixture, and toss gently. Spoon about ½ cup meat mixture on bottom half of each bun; top each with ¼ cup cabbage mixture and a remaining bun half. **Makes** 12 servings.

Barbecue Roast

Prep: 15 min.; Cook: 2 hrs., 15 min.

This roast has a sweet side due to brown sugar, ketchup, and cola in the recipe. Pair it with Simple Southern Iced Tea, page 50, with a squirt of lemon.

1 (3-lb.) boneless chuck roast
1 tsp. salt
½ tsp. pepper
¼ cup firmly packed brown sugar, divided
2 cups water
2 cups ketchup
¾ cup cola soft drink
¼ cup liquid smoke
2 Tbsp. white vinegar
2 Tbsp. Worcestershire sauce
1 Tbsp. prepared mustard
½ tsp. hot sauce
8 to 10 hamburger buns

Sprinkle roast with salt and pepper, and rub with 2 Tbsp. brown sugar. Place in a Dutch oven, and add 2 cups water. Cook, partially covered, over low heat 2 hours or until tender. Remove roast, and shred with 2 forks.

Bring remaining 2 Tbsp. brown sugar, ketchup, and next 6 ingredients to a boil in a large heavy saucepan. Reduce heat, and simmer 15 minutes or until thickened. Stir in shredded roast. Serve on hamburger buns. **Makes** 8 to 10 servings.

Four-Hour Barbecue
Prep: 15 min.; Cook: 4 hrs., 10 min.

The longer and slower you cook this roast the more tender it will be. Four hours for this roast makes it melt in your mouth and leaves you lots of free time for other activities.

1 (3-lb.) boneless chuck roast, trimmed
2 Tbsp. vegetable oil
2 cups water
1 cup ketchup
2 small onions, chopped
1 garlic clove, minced
¼ cup white vinegar
¼ cup Worcestershire sauce
1 Tbsp. chili powder
2 tsp. salt
1 tsp. pepper

Brown roast on all sides in hot oil in a Dutch oven over medium-high heat. Stir together 2 cups water and next 8 ingredients. Pour over roast.
Bake, covered, at 325° for 4 hours. Cool meat, and shred with 2 forks. Stir together shredded meat and sauce. **Makes** 6 to 8 servings.

Savory Onion Brisket
Prep: 15 min., Cook: 3 hrs.

1 (4½-lb.) beef brisket, untrimmed
3 Tbsp. olive oil
¼ cup white wine vinegar
2 Tbsp. vegetable oil
2 Tbsp. ketchup
1 tsp. salt
2 tsp. garlic powder
2 tsp. pepper
1 (1.4-oz.) envelope dry onion soup mix
1 cup water

Brown brisket in hot oil over high heat 5 minutes on each side. Place in a lightly greased 13- x 9-inch pan.
Stir together vinegar and next 6 ingredients; pour over brisket. Add 1 cup water to pan.
Bake, covered, at 350° for 2 hours, basting every hour. Reduce oven temperature to 300°, and bake 1 more hour. Skim fat from drippings, discarding fat; serve drippings with brisket. **Makes** 6 to 8 servings.

editor's favorite
Quickest Brisket Sandwiches
Prep: 15 min.; Cook: 1 hr., 20 min.

Cooking this brisket in the pressure cooker speeds up the process so you can have barbecue in record time.

1 cup sliced onion, separated into rings
¾ cup bottled chili sauce
½ cup beer
1 Tbsp. Worcestershire sauce
1 (2½-lb.) beef brisket
1 tsp. pepper
4 garlic cloves, minced
¼ cup packed brown sugar
8 (2½-oz.) submarine rolls

Combine first 4 ingredients in a 6-qt. pressure cooker. Bring to a boil; reduce heat, and simmer 5 minutes. Remove ½ cup mixture from cooker.
Trim fat from brisket. Cut brisket in half crosswise. Rub brisket with pepper and garlic. Place in cooker. Spoon ½ cup chili sauce mixture over brisket. Close lid securely; bring to high pressure over high heat (about 5 minutes). Adjust the heat to medium or level needed to maintain high pressure; cook 1 hour.
Remove from heat; place cooker under cold running water. Remove lid. Remove brisket from cooker, and set aside. Add brown sugar to chili sauce mixture in cooker; bring to a boil. Reduce heat, and simmer, uncovered, 5 minutes, stirring frequently.
Shred brisket with 2 forks. Return meat to sauce in pressure cooker; cook until thoroughly heated. Spoon 1 cup meat with sauce over bottom of each roll, and cover with a remaining roll half. **Makes** 8 servings.

Quick Tip: *Brisket is an essential cut of beef because it adapts easily to many different styles and flavors of barbecue. If you like sweet barbecue, try Ketchup 'n' Cola Brisket (page 154); if you like spicy, try Chili-Spiced Brisket (page 153). You can find interesting flavors paired with brisket such as Coffee-Baked Brisket (page 154) and Lone Star Brisket in Chili Sauce and Beer (page 152). Some of our recipes call for untrimmed brisket—the fat helps keep the meat from drying out when cooking.*

Quickest Brisket
Sandwiches

Saucy Brisket and Potatoes
Prep: 10 min., Cook: 3 hrs.

1 (4- to 5-lb.) beef brisket
2 Tbsp. vegetable oil
1 (8-oz.) package sliced fresh mushrooms
½ cup firmly packed brown sugar
½ cup barbecue sauce
½ cup ketchup
½ cup cider vinegar
½ cup duck sauce
1 (1.0-oz.) envelope dry onion soup mix
1 cup water
4 bay leaves
4 large baking potatoes, each cut into 8 wedges
    (optional)

Brown brisket on both sides in hot oil in a Dutch oven over medium-high heat; place in a large roasting pan. Stir together mushrooms and next 6 ingredients; spread over brisket.
Bake, covered, at 350° for 1 hour. Add 1 cup water and bay leaves, and bake, covered, 1½ hours. Add potato, if desired, and bake, uncovered, 30 minutes or until potato is tender. Remove and discard bay leaves. Cut brisket diagonally across the grain into thin slices. Serve with sauce and potato. **Makes** 8 servings.

Lone Star Brisket in Chili Sauce and Beer
Prep: 15 min.; Cook: 5 hrs., 30 min.

1 (5- to 7-lb.) beef brisket, trimmed
2½ tsp. seasoned salt
1 tsp. pepper
2 garlic cloves, minced
2 medium-size red onions, thinly sliced and
    separated into rings
2 celery ribs, chopped
1 (12-oz.) bottle chili sauce
¼ cup water
1 (12-oz.) can beer

Sprinkle brisket with salt, pepper, and garlic. Place half each of onion rings and celery in bottom of a lightly greased roasting pan.
Place brisket, fat side up, over vegetables. Top with remaining onion rings and celery. Pour chili sauce and ¼ cup water over top.
Bake at 300° for 1½ hours, basting every 30 minutes. Pour beer over brisket. Tightly cover pan with double-layered heavy-duty aluminum foil, and bake 3 to 4 more hours. **Makes** 10 to 14 servings.

> "Most of the South considers barbecue to be all about pork, but in the Lone Star State, barbecue means one thing—brisket. If you've never tried this Southern favorite, you're missing a real treat."

—Troy Black, *Southern Living* Contributor

Brisket with Veggies

Prep: 10 min., Cook: 4 hrs.

1 (5-lb.) beef brisket
½ tsp. salt
½ tsp. pepper
1 lb. carrots, cut into chunks
4 lb. small new potatoes
2 cups water
¼ cup Worcestershire sauce
1 (1.0-oz.) envelope dry onion soup mix

Trim fat from brisket; place brisket in a large Dutch oven. Sprinkle with salt and pepper. Add carrot chunks and next 3 ingredients; sprinkle with soup mix.
Bake, covered, at 350° for 4 hours. **Makes** 10 to 12 servings.

freezer friendly
Baked Brisket Au Jus

Prep: 10 min., Cook: 5 hrs., Other: 20 min.

1 (5-lb.) beef brisket
2 tsp. salt
¼ tsp. pepper
1 large onion, sliced
4 celery ribs
½ cup tomato paste
½ cup tomato sauce
1 Tbsp. Worcestershire sauce
1 cup brewed coffee
¼ cup water (optional)

Place brisket, fat side up, in a roasting pan. Sprinkle with salt and pepper. Top with onion and celery.
Stir together tomato paste, tomato sauce, and Worcestershire sauce; pour over beef.
Bake brisket at 325° for 1 hour. Cover and bake 2 more hours, basting with pan juices occasionally. Add coffee; cover and bake 2 more hours, checking every 30 minutes for dryness. Add ¼ cup water, if necessary.
Remove brisket from pan; let stand 20 minutes. Cut brisket across grain into thin slices using a sharp knife.
Strain pan drippings, and serve with sliced brisket.
Makes 8 to 10 servings.

Chili-Spiced Brisket

Prep: 10 min., Cook: 4 hrs.

The pan juices from this brisket provide a flavorful topping for mashed potatoes.

1 (4-lb.) beef brisket
1 Tbsp. vegetable oil
¼ tsp. salt
¼ tsp. ground pepper
4 black peppercorns, crushed
1 bay leaf
1 cup chili sauce
1½ cups chopped onion
1 (10½-oz.) can beef broth
1½ Tbsp. brown sugar
1 Tbsp. Worcestershire sauce
⅛ tsp. garlic salt

Trim excess fat from brisket. Brown brisket in hot oil in a large Dutch oven on all sides. Add salt and next 5 ingredients to Dutch oven. Combine beef broth and remaining 3 ingredients; stir well. Pour over brisket. Cover and bake at 350° for 4 hours or until tender. Remove meat to a serving platter; keep warm.
Pour pan juices through a wire-mesh strainer into a bowl, discarding solids. Slice meat across grain into thin slices, and serve with pan juices. **Makes** 8 to 10 servings.

5-Ingredient Brisket

Prep: 15 min., Cook: 3 hrs., Other: 20 min.

2 cups ketchup
1¼ cups cola soft drink
1 cup chili sauce
1 (1.4-oz.) envelope dry onion soup mix
1 (3- to 4-lb.) beef brisket, trimmed

Stir together first 4 ingredients in a small bowl.
Place brisket, fat side up, in an aluminum foil-lined 13- x 9-inch baking dish. Pour chili sauce mixture over brisket. Cover with foil, and seal.
Bake at 350° for 3 hours. Remove from oven; let stand 20 minutes. Slice meat, and pour sauce over slices.
Makes 6 to 8 servings.

Carolina Blond
Open-Faced Sandwiches
Prep: 15 min., Cook: 12 min.

1 (12-oz.) bag coleslaw
⅓ cup light coleslaw dressing (we tested with Marzetti)
¼ tsp. celery seeds
1 cup ketchup
½ cup water
¼ cup cider vinegar
2 Tbsp. instant minced onion
2 Tbsp. dark brown sugar
1 Tbsp. prepared mustard
1 tsp. pepper
1 tsp. hot sauce
½ tsp. garlic powder
1½ cups (¾ lb.) skinned, shredded roasted chicken
    breast (we tested with Tyson)
4 (2-oz.) slices Texas toast, lightly toasted

Combine first 3 ingredients in a bowl; toss well to coat. Combine ketchup and next 8 ingredients in a medium saucepan; bring to a boil. Reduce heat; simmer 5 minutes or until mixture begins to thicken. Stir in chicken, and cook 4 minutes or until roasted chicken is thoroughly heated.
Top each toasted bread slice with ½ cup chicken and ½ cup coleslaw mixture. **Makes** 4 servings.

Barbecue Turkey Sandwiches
Prep: 10 min., Cook: 10 min.

¾ lb. freshly ground raw turkey breast
1 medium onion, chopped
1 (8-oz.) can tomato sauce
1 (7-oz.) jar roasted red peppers, drained and chopped
¼ tsp. salt
¼ tsp. pepper
2 tsp. liquid mesquite smoke (optional)
4 whole wheat or plain Kaiser rolls

Cook turkey and onion in a nonstick skillet over medium-high heat 4 to 5 minutes or until onion is tender and turkey is done, stirring until turkey crumbles. Stir in sauce and peppers; simmer 5 minutes.
Stir in salt, pepper, and, if desired, liquid smoke. Spoon turkey mixture evenly onto bottom halves of rolls; top with remaining halves. **Makes** 4 servings.

editor's favorite
Warm Barbecue Chicken Salad
Prep: 40 min., Cook: 35 min.

3 cups shredded cooked chicken
Barbecue Dressing, divided
1 cup frozen whole kernel corn, thawed
2 bacon slices, cooked and crumbled
6 cups torn leaf lettuce (about 1 head)
4 plum tomatoes, chopped
⅓ large red onion, sliced and separated into rings
⅔ cup shredded mozzarella cheese

Stir together chicken and 1 cup Barbecue Dressing in a lightly greased 9-inch square pan.
Bake, covered, at 350° for 35 minutes or until warm. Cook corn in boiling water to cover 3 to 4 minutes; drain.
Toss together corn, bacon, and next 3 ingredients. Top with warm chicken mixture, and sprinkle with cheese. Serve immediately with remaining dressing. **Makes** 6 servings.

Barbecue Dressing
Prep: 10 min., Cook: 15 min.

1 (18-oz.) bottle barbecue sauce
⅓ cup firmly packed light brown sugar
½ cup honey
⅓ cup ketchup
1 Tbsp. butter or margarine
1 Tbsp. Worcestershire sauce
½ tsp. seasoned salt
1 tsp. lemon pepper

Bring all ingredients to a boil; reduce heat, and simmer, stirring occasionally, 10 minutes. Store in refrigerator up to 3 months, if desired. **Makes** 3 cups.

Barbecue Chicken Pizza

Barbecue Chicken Pizza

Prep: 25 min., Cook: 10 min.

For even more flavor, sprinkle pizza with chopped cooked bacon and chopped fresh cilantro before adding the cheese.

1 small onion, chopped
½ red bell pepper, chopped
½ tsp. salt
¼ tsp. pepper
1 tsp. olive oil
1 (13.8-oz.) can refrigerated pizza crust
½ cup hickory smoke barbecue sauce
2 (6-oz.) packages grilled boneless, skinless chicken breast strips
2 cups (8 oz.) shredded Monterey Jack cheese with peppers
Garnish: chopped fresh parsley
Additional hickory smoke barbecue sauce

Sauté first 4 ingredients in hot oil in a large skillet over medium-high heat 8 to 10 minutes or until vegetables are tender. Drain well.
Unroll pizza crust; press or pat into a lightly greased 13- x 9-inch pan.
Bake crust at 400° for 12 to 14 minutes. Spread ½ cup barbecue sauce evenly over top of pizza crust in pan. Arrange chicken strips evenly over barbecue sauce, top with onion mixture, and sprinkle evenly with cheese.
Bake at 400° for 8 to 10 minutes or until cheese melts. Garnish, if desired. Serve with extra sauce for dipping. **Makes** 6 servings.

Quick 'n' Easy Barbecue Chicken Pizza

Prep: 5 min., Cook: 15 min., Other: 15 min.

2 cups chopped cooked chicken
¾ cup barbecue sauce
1 (14-oz.) package prebaked Italian pizza crust (we tested with Boboli)
1 cup (4 oz.) shredded mozzarella cheese
¼ medium-size red onion, thinly sliced
2 green onions, chopped

Combine chicken and barbecue sauce; let stand 15 minutes.
Place pizza crust on a baking sheet. Spread chicken mixture over pizza crust. Top with remaining ingredients.
Bake at 450° for 15 minutes or until cheese melts.
Makes 4 servings.

Tex-Mex Chicken-and-Bacon Pizza

Prep: 20 min., Bake: 19 min.

1 (13.8-oz.) can refrigerated pizza crust
½ tsp. ground cumin
1 cup black bean-and-corn salsa
1 cup (4 oz.) shredded sharp Cheddar cheese
1 cup diced cooked chicken
4 fully cooked bacon slices, diced
½ red onion, thinly sliced and separated into rings
½ cup diced seeded plum tomatoes
1 cup (4 oz.) shredded four-cheese blend
2 small jalapeño peppers, sliced and seeded
1 ripe avocado
1 lime, halved
Sour cream
Chopped fresh cilantro

Coat a 14-inch pizza pan lightly with cooking spray. Unroll pizza crust; press or pat onto prepared pan. Lightly coat dough with cooking spray; sprinkle with cumin.
Bake at 425° for 7 minutes or just until crust begins to brown. Remove from oven, and reduce oven temperature to 375°.
Spread salsa evenly over crust; sprinkle evenly with Cheddar cheese. Layer with chicken and next 5 ingredients in order listed.
Bake at 375° for 9 to 12 minutes or until cheese melts.
Slice avocado. Squeeze lime over slices. Arrange slices in a spoke design on pizza; dollop with sour cream, and sprinkle evenly with chopped cilantro. **Makes** 6 servings.

Barbecue Baked Catfish
Prep: 20 min., Cook: 12 min.

¾ cup ketchup
¼ cup butter or margarine
1 Tbsp. balsamic vinegar
1 Tbsp. Worcestershire sauce
1 tsp. Dijon mustard
½ tsp. Jamaican jerk seasoning
1 garlic clove, minced
10 (3- to 4-oz.) catfish fillets
⅛ tsp. pepper
Garnish: chopped fresh parsley

Stir together first 7 ingredients in a small saucepan over medium-low heat; cook mixture 10 minutes, stirring occasionally.

Sprinkle catfish with pepper; arrange in an even layer in a lightly greased aluminum foil-lined broiler pan. Pour sauce over catfish.

Bake catfish at 400° for 10 to 12 minutes or until fish flakes with a fork. Garnish, if desired. **Makes** 5 servings.

Barbecue Roasted Salmon
Prep: 10 min., Cook: 12 min., Other: 1 hr.

¼ cup pineapple juice
2 Tbsp. fresh lemon juice
4 (6-oz.) salmon fillets
2 Tbsp. brown sugar
4 tsp. chili powder
2 tsp. grated lemon rind
¾ tsp. ground cumin
½ tsp. salt
¼ tsp. ground cinnamon
Lemon wedges (optional)

Combine first 3 ingredients in a zip-top freezer bag; seal and marinate in refrigerator 1 hour, turning occasionally.

Remove fish from bag; discard marinade. Combine sugar and next 5 ingredients in a bowl. Rub over fish; place in an 11- x 7-inch baking dish coated with cooking spray. Bake at 400° for 12 minutes or until fish flakes easily when tested with a fork. Serve with lemon, if desired. **Makes** 4 servings.

Barbecue Roasted Salmon

Barbecue Shrimp and Cornbread-Stuffed Peppers
Prep: 45 min., Cook: 20 min.

This restaurant-style masterpiece was created by Chef John I. Akhile from the Waverly Grill at the Renaissance Waverly Hotel in Atlanta. He grills his shrimp over medium-high heat for 5 minutes; we broiled them indoors for simplicity while the peppers baked. The recipe is perfect for combining Southern barbecue flavors with a more formal setting, such as a bridal shower.

16 unpeeled, large fresh shrimp
½ tsp. kosher salt, divided
½ tsp. pepper, divided
1 (6-oz.) package Mexican cornbread mix
½ cup diced onion
½ cup diced celery
1 yellow bell pepper, diced
½ cup diced country ham
1 Tbsp. olive oil
½ cup milk
½ cup buttermilk
1 Tbsp. chopped fresh thyme
2 large eggs, lightly beaten
1¼ cups chopped pecans, toasted
8 medium-size red bell peppers
⅓ cup butter or margarine, cut into pieces
1 (8-oz.) bottle barbecue sauce
1 (4-oz.) jar chipotle pepper sauce
Green Bell Pepper Sauce

Peel shrimp, and devein, if desired. Sprinkle evenly with ¼ tsp. salt and ¼ tsp. pepper; cover and chill.
Prepare cornbread according to package directions; cool on a wire rack. Crumble.
Sauté onion and next 3 ingredients in hot oil in a large skillet until vegetables are tender. Reduce heat, and stir in crumbled cornbread, milk, buttermilk, and thyme. Remove from heat, and stir in eggs, pecans, remaining ¼ tsp. salt, and remaining ¼ tsp. pepper.
Cut bell peppers in half crosswise; remove and discard seeds and membranes. Stuff bell pepper shells evenly with cornbread mixture. Top each evenly with butter, and place in a 13- x 9-inch pan.
Bake at 375° for 15 to 20 minutes. Remove from oven, and keep warm.
Meanwhile, stir together barbecue sauce and chipotle pepper sauce. Toss shrimp in sauce mixture; reserve remaining sauce.

Place shrimp on rack coated with cooking spray; place rack in broiler pan. Broil shrimp 5½ inches from heat for 4 minutes or until shrimp turn pink, basting twice. Set aside.
Spoon Green Bell Pepper Sauce onto individual serving plates; place stuffed peppers in center, and top with shrimp. **Makes** 8 servings.

Green Bell Pepper Sauce
Prep: 10 min., Cook: 15 min.

2 green bell peppers, diced
½ medium onion, diced
1½ tsp. minced garlic
1 Tbsp. olive oil
2 cups chicken broth, divided
2 cups loosely packed fresh spinach leaves
1 tsp. salt
1 tsp. pepper

Sauté first 3 ingredients in hot oil in a large saucepan until tender. Add 1 cup chicken broth. Bring to a boil over medium heat; reduce heat, and simmer, stirring occasionally, 7 minutes. Add spinach leaves, and simmer 3 minutes. Remove from heat; cool slightly.
Process bell pepper mixture in a blender until very smooth. Stir in enough remaining chicken broth to reach sauce consistency, if necessary. Pour through a wire-mesh strainer into a bowl, discarding solids; stir in salt and pepper. **Makes** 4 cups.

quick & easy
Cajun-Barbecue Shrimp
Prep: 10 min., Cook: 10 min.

16 unpeeled, jumbo fresh shrimp (1¼ lb.)
½ cup unsalted butter, sliced
¼ cup Worcestershire sauce
3 garlic cloves, chopped
2 Tbsp. lemon juice
1 Tbsp. Creole seasoning
1 Tbsp. coarsely ground pepper
1 lemon, cut into 4 wedges

Stir all ingredients in an ovenproof skillet.
Bake at 450° for 10 minutes or just until shrimp turn pink. Serve with crusty bread. **Makes** 2 servings.

Chuck Roast Barbecue

Prep: 10 min., Cook: 6 hrs.

1 (2- to 2½-lb.) boneless chuck roast, trimmed
2 medium onions, chopped
¾ cup cola soft drink
¼ cup Worcestershire sauce
1 Tbsp. apple cider vinegar
1 tsp. beef bouillon granules
½ tsp. dry mustard
½ tsp. chili powder
¼ tsp. ground red pepper
2 garlic cloves, minced
½ cup ketchup
2 tsp. butter or margarine
6 hamburger buns
Potato chips (optional)
Pickle spears (optional)

Combine roast and chopped onion in a 4-qt. slow cooker.

Combine cola and next 7 ingredients; reserve ½ cup in refrigerator. Pour remaining mixture over roast and onion.

Cover and cook on HIGH 6 hours or until roast is very tender; drain and shred roast in slow cooker. Keep warm.

Combine reserved ½ cup cola mixture, ketchup, and butter in a small saucepan; cook mixture over medium heat, stirring constantly, just until thoroughly heated. Pour over shredded roast, stirring gently.

Spoon onto buns; serve with potato chips and pickle spears, if desired. **Makes** 6 servings.

make ahead
Barbecue Beef Sandwiches
Prep: 10 min., Cook: 7 hrs.

Make your favorite creamy coleslaw to serve with or on these barbecue sandwiches. Freeze leftover meat up to one month.

1 (3½-lb.) eye of round roast, cut in half vertically
2 tsp. salt, divided
2 garlic cloves, pressed
1 (10½-oz.) can condensed beef broth
1 cup ketchup
½ cup firmly packed brown sugar
½ cup lemon juice
3 Tbsp. steak sauce
1 tsp. coarse ground pepper
1 tsp. Worcestershire sauce
12 Kaiser rolls or sandwich buns
Dill pickle slices

Sprinkle beef evenly with 1 tsp. salt.
Stir together remaining 1 tsp. salt, garlic, and next 7 ingredients. Pour half of mixture into a 5½-qt. slow cooker. Place beef in slow cooker, and pour remaining mixture over beef.
Cover and cook on HIGH 7 hours.
Shred beef in slow cooker with 2 forks. Serve on rolls or buns with dill pickle slices. **Makes** 12 servings.

Guinness-Braised Beef Brisket
Prep: 5 min., Cook: 8 hrs.

Tender from gentle cooking, this entrée is a classic preparation made without the usual pot watching. Serve it with grainy, coarse-ground mustard. Use the leftovers in Reuben sandwiches.

2 cups water
1 cup chopped onion
1 cup chopped carrot
1 cup chopped celery
1 cup Guinness stout
⅔ cup packed brown sugar
¼ cup chopped fresh or 1 Tbsp. dried dill
¼ cup tomato paste
1 (14-oz.) can low-sodium beef broth
6 black peppercorns
2 whole cloves
1 (3-lb.) cured corned beef brisket, trimmed

Combine first 11 ingredients in a 5- to 6-qt. slow cooker, stirring until well blended; top with beef. Cover and cook on HIGH 8 hours or until beef is tender. Remove beef; cut diagonally across grain into ¼-inch slices. Discard broth mixture. **Makes** 6 servings.

Knife-and-Fork Barbecued Brisket Sandwiches
Prep: 10 min., Cook: 5 hrs.

2 large onions, thinly sliced
1 (3-lb.) beef brisket
1 tsp. ground pepper
¼ tsp. salt
2 Tbsp. all-purpose flour
1 (12-oz.) bottle chili sauce
½ cup light beer
2 Tbsp. brown sugar
1 Tbsp. prepared horseradish
1 Tbsp. minced garlic (about 6 cloves)
5 submarine rolls, split and toasted

Place half of onion slices in a 4-qt. slow cooker. Trim fat from meat, and cut meat into large pieces to fit in slow cooker; sprinkle with pepper and salt. Dredge meat in flour; place on top of onion, sprinkling with any remaining flour. Add remaining half of onion.
Combine chili sauce and next 4 ingredients in a medium bowl, stirring well. Pour over meat mixture. Cover and cook on HIGH 4 to 5 hours or until meat is tender. Remove brisket, and replace slow cooker cover.
Shred beef with 2 forks; return meat to hot liquid in slow cooker, stirring well. Spoon meat mixture over toasted roll halves. **Makes** 10 servings.

Quick Tip: *Meat shreds easier while it's still warm. Barbecued meat can be refrigerated up to two days; reheat in the microwave to serve.*

Spiced Beef Barbecue
Prep: 15 min., Cook: 9 hrs.

Cinnamon and cloves add an exotic spiciness to the traditional barbecue sandwich. You can freeze leftover meat for later use.

4 lb. beef stew meat, cubed
2 (8-oz.) cans tomato sauce
1 medium onion, chopped
½ cup white vinegar
¼ cup firmly packed brown sugar
2 tsp. salt
1 tsp. minced garlic
1½ tsp. ground cinnamon (optional)
¾ tsp. ground cloves (optional)
12 sandwich buns

Place beef in 5-qt. slow cooker. Combine tomato sauce, next 5 ingredients, and, if desired, cinnamon and cloves; pour over beef. Cover and cook on HIGH 1 hour; reduce heat to LOW and cook 7 to 8 hours.
Remove beef from slow cooker; shred with 2 forks. Return beef to slow cooker, and stir into sauce. Serve on buns. **Makes** 12 servings.

Beef and Pork Barbecue
Prep: 5 min., Cook: 8 hrs.

1½ lb. beef stew meat
1½ lb. lean cubed pork
1 medium-size green bell pepper, chopped
1 small onion, chopped (about 1 cup)
1 (6-oz.) can tomato paste
½ cup firmly packed brown sugar
¼ cup white vinegar
1 Tbsp. chili powder
2 tsp. salt
1 tsp. dry mustard
2 tsp. Worcestershire sauce

Combine all ingredients in a 5-qt. slow cooker. Cover and cook on HIGH 8 hours. Shred meat before serving. **Makes** 6 servings.

Saucy Chipotle Barbecue Pork
Prep: 15 min., Cook: 7 hrs.

2 tsp. dry mustard
1 tsp. salt
½ tsp. ground red pepper
1 (4- to 5-lb.) boneless pork butt roast, cut in half
2 Tbsp. butter
1 large onion, chopped (about 2½ cups)
1 (18-oz.) bottle spicy original barbecue sauce (we tested with KC Masterpiece)
1 (12-oz.) bottle Baja chipotle marinade (we tested with Lawry's)
Garnish: sliced green onions

Rub first 3 ingredients evenly over pork. Melt butter in a large nonstick skillet over medium-high heat.
Add pork; cook 10 minutes or until browned on all sides.
Place onion and pork in a 5-qt. slow cooker. Add barbecue sauce and marinade.
Cover and cook on HIGH 7 hours or until pork is tender and shreds easily.
Remove pork to a large bowl, reserving sauce; shred pork. Stir shredded pork into sauce in slow cooker. Serve as is, over a cheese-topped baked potato, in a sandwich, or over a green salad. Garnish, if desired. **Makes** 8 servings.

3-Ingredient BBQ Pork
Prep: 5 min., Cook: 8 hrs.

This supersimple recipe delivers big flavor with the addition of cola. Serve on buns with slaw or over hot toasted cornbread.

1 (3- to 4-lb.) shoulder pork roast
1 (18-oz.) bottle barbecue sauce (we tested with Kraft Original)
1 (12-oz.) can cola soft drink

Place pork roast in a 6-qt. slow cooker; pour barbecue sauce and cola over roast.
Cover and cook on HIGH 8 hours or until meat is tender and shreds easily. **Makes** 6 servings.

Easy Barbecue Pork Chops
Prep: 10 min., Cook: 4 or 8 hrs.

8 (5-oz.) center-cut pork chops (½ inch thick)
¼ tsp. pepper
½ cup thick-and-spicy honey barbecue sauce
1 (14½-oz.) can stewed tomatoes, undrained
1 (10-oz.) package frozen vegetable seasoning
    blend

Trim fat from chops; sprinkle chops with pepper. Coat a large nonstick skillet with cooking spray; place over medium-high heat until hot.

Add chops, in 2 batches, and cook until browned on both sides.
Coat a 3½- or 4-qt. slow cooker with cooking spray. Place chops in cooker.
Combine barbecue sauce, stewed tomatoes, and frozen vegetable blend, stirring well; pour mixture over chops.
Cover and cook on HIGH 4 hours; or cover and cook on HIGH 1 hour and then on LOW 7 hours. **Makes** 8 servings.

Spicy-Sweet Ribs and Beans
Prep: 30 min., Cook: 6 or 10 hrs., Other: 20 min.

Slow cookers don't brown food, so here we broil the ribs for extra flavor before adding them to the pot. Serve with cornbread and a simple green salad with creamy Italian or Ranch dressing.

2 (16-oz.) cans pinto beans, drained
4 lb. country-style pork ribs, trimmed
1 tsp. garlic powder
½ tsp. salt
½ tsp. pepper
1 medium onion, chopped
1 (10.5-oz.) jar red jalapeño jelly
1 (18-oz.) bottle hickory-flavored barbecue sauce (we tested with Kraft Thick 'n Spicy)
1 tsp. green hot sauce (we tested with Tabasco)

Place beans in a 5-qt. slow cooker; set aside.
Cut ribs apart; sprinkle with garlic powder, salt, and pepper. Place ribs on a roasting pan.
Broil 5½ inches from heat 18 to 20 minutes or until browned, turning once. Add ribs to slow cooker, and sprinkle with onion.
Combine jelly, barbecue sauce, and hot sauce in a saucepan; cook over low heat until jelly melts. Pour over ribs; stir gently.
Cover and cook on HIGH 5 to 6 hours or on LOW 9 to 10 hours.
Remove ribs. Drain bean mixture, reserving sauce. Skim fat from sauce.
Arrange ribs over bean mixture; serve with sauce.
Makes 8 servings.

So-Simple
Baby Back Ribs
Prep: 15 min., Cook: 8 hrs.

4 lb. pork back ribs
1 (18-oz.) bottle honey-mustard barbecue sauce

Cut ribs to fit in a 6-qt. slow cooker. Pour sauce over ribs; cover and cook on HIGH 8 hours or until tender. **Makes** 4 to 6 servings.

editor's favorite • make ahead
Country-Style Barbecue Ribs
Prep: 15 min., Cook: 7 hrs.

Put these on to cook before you leave for work, or cook them overnight and refrigerate until dinnertime. If you reheat in the microwave, use 50% power.

4 lb. bone-in country-style pork ribs
2 tsp. salt, divided
1 medium onion, chopped
1 cup firmly packed light brown sugar
1 cup apple butter
1 cup ketchup
½ cup lemon juice
½ cup orange juice
1 Tbsp. steak sauce (we tested with A.1. Steak Sauce)
1 tsp. coarse ground pepper
1 tsp. minced garlic
½ tsp. Worcestershire sauce

Cut ribs apart, if necessary, and trim; sprinkle 1 tsp. salt evenly over ribs, and set aside.
Stir together remaining 1 tsp. salt, chopped onion, and remaining 9 ingredients until blended. Pour half of mixture into a 5-qt. slow cooker. Place ribs in slow cooker; pour remaining mixture over ribs.
Cover and cook on HIGH 6 to 7 hours. **Makes** 6 to 8 servings.

Debate Barbecue Sandwiches
Prep: 8 min., Cook: 8 hrs.

A Test Kitchen staffer reports that his mother-in-law sold these at his debate team meetings to pay for his travel.

1 (3-lb.) boneless pork loin roast, trimmed
1 cup water
1 (18-oz.) bottle barbecue sauce
¼ cup firmly packed brown sugar
2 Tbsp. Worcestershire sauce
1 to 2 Tbsp. hot sauce
1 tsp. salt
1 tsp. pepper
Hamburger buns
Coleslaw

Place roast in a 4-qt. slow cooker; add 1 cup water.
Cover and cook on HIGH 7 hours or until tender; shred meat with a fork. Add barbecue sauce and next 5 ingredients. Reduce to LOW; cook, covered, 1 hour. Serve on buns with coleslaw. **Makes** 20 servings.

Shredded Barbecue Chicken
Prep: 22 min., Cook: 7 hrs.

1½ lb. skinned and boned chicken thighs
1 Tbsp. olive oil
1 cup ketchup
¼ cup dark brown sugar
1 Tbsp. Worcestershire sauce
1 Tbsp. cider vinegar
1 Tbsp. yellow mustard
1 tsp. ground red pepper
½ tsp. garlic salt
6 hamburger buns
Dill pickle slices

Brown chicken 4 minutes on each side in 1 Tbsp. hot oil in a large skillet over medium-high heat. Remove from heat, and place in a 4-qt. slow cooker. Combine ketchup and next 6 ingredients. Pour over chicken.
Cover and cook on HIGH 1 hour. Reduce heat to LOW, and cook 5 to 6 hours. Remove chicken from sauce; shred chicken. Stir shredded chicken into sauce.
Spoon mixture evenly onto buns, and top with pickle slices. **Makes** 6 servings.

Spicy Pickled Okra,
page 202

Sauces, Marinades, and More

Every barbecuer depends on a great
collection of sauces and marinades.
Whether you favor sweet or tangy
flavors for basting, marinating, and
dipping, you'll find a complement
here. Condiments, such as pickles
and relishes, continue the
play on flavors.

Predominantly sweet with a mild tang, these sauces are perfect for pleasing families with kids as well as those who prefer milder flavors.

quick & easy
Thick 'n' Sweet Barbecue Sauce
Prep: 8 min., Cook: 20 min.

½ cup chopped onion
1 garlic clove, minced
¼ cup vegetable oil
1 (8-oz.) can tomato sauce
¼ cup firmly packed brown sugar
1½ tsp. grated lemon rind
¼ cup fresh lemon juice
2 Tbsp. Worcestershire sauce
2 Tbsp. prepared mustard
1 Tbsp. chopped fresh parsley

Cook onion and garlic in oil in a medium skillet over medium-high heat, stirring constantly, until tender. Add tomato sauce and remaining ingredients. Bring to a boil; reduce heat, and simmer 20 minutes or until thickened, stirring often. Use as a basting sauce for burgers, chicken, or ribs. **Makes** 1½ cups.

editor's favorite • quick & easy
Sweet and Simple Barbecue Sauce
Prep: 3 min., Cook: 6 min.

2 garlic cloves, crushed
2 Tbsp. butter or margarine, melted
1 cup ketchup
1 cup water
¾ cup chili sauce
¼ cup firmly packed brown sugar
2 Tbsp. prepared mustard
2 Tbsp. Worcestershire sauce
1½ tsp. celery seeds
½ tsp. salt
2 dashes of hot sauce

Sauté garlic in butter 4 to 5 minutes in a saucepan. Add ketchup and remaining ingredients; bring to a boil. Use to baste pork or chicken during cooking. **Makes** 3½ cups.

quick & easy
Honey-Barbecue Sauce
Prep: 5 min., Cook: 5 min.

Bold, distinct gallberry honey holds its own in this zesty sauce.

2 cups ketchup
½ cup white vinegar
½ cup honey (we tested with gallberry honey)
½ cup water
2 tsp. dried crushed green pepper
1 Tbsp. minced onion
2 Tbsp. Worcestershire sauce
¼ tsp. ground black pepper
Dash of garlic powder
Dash of ground red pepper

Bring all ingredients to a boil in a large saucepan over medium-high heat, stirring often. Serve with pork or poultry. **Makes** 3½ cups.

Molasses, the cooked-down syrup from sugarcane or sugar beets, adds the characteristic flavor to gingerbread. This sweet syrup, with its acidic taste, also pertly flavors savory sauces and meat glazes like the two sauces that follow.

Citrus-Spiced Barbecue Sauce

Prep: 5 min., Cook: 40 min.

The sweet, citrusy twang of this sauce pairs well with grilled shrimp, poultry, or pork ribs.

1 medium onion, chopped
2 Tbsp. grated orange rind
½ cup molasses
½ cup ketchup
⅓ cup fresh orange juice
2 Tbsp. olive oil
1 Tbsp. white vinegar
1 Tbsp. steak sauce
½ tsp. Worcestershire sauce
½ tsp. prepared mustard
¼ tsp. garlic powder
¼ tsp. salt
¼ tsp. ground red pepper
¼ tsp. hot sauce
⅛ tsp. ground cloves
¼ cup bourbon

Cook first 15 ingredients in a medium saucepan over low heat 30 minutes. Add bourbon, and simmer 10 minutes. **Makes** about 2 cups.

Maple-Molasses Barbecue Sauce

Prep: 10 min., Cook: 10 min.

½ cup finely chopped onion
2 garlic cloves, minced
2 Tbsp. vegetable oil
1 Tbsp. cornstarch
½ cup maple syrup
½ cup water
¼ cup soy sauce
¼ cup molasses
3 Tbsp. cider vinegar
1 tsp. dried crushed red pepper
1 tsp. peeled, minced fresh ginger
¼ cup creamy peanut butter

Sauté onion and garlic in hot oil in a medium saucepan 3 minutes or until tender.
Combine cornstarch and next 7 ingredients; stir well. Add to onion mixture; bring to a boil.
Cook 3 minutes, stirring frequently. Add peanut butter; cook, stirring constantly, 2 minutes or until peanut butter melts. **Makes** 1¾ cups.

Since it came on the market in 1886, Coca-Cola® has been a thirst cure. But this fizzy drink is good for more than quenching thirsts—from flavoring sauces to salads, dinner to dessert. And it's especially good in the next 3 sauces.

Smoky Sweet Barbecue Sauce

Prep: 5 min., Cook: 30 min.

2 cups Worcestershire sauce
1¼ cups ketchup
1 cup cola soft drink
½ cup butter or margarine
1½ Tbsp. sugar
1 Tbsp. salt
2 tsp. freshly ground pepper

Combine all ingredients in a medium saucepan. Bring to a boil; reduce heat, and simmer, stirring constantly, 30 minutes. **Makes** 3¼ cups.

Cola Barbecue Sauce

Prep: 10 min., Cook: 8 min.

This recipe was adapted from grillmaster Steven Raichlen's version in his book **Beer-Can Chicken**—*a necessary pairing for Basic Beer-Can Chicken (page 123).*

1 Tbsp. butter
½ small onion, minced
1 Tbsp. minced fresh ginger
1 garlic clove, minced
¾ cup cola soft drink
¾ cup ketchup
½ tsp. grated lemon rind
2 Tbsp. fresh lemon juice
2 Tbsp. Worcestershire sauce

2 Tbsp. steak sauce (we tested with A.1.)
½ tsp. liquid smoke
½ tsp. pepper
Salt to taste

Melt butter in a heavy saucepan over medium heat. Add onion, ginger, and garlic; sauté 3 minutes or until tender.

Stir in cola soft drink; bring mixture to a boil. Stir in ketchup and remaining ingredients; bring to a boil. Reduce heat, and simmer 5 minutes. Serve with poultry. **Makes** about 1½ cups.

These sauces please more adventuresome palates. The "tangy" comes from vinegars and lemon juice, and the "hot" comes from peppers.

editor's favorite
Sweet-and-Tangy Barbecue Sauce
Prep: 5 min., Cook: 1 hr.

Vinegar, chili sauce, and red pepper heat things up in this sweet cola-based barbecue sauce.

1 large onion, finely chopped
1 tsp. vegetable oil
¾ cup cola soft drink
¾ cup chili sauce
1 Tbsp. brown sugar
½ tsp. salt
1 Tbsp. dry mustard
1 Tbsp. paprika
⅛ tsp. ground red pepper
2 Tbsp. white vinegar

Cook onion in oil in a large saucepan over low heat, stirring often, 15 minutes or until onion is caramel-colored. Stir in cola and remaining ingredients. Bring to a boil over medium heat. Cover, reduce heat, and simmer, stirring occasionally, 45 minutes. Serve with beef or pork. **Makes** 2 cups.

make ahead • quick & easy
Fiery-Sweet Barbecue Sauce
Prep: 5 min., Cook: 6 min.

Using low-sugar marmalade helps prevent flare-ups on the grill.

1 cup low-sugar orange marmalade
1 cup ketchup
¼ cup cider vinegar
1 Tbsp. soy sauce
¾ tsp. celery seeds
½ tsp. ground red pepper

Combine all ingredients in a 1-qt. microwave-safe measuring cup, and stir well. Cover with wax paper. Microwave at HIGH 6 minutes or until mixture comes to a boil, stirring after 3 minutes. Use for basting chicken, beef, or pork while cooking. **Makes** 2½ cups.

quick & easy
Big "D" Barbecue Sauce
Prep: 10 min., Cook: 20 min.

This barbecue sauce is so darn good that it will become a permanent condiment in your refrigerator. Make an extra batch, and store in the refrigerator in an airtight container up to three weeks.

2 Tbsp. butter
1 Tbsp. olive oil
1 medium onion, finely chopped
½ green bell pepper, finely chopped
4 garlic cloves, minced
3 medium jalapeño peppers, seeded and minced
1 cup firmly packed brown sugar
1 cup cider vinegar
1 cup chili sauce
1 cup bottled barbecue sauce
1 Tbsp. mustard powder
1 Tbsp. paprika
3 Tbsp. fresh lemon juice
2 Tbsp. Worcestershire sauce
2 Tbsp. hot sauce
2 Tbsp. molasses
¼ tsp. salt

Melt butter with oil in a large Dutch oven over medium heat.
Add onion and next 3 ingredients, and sauté 5 to 6 minutes or until onion is tender.
Stir in brown sugar and remaining ingredients; bring to a boil. Reduce heat to medium-low, and simmer 10 minutes. Pour mixture through a wire-mesh strainer into a bowl, discarding solids. Serve with beef or pork. **Makes** about 3½ cups.

Tangy Sorghum Barbecue Sauce

Prep: 5 min., Cook: 10 min.

For a flavorful glaze, brush this sauce on ribs or pork chops during the last 15 minutes of cooking to prevent it from burning.

1 (8-oz.) can tomato sauce

¾ cup steak sauce

½ to ¾ cup sorghum

¼ cup ketchup

¼ cup lemon juice

2 Tbsp. brown sugar

2 Tbsp. Worcestershire sauce

2 to 4 dashes of hot sauce

Dash of seasoned salt

2 Tbsp. pineapple marmalade (optional)

Cook first 9 ingredients and, if desired, marmalade in a medium saucepan over low heat, stirring occasionally, 10 minutes or until thoroughly heated. Serve with pork or chicken. **Makes** about 3 cups.

Spiced Barbecue Sauce

Prep: 15 min.; Cook: 1 hr., 6 min.

2 Tbsp. vegetable oil
1 medium onion, chopped
4 garlic cloves, halved
1½ cups ketchup
1 cup fresh orange juice
½ cup water
⅓ cup fresh lemon juice
⅓ cup red wine vinegar
¼ cup firmly packed dark brown sugar
¼ cup honey
3 Tbsp. finely chopped crystallized ginger
2 Tbsp. chili powder
1 Tbsp. ground coriander
1 Tbsp. dry mustard
1 Tbsp. Worcestershire sauce
2 Tbsp. liquid smoke
2 Tbsp. dark molasses
1 tsp. salt
¼ tsp. hot sauce

Heat oil in a large saucepan over medium heat; add onion, and cook 5 minutes or until golden, stirring occasionally. Add garlic; cook 1 minute. Stir in ketchup and remaining ingredients; bring to a boil. Reduce heat, and simmer, uncovered, 1 hour or until sauce is thickened, stirring often. Pour mixture through a wire-mesh strainer into a container, discarding onion, garlic, and ginger. Cool to room temperature. Serve with pork or chicken. **Makes** 3¾ cups.

make ahead • quick & easy
Peppery Barbecue Sauce

Prep: 10 min.

2 cups firmly packed brown sugar
2 Tbsp. pepper
1 to 1½ tsp. salt
4 garlic cloves, minced
4 cups ketchup
1 cup white vinegar
2 Tbsp. vegetable oil
2 Tbsp. prepared mustard
2 Tbsp. Worcestershire sauce
2 Tbsp. hot sauce

Stir together all ingredients. Store in refrigerator up to 2 weeks. Serve with beef or pork. **Makes** 6 cups.

quick & easy
Peach of the Old South Barbecue Sauce for Ribs

Prep: 4 min., Cook: 20 min.

Bourbon lends a distinctive flavor to this peach-sweetened barbecue sauce.

2 cups tomato puree
½ cup fresh lemon juice
½ cup sweetened bourbon
½ cup peach preserves
½ cup Dijon mustard
¼ cup firmly packed light brown sugar
2 Tbsp. hot sauce
1 tsp. salt

Combine all ingredients in a saucepan; stir well. Bring to a boil; cover, reduce heat, and simmer 20 minutes, stirring occasionally. Use as a basting sauce for ribs. **Makes** 4 cups.

quick & easy
Apple Barbecue Sauce

Prep: 4 min., Cook: 25 min.

Apple jelly teams with vinegar and hot sauce to conjure up tangy-sweet flavors especially tasty on smoked pork.

½ cup apple jelly
1 (8-oz.) can tomato sauce
¼ cup white vinegar
2 Tbsp. light brown sugar
2 Tbsp. water
1 tsp. hot sauce

Bring all ingredients to a boil in a saucepan, stirring until smooth. Reduce heat, and simmer, stirring occasionally, 20 to 25 minutes. **Makes** 1⅓ cups.

Ranch Barbecue Sauce
Prep: 5 min., Cook: 20 min.

You can vary the flavor this recipe takes on by the brand of bottled sauce you select.

1 (18-oz.) bottle barbecue sauce (we tested with Stubb's
    Original)
1 (1-oz.) envelope Ranch dressing mix
¼ cup honey
½ tsp. dry mustard

Stir together all ingredients in a saucepan over medium-high heat; bring to a boil. Reduce heat, and simmer, stirring occasionally, 20 minutes. Serve with poultry. **Makes** about 1¼ cups.

Chipotle Barbecue Sauce
Prep: 5 min.

Fiery peppers crank up the heat in this simple sauce.

2 (18-oz.) bottles smoke-flavor barbecue sauce
6 Tbsp. fresh lime juice (about 2 limes)
2 Tbsp. minced garlic
3 canned chipotle peppers in adobo sauce, undrained
    and chopped
1 Tbsp. adobo sauce from can

Combine all ingredients, stirring well. Serve with beef or pork. **Makes** 3½ cups.

VINEGAR CONTROVERSY

Vinegar sauces rule in North Carolina. The following two vinegar-based sauces lend a taste of Lexington-style and Eastern-style pig pickin'.

Cider Vinegar Barbecue Sauce
Prep: 10 min., Cook: 7 min.

This sauce is often referred to as Lexington Style Dip, but there are many variations. Most folks can't resist adding their own touch by adjusting the sugar or spice. Bob Garner, author of **North Carolina Barbecue: Flavored by Time,** *likes to combine the best of eastern and western Carolina-style barbecue in this sweet vinegar-based sauce.*

1½ cups cider vinegar
⅓ cup firmly packed brown sugar
¼ cup ketchup
1 Tbsp. hot sauce (we tested with Texas Pete)
1 tsp. browning-and-seasoning sauce (we tested with
    Kitchen Bouquet)
½ tsp. salt
½ tsp. onion powder
½ tsp. pepper
½ tsp. Worcestershire sauce

Stir together all ingredients in a saucepan; cook over medium heat, stirring constantly, 7 minutes or until sugar dissolves. Serve with North Carolina Smoked Pork Shoulder (page 107). **Makes** 2 cups.

Zesty Barbecue Sauce

Prep: 8 min., Cook: 5 min.

½ cup lemon juice
⅓ cup cider vinegar
¼ cup water
¼ cup tomato juice
4 tsp. sugar
1 tsp. dry mustard
1 tsp. hot sauce
½ tsp. salt
½ tsp. onion powder
½ tsp. paprika
½ tsp. ground red pepper
½ tsp. black pepper
⅛ tsp. garlic powder
⅛ tsp. dried oregano

Combine all ingredients in a medium saucepan. Bring mixture to a boil.
Transfer mixture to a serving container; cover and chill. Serve with meat or poultry. **Makes** 1¼ cups.

quick & easy
Spicy-Sweet Mustard Sauce

Prep: 10 min, Cook: 20 min.

Smoked pork or grilled bratwursts welcome a gracious helping of this mustardy concoction.

½ cup butter or margarine
2 beef bouillon cubes
3 egg yolks, lightly beaten
½ cup sugar
½ cup prepared mustard
¼ cup cider vinegar
1 tsp. salt

Combine butter and bouillon cubes in top of a double boiler. Place over simmering water, and cook, whisking constantly, until butter melts and bouillon cubes dissolve. Gradually whisk in beaten egg yolks. Add sugar and remaining ingredients; cook, whisking often, 20 minutes. Cover and chill. **Makes** 1½ cups.

kids love it • quick & easy
Honey-Mustard Barbecue Sauce

Prep: 15 min., Cook: 18 min.

This is a thick, hearty sauce; if you prefer a thinner sauce, add ¼ cup water.

1 bacon slice, diced
1 small onion, diced
1 garlic clove, minced
1 cup cider vinegar
¾ cup prepared mustard
¼ cup firmly packed brown sugar
¼ cup honey
1 tsp. black pepper
1 tsp. Worcestershire sauce
¼ tsp. ground red pepper

Cook bacon in a medium saucepan until crisp; remove bacon, and drain on paper towels, reserving drippings in saucepan.
Sauté onion and garlic in hot drippings about 3 minutes or until tender. Stir in bacon, vinegar, and remaining ingredients; bring to a boil. Reduce heat, and simmer, stirring occasionally, 10 minutes. Serve with meat or poultry. **Makes** 1½ cups.

"'Low and slow' is the motto of North Carolina pitmaster Jim 'Trim' Tabb when it comes to barbecue. His succulent pork, Tabb's Barbecue Pork (page 110), is out of this world when drizzled with Honey-Mustard Barbecue Sauce, a South Carolina specialty."

—Scott Jones, *Southern Living* Staff

White Barbecue Sauce
Prep: 5 min.

1½ cups mayonnaise

¼ cup water

¼ cup white wine vinegar

1 Tbsp. coarsely ground pepper

1 Tbsp. Creole mustard

1 tsp. salt

1 tsp. sugar

2 garlic cloves, minced

2 tsp. prepared horseradish

Whisk together all ingredients until blended. Serve with chicken. **Makes** 2 cups.

ORIGIN OF WHITE SAUCE

The color spectrum of barbecue sauce is rich and diverse—one reason why sampling different styles from all over the South is so much fun and so delicious. Ask the average person the color of his or her favorite sauce, and you'll probably get an answer such as brick red, mahogany, or caramel.

Pose the same question to a resident of North Alabama, though, and you're sure to get only one answer: white.

"It's the only sauce we know here, because it's what everyone grows up on," says world barbecue champion Chris Lilly of Big Bob Gibson Bar-B-Q in Decatur, Alabama. Bob Gibson is credited with concocting white sauce back in 1925.

Today, this tangy, mayonnaise-based condiment, traditionally used to dress chicken, is as synonymous with the state of Alabama as legendary football coach Paul "Bear" Bryant. "We marinate with it, use it to baste, plus we use it as an all-purpose table sauce," explains Chris.

—Scott Jones, *Southern Living* Staff

SASSY SAUCES

Don't be afraid to sample unique flavors when you journey to the smoker. Try these playful flavors for your next barbecue.

Asian Barbecue Sauce
Prep: 3 min., Cook: 5 min.

1 cup ketchup

2 Tbsp. brown sugar

2 Tbsp. red wine vinegar

1 tsp. dry hot mustard

1 large garlic clove, minced

2 tsp. chili puree with garlic

Combine first 5 ingredients in a small saucepan. Bring to a boil; remove from heat. Stir in chili puree. Use as a basting sauce for chicken, beef, or pork. **Makes** 1⅓ cups.

Tomatillo Barbecue Sauce
Prep: 15 min., Cook: 2 hrs.

2½ lb. green tomatoes, coarsely chopped

1½ lb. tomatillos, husked and coarsely chopped

2 garlic cloves, pressed

½ to 1 cup sugar

1 cup white vinegar

1 large sweet onion, coarsely chopped (about 1½ cups)

1 Tbsp. dry mustard

1 tsp. salt

½ tsp. dried crushed red pepper

Cook all ingredients in a large stockpot over medium-low heat 2 hours or until green tomatoes and tomatillos are tender. Cool.

Process mixture, in batches, in a food processor or blender until smooth, stopping to scrape down sides. Serve over grilled chicken, fish, or shrimp. **Makes** 3 cups.

Tomatillo Sauce

Prep: 10 min., Cook: 20 min., Other: 8 hrs.
(pictured on page 191)

1¼ lb. small tomatillos (about 30)
1 medium onion, chopped
1 Tbsp. olive oil
4 tsp. minced garlic
1 cup water
1 jalapeño pepper, minced
½ cup chopped fresh cilantro
1 Tbsp. fresh lime juice
1 tsp. salt

Remove husks from tomatillos; wash thoroughly.
Sauté onion in hot olive oil in a large saucepan over medium-high heat 5 minutes or until softened. Add garlic, and sauté 1 minute. Stir in tomatillos, 1 cup water, and jalapeño; bring to a boil. Reduce heat to medium; cover and simmer, stirring occasionally, 10 to 12 minutes or until tomatillos are softened. Remove from heat; cool slightly.
Process tomatillo mixture, cilantro, lime juice, and salt in a food processor or blender until smooth. Cover; chill at least 8 hours. Serve with chicken, fish, or shrimp. **Makes** about 3½ cups.

kids love it • quick & easy
Blueberry-Balsamic Barbecue Sauce

Prep: 5 min., Cook: 15 min.

Try this sweet and tangy sauce the next time you grill chicken, pork, or tuna. If fresh blueberries aren't available, use 2 cups thawed frozen blueberries.

2 cups fresh blueberries
¼ cup balsamic vinegar
3 Tbsp. sugar
3 Tbsp. ketchup
½ tsp. garlic powder
¼ tsp. salt

Place all ingredients in a saucepan. Bring to a boil; reduce heat, and simmer 15 minutes or until slightly thick. Remove from heat; cool. Place blueberry mixture in a blender; process until smooth. **Makes** about 1½ cups.

Blueberry Barbecue Sauce

Prep: 15 min., Cook: 15 min.

The combination of fresh blueberries with mustard and butter makes this sauce delectable on chicken or pork.

2 Tbsp. minced onion
1½ tsp. chopped fresh jalapeño pepper
1½ tsp. olive oil
1 cup fresh blueberries
2 Tbsp. rice vinegar
2 Tbsp. ketchup
1½ Tbsp. brown sugar
1½ Tbsp. Dijon mustard
½ tsp. hot sauce
2 Tbsp. unsalted butter
⅛ tsp. salt
⅛ tsp. freshly ground pepper

Cook onion and jalapeño pepper in hot oil in a medium saucepan over medium-high heat, stirring constantly, until tender. Add blueberries and next 5 ingredients; bring to a boil. Reduce heat, and simmer, uncovered, 15 minutes, stirring often.
Pour blueberry mixture into container of an electric blender; process until smooth, stopping once to scrape down sides. Pour blueberry mixture through a wire-mesh strainer into a small saucepan, pressing against strainer with back of a spoon to press out any remaining liquid.
Add butter, salt, and pepper to blueberry mixture; cook over medium heat until butter melts, stirring occasionally. **Makes** ⅔ cup.

Raspberry Barbecue Sauce

Prep: 5 min., Cook: 7 min.

1 (10-oz.) jar seedless raspberry preserves
⅓ cup bottled barbecue sauce (we tested with KC Masterpiece)
2 Tbsp. raspberry vinegar
2 Tbsp. Dijon mustard
1½ tsp. hot sauce

Bring first 4 ingredients to a boil in a small saucepan. Reduce heat to medium, and cook 2 minutes or until slightly thickened. Stir in hot sauce. Serve with pork or chicken. **Makes** 1 cup.

Fragrant Ginger-Hot Pepper Sauce
Prep: 5 min., Cook: 5 min.

A little of this mighty Asian seasoning blend goes a long way. Serve with smoked pork or chicken.

1 Tbsp. vegetable oil
¼ cup minced peeled fresh ginger
2 tsp. dried crushed red pepper
2 large garlic cloves, minced
¼ cup chopped fresh cilantro
¼ cup minced green onions
2½ Tbsp. water
½ tsp. salt

Heat vegetable oil in a small skillet over medium heat. Add minced fresh ginger, red pepper, and garlic; sauté 2 minutes. Remove from heat; spoon into a small bowl, and stir in remaining ingredients. **Makes** ½ cup.

Mango-Pineapple Hot Sauce
Prep: 10 min., Cook: 30 min., Other: 1 hr.

This potent blend offers a sweet-hot finish for smoked fish and pork. Or to make a quick appetizer for a last-minute barbecue, pour some of the sauce over a block of cream cheese and serve with assorted crackers. Always handle habaneros with kitchen gloves. If you prefer a milder finish, use only one habanero.

1 cup mango nectar
1 cup pineapple juice
5 Tbsp. cider vinegar
4 garlic cloves, minced
1 to 2 habanero peppers, seeded and chopped
1¼ tsp. salt
1 tsp. ground turmeric

Stir together all ingredients in a 1-qt. saucepan over medium-high heat; bring to a boil, stirring often. Cover, reduce heat to low, and simmer 30 minutes. Remove pan from heat, and let stand at room temperature 1 hour or until completely cool. **Makes** 1⅔ cups.

Smoky Hot Sauce
Prep: 10 min., Cook: 35 min., Other: 8 hrs.

1 large onion, chopped
1 Tbsp. olive oil
4 tsp. minced garlic
5 medium tomatoes, coarsely chopped (about 1½ lb.)
¾ cup water
1 chicken bouillon cube
1 canned chipotle pepper in adobo sauce
2 Tbsp. adobo sauce from can
1 Tbsp. balsamic vinegar
1 tsp. hot sauce
¼ tsp. salt

Sauté onion in hot oil in a large saucepan over medium-high heat 5 minutes or until softened. Add garlic; sauté 1 minute. Stir in tomatoes and remaining ingredients. Bring to a boil. Reduce heat; simmer, stirring occasionally, 25 minutes. Remove from heat; cool slightly.
Remove chipotle pepper, if desired. Process tomato mixture in a food processor or blender until smooth.
Cover and chill at least 8 hours. Serve with chicken or fish. **Makes** about 3 cups.

Herbed Lemon Barbecue Sauce
Prep: 5 min.

¾ cup lemon juice
2 garlic cloves, peeled
1 Tbsp. onion powder
1½ tsp. salt
1½ tsp. paprika
1½ cups vegetable oil
1 Tbsp. dried basil
1 tsp. dried thyme, crushed

Process first 5 ingredients in a blender 1 minute. With blender on high, add oil in a slow, steady stream; process 1 minute. Add basil and thyme; process on low 30 seconds. Serve with fish or chicken. **Makes** 2 cups.

Smoky Hot Sauce,
at left

Tomatillo Sauce,
page 189

A rub is a blend of seasonings—usually dried herbs and spices—applied to meat, seafood, or poultry before cooking.

■ A rub is often left on the food for a while before cooking to allow the flavors to penetrate.

■ When a small amount of liquid—such as olive oil or crushed garlic with its juice—is added to a rub, it becomes a wet rub paste. A wet rub is easy to apply to meat because it clings well to the food.

■ For maximum flavor, you can apply a dry rub or wet rub to food up to 24 hours before cooking.

■ Dry rubs can be stored in an airtight container in a cool, dry place up to 6 months.

■ Wet rubs can be stored in an airtight container in the refrigerator up to 1 week.

Sweet 'n' Spicy Barbecue Rub
Prep: 10 min.

1¼ cups firmly packed dark brown sugar
⅓ cup kosher salt
¼ cup granulated garlic
¼ cup paprika
1 Tbsp. chili powder
1 Tbsp. ground red pepper
1 Tbsp. ground cumin
1 Tbsp. lemon pepper
1 Tbsp. onion powder
2 tsp. dry mustard
2 tsp. ground black pepper
1 tsp. ground cinnamon

Combine all ingredients. Store in an airtight container up to 6 months. **Makes** about 2½ cups.

Garlic-Pepper Brisket Rub
Prep: 5 min.

¼ cup kosher salt
¼ cup sugar
¼ cup black pepper
¾ cup paprika
2 Tbsp. garlic powder
2 Tbsp. garlic salt
2 Tbsp. onion powder
2 Tbsp. chili powder
2 tsp. ground red pepper

Combine all ingredients. Store in an airtight container up to 6 months. **Makes** 2 cups.

make ahead
Southwestern Spice Blend
Prep: 5 min.

1 Tbsp. salt
2 tsp. garlic powder
2 tsp. chili powder
2 tsp. ground cumin
2 tsp. pepper
½ tsp. unsweetened cocoa

Combine all ingredients. Store in airtight container up to 6 months. Use as a meat or poultry rub or to flavor chilis and soups. **Makes** ¼ cup.

All-Purpose Barbecue Rub
Prep: 5 min.

¼ cup coarse salt
¼ cup dark brown sugar
¼ cup sweet paprika
2 Tbsp. pepper

Combine all ingredients. Store in an airtight jar, away from heat, up to 6 months. **Makes** about ¾ cup.

Chipotle Rub
Prep: 5 min.

2 to 3 canned chipotle peppers in adobo sauce
¼ cup firmly packed brown sugar
1 Tbsp. chili powder
1 tsp. salt

Chop chipotle peppers; stir together peppers, brown sugar, chili powder, and salt to form a paste. Store in refrigerator up to a week. **Makes** ⅓ cup.

MARINADE PRIMER

A marinade is a seasoned liquid added to uncooked food for flavor and sometimes tenderizing. Most contain an acid—such as wine, citrus juice, or vinegar—that helps tenderize meat. The more acid a recipe contains, the more tenderizing ability it has.

■ Marinate food in such nonmetal containers as glass dishes, plastic bowls, or heavy-duty plastic bags that won't react with acidic components in the marinade.

■ Allow about ½ cup marinade for every pound of meat, poultry, or seafood.

■ Always marinate food, covered, in the refrigerator, turning occasionally.

■ To simply add flavor, marinate most foods 30 minutes to 2 hours.

■ To tenderize meat, marinating 8 hours is ideal, but you can marinate large cuts of meat up to 24 hours with good results. Meat that marinates longer than that can become mushy.

■ Never reuse a marinade in which raw meat, fish, or poultry has been soaked until you first bring it to a boil. This kills any bacteria that may have been transferred from the raw food.

Beer Marinade
Prep: 5 min.

Red beer is actually a medium dark beer or ale. The name comes from the reddish tint it gets from aging in redwood barrels.

1 (12-oz.) can red beer
¼ cup ketchup
2 tsp. dry mustard
¼ tsp. salt
¼ tsp. pepper
1 garlic clove, crushed

Combine all ingredients; stir well. Use to marinate chicken or pork. **Makes** 1¾ cups.

Horseradish Marinade
Prep: 5 min.

¼ cup dry red wine
2 Tbsp. minced fresh thyme
2 Tbsp. Worcestershire sauce
2 Tbsp. red wine vinegar
2 Tbsp. prepared horseradish
2 Tbsp. tomato paste
1½ tsp. freshly ground pepper
4 garlic cloves, minced

Combine all ingredients; stir well. Use to marinate beef. **Makes** ¾ cup.

Browned Garlic and Burgundy Marinade
Prep: 10 min., Cook: 5 min.

1 Tbsp. olive oil
3 garlic cloves, thinly sliced
¾ cup dry red wine
3 Tbsp. soy sauce
1 tsp. dried tarragon

Heat oil in a small nonstick skillet over medium-high heat until hot. Add garlic; sauté 3 minutes or until brown. Remove from heat; stir in wine, soy sauce, and tarragon. Use to marinate beef. **Makes** 1 cup.

Red Wine-Mustard Marinade
Prep: 5 min.

½ cup dry red wine
¼ cup finely chopped shallot
3 Tbsp. green peppercorn mustard with white wine
1 Tbsp. freshly ground pepper
1 Tbsp. balsamic vinegar
1½ tsp. chopped fresh rosemary
1 large garlic clove, minced

Combine all ingredients; stir well. Use to marinate beef, pork, or lamb. **Makes** 1 cup.

Green Tomato Pickles

Chipotle Caesar Salad
Prep: 20 min.

Add a chipotle pepper or two to a bottled Caesar dressing for a quicker take on this salad.

1 large jícama
2 heads romaine lettuce, torn
1 large red bell pepper, thinly sliced
Chipotle Caesar Dressing

Cut jícama into thin slices. Cut each slice into a star using a 1½-inch star-shaped cookie cutter (about 15 stars).
Toss together lettuce, bell pepper, and desired amount of dressing in a large bowl. Top with jícama stars. **Makes** 8 servings.

Chipotle Caesar Dressing
Prep: 10 min.

2 garlic cloves
1 to 2 canned chipotle peppers
½ tsp. salt
⅓ cup fresh lemon juice
⅓ cup egg substitute
⅓ cup shredded Parmesan cheese
½ cup olive oil

Pulse first 3 ingredients in a food processor 3 to 4 times or until garlic is minced. Add lemon juice, egg substitute, and Parmesan cheese. With food processor running, pour oil through food chute in a slow, steady stream; process until smooth. Cover and chill until ready to serve. **Makes** 1¼ cups.

Grilled Romaine Salad with Buttermilk-Chive Dressing

Prep: 10 min., Cook: 5 min.

Nestle romaine halves on the grill next to the barbecue for a warm and wilted salad to start the meal.

4 bunches romaine hearts
1 red onion
1 to 2 Tbsp. olive oil
Buttermilk-Chive Dressing
Kosher salt to taste
Freshly ground pepper to taste
½ cup freshly shaved or shredded Parmesan cheese

Cut romaine hearts in half lengthwise, keeping leaves intact. Cut red onion crosswise into ½-inch slices, keeping rings intact; brush romaine and onions with olive oil, and set aside.

Coat food grate evenly with vegetable cooking spray, or brush lightly with vegetable oil. Place food on grate; grill over medium heat (300° to 350°).

Place romaine halves, cut sides down, on food grate. Grill, uncovered, 3 to 5 minutes or until just wilted. If desired, rotate halves once to get crisscross grill marks. Brush warm romaine halves with Buttermilk-Chive Dressing, coating lightly.

Place 2 romaine halves on each of 4 salad plates. Sprinkle with salt and pepper to taste. Top each evenly with onion slices and freshly shaved Parmesan cheese. Serve immediately with remaining Buttermilk-Chive Dressing. **Makes** 4 servings.

Buttermilk-Chive Dressing

Prep: 5 min.

¾ cup buttermilk
½ cup mayonnaise
2 Tbsp. chopped fresh chives
1 Tbsp. minced green onions
1 garlic clove, minced
½ tsp. salt
¼ tsp. freshly ground pepper

Whisk together all ingredients. Cover; chill until ready to use. **Makes** 1¼ cups.

Mixed Salad Greens with Warm Goat Cheese

Prep: 15 min., Cook: 5 min.

Pecan-encrusted slices of creamy goat cheese crown a fresh mix of five salad greens. Buy bags of washed, torn salad greens to save preparation time and effort.

2 heads Boston lettuce, torn
2 heads Bibb lettuce, torn
2 heads romaine lettuce, torn
3 bunches arugula, torn
2 bunches watercress, torn
3 cups seedless red grapes
1 (1-lb.) log goat cheese
1⅔ cups chicken broth, divided
1 to 1½ cups ground pecans
½ cup chopped fresh parsley
⅓ cup red wine vinegar
3 Tbsp. fresh lemon juice
3 Tbsp. walnut oil
2 Tbsp. safflower oil
1 Tbsp. Dijon mustard
2 green onions, chopped
1 garlic clove, minced
1 Tbsp. sugar
¼ tsp. salt
¼ tsp. freshly ground pepper

Combine first 6 ingredients in a large bowl, tossing gently; cover and chill thoroughly.

Cut goat cheese into ¼-inch rounds. Dip each round in 1 cup broth; roll in pecans and then in parsley. Place on a lightly greased baking sheet. Bake, uncovered, at 325° for 5 minutes or until toasted.

Combine remaining ⅔ cup broth, vinegar, and remaining 9 ingredients in container of an electric blender; process 1 minute. Drizzle over salad greens, and toss gently; place cheese on top of salad. Serve immediately. **Makes** 8 servings.

Garden Salad with Buttermilk Dressing
Prep: 8 min., Other: 2 hrs.

¾ cup mayonnaise or salad dressing
½ cup buttermilk
1 Tbsp. chopped fresh parsley
1 Tbsp. finely chopped onion
1 garlic clove, minced
¼ tsp. salt
Dash of pepper
4 cups mixed salad greens

Combine first 7 ingredients; stir with a wire whisk until blended. Cover and chill at least 2 hours. Serve with greens. **Makes** 4 servings.

Tossed Spinach Salad
Prep: 20 min.

1 (10-oz.) package fresh spinach*
1 medium-size red onion, thinly sliced
2 large hard-cooked eggs, chopped
1 cup garlic-seasoned croutons
2 Tbsp. grated Parmesan cheese
Zesty Lemon Dressing

Toss first 5 ingredients in a large bowl; serve with Dressing. **Makes** 6 servings.

*Substitute 1 (10-oz.) package salad greens for spinach, if desired.

Zesty Lemon Dressing
Prep: 10 min.

¼ cup lemon olive oil (we tested with Stutz Limonato California Extra Virgin Lemon and Olive Oil)
3 Tbsp. lemon juice
1 Tbsp. red wine vinegar
1 tsp. Dijon mustard
½ tsp. salt
¼ tsp. freshly ground pepper
6 oz. Canadian bacon, cut into thin strips

Whisk together first 6 ingredients. Add Canadian bacon just before serving. **Makes** ½ cup.

Black Bean and Black-Eyed Pea Salad
Prep: 20 min., Other: 30 min.

1 tsp. grated lime rind
½ cup fresh lime juice (about 4 limes)
¼ cup olive oil
1 tsp. brown sugar
1 tsp. chili powder
½ tsp. ground cumin
½ to 1 tsp. salt
1 (15-oz.) can black beans, rinsed and drained
1 (15.5-oz.) can black-eyed peas, rinsed and drained
1½ cups frozen whole kernel corn, thawed
½ small green bell pepper, chopped
⅓ cup chopped fresh cilantro
Romaine lettuce
2 large avocados, sliced
Garnishes: lime wedges, fresh cilantro sprigs

Whisk together first 7 ingredients in a large bowl. Add black beans and next 4 ingredients, tossing to coat. Cover and chill at least 30 minutes. **Serve** over lettuce; arrange avocado slices around salad. Garnish, if desired. **Makes** 6 servings.

Pea Salad
Prep: 10 min.

1 (16-oz.) can small sweet peas, drained
1 (16-oz.) can medium-size sweet peas, drained
6 green onions, sliced
2 large hard-cooked eggs, chopped
¾ cup diced sharp Cheddar cheese
½ cup mayonnaise
1 tsp. sugar
1 tsp. fresh dill, minced
1 tsp. lemon juice
¼ tsp. salt
¼ tsp. pepper

Stir together all ingredients in a large bowl. **Makes** 4 to 6 servings.

Fresh Mozzarella-
Tomato-Basil Salad

Fresh Mozzarella-Tomato-Basil Salad
Prep: 10 min., Other: 4 hrs.

For an extra sprinkling of color, use multicolored peppercorns and grind them over the salad just before serving.

½ lb. fresh mozzarella cheese
2 large red tomatoes, sliced
1 large yellow tomato, sliced
½ tsp. salt
3 Tbsp. extra-virgin olive oil
Freshly ground pepper
½ cup shredded or chopped fresh basil

Remove cheese from brine, and cut into 12 slices; sprinkle tomato slices evenly with salt. Alternate tomato and cheese slices on a platter; drizzle with olive oil. Cover and chill 4 hours. Just before serving, sprinkle with freshly ground pepper and shredded basil. **Makes** 6 servings.

Note: Fresh mozzarella is a soft white cheese available at gourmet grocery stores or cheese shops. It's usually packed in brine, a strong solution of water and salt used for pickling or preserving foods.

Italian Tomato Salad
Prep: 20 min., Other: 8 hrs.

6 plum tomatoes, chopped*
1 small red onion, thinly sliced (optional)
1 Tbsp. minced fresh basil
1 Tbsp. minced fresh oregano
1 garlic clove, minced
¼ tsp. salt
⅛ tsp. pepper
3 Tbsp. olive oil
3 Tbsp. red wine vinegar
¼ cup crumbled Gorgonzola cheese
Garnish: croutons

Combine chopped tomato and, if desired, onion in a large bowl.
Combine basil and next 6 ingredients in a small bowl; add to tomato mixture, tossing to coat. Sprinkle with cheese. Chill 8 hours. Garnish, if desired. **Makes** 4½ cups.

*Substitute 3 large tomatoes, if desired.

Asparagus, Roasted Beet, and Goat Cheese Salad
Prep: 15 min., Cook: 47 min.

18 small fresh beets (about 6 lb.)
1 cup olive oil
⅓ cup red wine vinegar
½ tsp. salt, divided
½ tsp. freshly ground pepper, divided
60 small fresh asparagus
1 (11-oz.) log goat cheese
1 Tbsp. chopped fresh chives
Cracked pepper (optional)
Chopped fresh chives (optional)
Gourmet mixed salad greens (optional)

Arrange beets in a single layer on a lightly greased baking sheet; bake at 425° for 40 to 45 minutes or until tender, stirring every 15 minutes. Cool beets completely.
Whisk together oil, vinegar, ¼ tsp. salt, and ¼ tsp. ground pepper in a small bowl.
Peel beets, and cut into wedges. Toss together beets, ½ cup vinaigrette, remaining ¼ tsp. salt, and remaining ¼ tsp. ground pepper; set aside.
Snap off tough ends of asparagus, discarding ends; cook asparagus in boiling water to cover 1 to 2 minutes or until crisp-tender. Plunge into ice water to stop the cooking process, and drain. Combine asparagus and ½ cup vinaigrette; set aside.
Cut cheese into 6 equal slices. Place 1 cheese slice in a 3-inch round cutter or ring mold; sprinkle with ½ tsp. chives. Press chives into cheese; remove cutter. Repeat procedure with remaining cheese and 2½ tsp. chives.
Arrange asparagus over cheese. Surround with beets, and drizzle with remaining vinaigrette. Sprinkle with cracked pepper and chives, if desired; serve with salad greens, if desired. **Makes** 6 servings.

Cucumber Salad with Roasted Red Bell Pepper Dressing
Prep: 5 min.

8 cups gourmet mixed salad greens
2 cucumbers, diced
1 small red onion, sliced
Roasted Red Bell Pepper Dressing

Combine salad greens, diced cucumbers, and onion; serve with Roasted Red Bell Pepper Dressing. **Makes** 6 to 8 servings.

Roasted Red Bell Pepper Dressing
Prep: 5 min.

1 (7-oz.) jar roasted red bell peppers, drained
2 large garlic cloves, chopped
1 cup fat-free yogurt
1 tsp. salt

Pulse ingredients in a blender 5 to 6 times or until smooth. **Makes** about 2 cups.

Avocado Salad
Prep: 10 min., Other: 1 hr.

2 large ripe avocados, coarsely chopped
4 large radishes, chopped
2 celery ribs, chopped
2 green onions, chopped
2 Tbsp. fresh lemon juice
2 Tbsp. olive oil
½ tsp. salt
¼ to ½ tsp. freshly ground pepper

Combine all ingredients. Cover and chill 1 hour. **Makes** 2½ cups.

Fried Okra Salad
Prep: 25 min., Cook: 4 min. per batch, Other: 20 min.

Crispy fried small whole pods of okra perch atop greens and tomato slices for a distinctly Southern take on salad.

1 lb. small fresh okra
2 cups buttermilk
1 lb. bacon, chopped
1 cup cornmeal
1 cup all-purpose flour
1¼ tsp. salt, divided
¾ tsp. pepper, divided
Canola oil
½ small onion, coarsely chopped
¼ cup canola oil
3 Tbsp. red wine vinegar
3 Tbsp. honey
1½ Tbsp. Dijon mustard
1 tsp. paprika
1 lb. Bibb lettuce
6 tomatoes, sliced
Garnish: fresh basil sprigs

Stir together okra and buttermilk in a large bowl; let stand 20 minutes. Drain okra.

Cook chopped bacon in a large skillet over medium heat until crisp; drain on paper towels. Reserve ¼ cup bacon drippings.

Combine cornmeal, flour, 1 tsp. salt, and ½ tsp. pepper in a large zip-top freezer bag; add okra a few at a time, sealing and shaking to coat each batch.

Pour oil to a depth of ½ inch into a large heavy skillet. Fry okra in batches in hot oil 2 minutes on each side or until golden. Drain well on paper towels.

Process reserved ¼ cup drippings, remaining ¼ tsp. salt, remaining ¼ tsp. pepper, onion, and next 5 ingredients in a blender or food processor until smooth, stopping once to scrape down sides. Pour into a 1-cup glass measuring cup.

Microwave dressing mixture at HIGH 30 to 45 seconds or until thoroughly heated.

Line a large serving platter with lettuce; arrange tomato and okra on top. Sprinkle with bacon, and drizzle with warm dressing. Garnish, if desired. Serve immediately. **Makes** 6 main-dish or 10 side-dish servings.

Kentucky Bibb Salad with Fried Green Tomatoes
Prep: 20 min., Cook: 8 min. per batch

½ cup cornmeal
1 tsp. dried mint
1 tsp. ground cumin
½ tsp. salt
½ cup buttermilk
3 large green tomatoes, cut into ¼-inch-thick slices
Vegetable or peanut oil
2 large heads Bibb lettuce, rinsed and torn
½ cup toasted walnuts
Rose Vinaigrette
Garnishes: gourmet edible petite rose petals; chopped
    green, red, and yellow bell peppers; chopped red
    onion

Whisk together first 5 ingredients in a bowl until smooth; dip tomato slices evenly in batter.
Pour oil to a depth of 2 inches into a large heavy skillet. Fry tomato slices, in batches, in hot oil over medium-high heat 4 minutes on each side or until slices are golden.
Arrange lettuce evenly on 6 plates; top each with 2 tomato slices. Sprinkle evenly with walnuts; drizzle with Rose Vinaigrette. Garnish, if desired. **Makes** 6 servings.

Note: For extra-crispy fried tomatoes, dip in batter twice.

Rose Vinaigrette
Prep: 10 min.

3 large shallots, finely chopped
¼ tsp. salt
1 Tbsp. honey
⅓ cup red wine vinegar
2 tsp. rose water (optional)
⅓ cup vegetable oil
3 Tbsp. walnut oil*

Stir together first 4 ingredients and, if desired, rose water; whisk in oils. **Makes** ¾ cup.

*Substitute 3 Tbsp. vegetable oil for walnut oil, if desired.

Bacon-Mandarin Salad

Bacon-Mandarin Salad

Prep: 15 min., Cook: 18 min.

Wash the lettuces the night before. Wrap in a damp paper towel, and chill in zip-top plastic bags; cook the bacon, and toast the almonds, too. Assemble and dress right before serving.

½ cup olive oil

¼ cup red wine vinegar

¼ cup sugar

1 Tbsp. chopped fresh basil

⅛ tsp. hot sauce

2 (15-oz.) cans mandarin oranges, drained and chilled*

1 bunch Red Leaf lettuce, torn

1 head romaine lettuce, torn

1 lb. bacon, cooked and crumbled

1 (4-oz.) package sliced almonds, toasted

Whisk together first 5 ingredients in a large bowl, blending well. Add oranges and lettuces, tossing gently to coat. Sprinkle with crumbled bacon and sliced almonds. Serve immediately. **Makes** 12 servings.

*Substitute fresh orange segments for canned mandarin oranges, if desired.

Orange-Walnut Salad

Prep: 20 min., Cook: 6 min.

2 heads Bibb lettuce, torn into bite-size pieces

1 (10-oz.) package fresh spinach, torn

2 oranges, peeled, seeded, and sectioned

½ medium onion, sliced and separated into rings

½ cup coarsely chopped walnuts

2 tsp. butter or margarine, melted

Sweet-and-Sour Dressing

Place first 4 ingredients in a large salad bowl. Sauté walnuts in butter in a small skillet over medium heat until toasted; add to salad. Toss with Sweet-and-Sour Dressing. **Makes** 6 servings.

Sweet-and-Sour Dressing

Prep: 2 min.

1 cup vegetable oil

½ cup white vinegar

½ cup sugar

1 tsp. salt

1 tsp. dry mustard

1 tsp. paprika

1 tsp. grated onion

1 tsp. celery seeds

Process first 7 ingredients in a blender until smooth. Stir in celery seeds. Cover and chill until ready to serve. Stir again just before serving. **Makes** 1¾ cups.

Cantaloupe-Spinach Salad with Pistachio-Lime Vinaigrette
Prep: 15 min.

1 large cantaloupe
6 cups torn fresh spinach leaves
½ cup pistachios, coarsely chopped
Pistachio-Lime Vinaigrette

Peel, seed, and cut cantaloupe into thin wedges; cut wedges vertically into ½-inch slices.
Place spinach on individual serving plates; arrange cantaloupe on top, and sprinkle with pistachios. Serve with Pistachio-Lime Vinaigrette. **Makes** 6 to 8 servings.

Pistachio-Lime Vinaigrette
Prep: 5 min.

⅓ cup fresh lime juice
⅓ cup honey
¼ cup chopped red onion
1 tsp. dried crushed red pepper
½ tsp. salt
¼ cup chopped fresh cilantro
¾ cup vegetable oil
1 cup pistachios

Process first 6 ingredients in a blender until smooth. With blender running, add oil in a slow, steady stream. Turn blender off; add pistachios, and pulse until pistachios are finely chopped. Store in refrigerator. **Makes** about 2 cups.

Strawberry Salad with Cinnamon Vinaigrette
Prep: 20 min.

This salad's dressing offers a wonderful balance of tastes. It's so delicious, we gave it our highest rating.

1 (11-oz.) can mandarin oranges, drained
1 pt. fresh strawberries, stemmed and quartered
1 small red onion, thinly sliced
½ cup coarsely chopped pecans, toasted
1 ripe avocado, sliced
1 (10-oz.) package romaine lettuce
Cinnamon Vinaigrette

Combine first 6 ingredients in a large bowl. Drizzle with half of Cinnamon Vinaigrette, tossing to coat. Serve remaining vinaigrette with salad. **Makes** 6 to 8 servings.

Cinnamon Vinaigrette
Prep: 5 min., Other: 2 hrs.

⅓ cup olive oil
⅓ cup raspberry vinegar
1 Tbsp. sugar
½ tsp. salt
½ tsp. ground cinnamon
¼ tsp. pepper
½ tsp. hot sauce

Combine all ingredients in a jar; cover tightly, and shake vigorously. Chill at least 2 hours. Shake well before serving. **Makes** ⅔ cup.

quick & easy
Cranberry-Gorgonzola Green Salad
Prep: 20 min.

⅓ cup vegetable oil
¼ cup seasoned rice vinegar
¾ tsp. Dijon mustard
1 garlic clove, pressed
1 small head Bibb lettuce, torn
1 bunch Green Leaf lettuce, torn
1 Granny Smith or pippin apple, diced
⅓ cup coarsely chopped walnuts, toasted
⅓ cup dried cranberries
⅓ cup crumbled Gorgonzola cheese

Combine first 4 ingredients; stir with a wire whisk until blended. Set aside.
Just before serving, combine Bibb lettuce and remaining 5 ingredients in a large bowl. Pour dressing over salad; toss gently. **Makes** 8 servings.

Cranberry-Strawberry-Jícama Salad

Prep: 30 min.

The raw jícama in this salad adds flavor and crunch. Sometimes referred to as the Mexican potato, jícama has a sweet, nutty taste and can be eaten raw or cooked.

½ cup olive oil
½ cup orange juice
¼ cup cranberry-orange relish (we tested with Ocean Spray Cran-Fruit Crushed Fruit For Chicken)
1 small shallot, peeled and chopped
2 Tbsp. balsamic vinegar
¼ tsp. ground red pepper
¼ tsp. salt
¼ tsp. freshly ground black pepper
1 large jícama, peeled
2 (5-oz.) packages gourmet mixed salad greens
2 cups sliced fresh strawberries
½ cup sweetened dried cranberries, finely chopped
2 large navel oranges, peeled and sectioned (optional)
Garnish: shaved Pecorino Romano or Parmesan cheese

Process first 8 ingredients in a blender until smooth, stopping to scrape down sides.

Cut jícama into cubes (or, if desired, cut into ¼-inch-thick slices; cut with a 1½-inch star-shaped cutter).

Place jícama, salad greens, strawberries, cranberries, and, if desired, orange sections in a large bowl. Drizzle with vinaigrette, and gently toss to coat. Garnish, if desired. **Makes** 8 to 10 servings.

Watermelon-Prosciutto Salad

Prep: 20 min., Cook: 5 min.

¼ lb. prosciutto, cut into thin strips
1 Tbsp. chopped fresh basil
3 Tbsp. white balsamic vinegar
2 tsp. honey
⅛ tsp. paprika
⅓ cup olive oil
3 cups seeded and cubed watermelon
2 bunches watercress
½ tsp. freshly ground pepper
Garnish: watermelon wedges

Brown prosciutto in a small nonstick skillet over medium heat 5 minutes. Remove prosciutto, and set aside.

Whisk together basil and next 3 ingredients; gradually whisk in oil until blended.

Arrange watermelon cubes over watercress. Sprinkle with prosciutto and pepper, and drizzle with vinaigrette. Garnish, if desired. Serve immediately. **Makes** 4 servings.

quick & easy

Fruit Salad with Honey-Pecan Dressing

Prep: 5 min.

2½ cups fresh orange sections
2½ cups fresh grapefruit sections
1 ripe avocado, sliced
3⅓ cups sliced strawberries
10 cups Bibb lettuce leaves
Honey-Pecan Dressing

Arrange fresh orange and grapefruit sections, sliced avocado, and sliced strawberries over Bibb lettuce leaves; drizzle with Honey-Pecan Dressing. **Makes** 6 to 8 servings.

Honey-Pecan Dressing

Prep: 5 min.

3 Tbsp. sugar
1 Tbsp. chopped sweet onion
½ tsp. dry mustard
¼ tsp. salt
½ cup honey
¼ cup red wine vinegar
1 cup vegetable oil
1 cup chopped pecans, toasted

Pulse first 6 ingredients in a blender 2 to 3 times until blended. With blender running, pour oil through food chute in a slow, steady stream; process until smooth. Stir in pecans. **Makes** 2½ cups.

Summer Fruit Salad with Blueberry Vinaigrette

Prep: 10 min., Other: 1 hr.

2 cups fresh or frozen blueberries
1 cup fresh strawberries, halved
2 nectarines, sliced
8 cups mixed salad greens
Blueberry Vinaigrette
½ cup slivered almonds, toasted (optional)

Combine first 4 ingredients in a large bowl. Cover and chill 1 hour.
Drizzle ⅓ cup Blueberry Vinaigrette over blueberry mixture, tossing to coat.
Sprinkle with slivered almonds, if desired. **Makes** 4 servings.

Blueberry Vinaigrette

Prep: 5 min.

¼ cup Blueberry Chutney
¼ cup minced onion
⅓ cup balsamic vinegar
1 tsp. salt
½ tsp. pepper
⅔ cup vegetable oil

Whisk together first 5 ingredients. Gradually whisk in oil until blended. Refrigerate leftover vinaigrette up to 2 weeks. **Makes** 1½ cups.

Blueberry Chutney

Prep: 15 min., Cook: 40 min.

1 large Granny Smith apple, peeled and diced
½ cup sugar
½ cup orange juice
1 Tbsp. grated orange rind
1 tsp. ground ginger
¼ to ½ tsp. dried crushed red pepper
¼ tsp. ground black pepper
4 cups fresh or frozen blueberries
3 Tbsp. balsamic vinegar

Bring first 7 ingredients to a boil in a medium saucepan. Reduce heat to low; simmer, stirring occasionally, 15 minutes or until apple is tender. Stir in blueberries and vinegar; bring to a boil.
Reduce heat to medium; cook, stirring occasionally, 40 minutes or until thickened. **Makes** 3 cups.

Fruity Spring Mix Salad
Prep: 15 min.

You can make the salad dressing and sugared almonds several days ahead and store in airtight containers.

1 head Bibb lettuce, torn
10 oz. gourmet mixed salad greens*
2 cups fresh chopped pineapple (1-inch cubes)
2 kiwifruit, peeled and sliced
1 (11-oz.) can mandarin oranges, drained and chilled
16 seedless green or red grapes, cut in half lengthwise
Sweet-Hot Vinaigrette
Sugared Almonds

Toss first 6 ingredients together in a large glass bowl. Drizzle evenly with Sweet-Hot Vinaigrette, and sprinkle with Sugared Almonds. **Makes** 6 to 8 servings.

*Substitute 10 cups of your favorite salad greens, loosely packed and torn, if desired.

Sweet-Hot Vinaigrette
Prep: 5 min., Other: 30 min.

¼ cup vegetable oil
¼ cup balsamic vinegar
2 Tbsp. sugar
¼ tsp. salt
¼ tsp. pepper
¼ tsp. hot sauce

Whisk together all ingredients. Cover; chill 30 minutes. **Makes** ½ cup.

Sugared Almonds
Prep: 2 min., Cook: 10 min., Other: 20 min.

1 cup slivered almonds
½ cup sugar

Stir together all ingredients in a heavy saucepan over medium heat, and cook, stirring constantly, 10 minutes or until golden. Spread mixture in an even layer on lightly greased wax paper, and cool 20 minutes. Break into pieces, and store in an airtight container. **Makes** 1 cup.

Look for prepackaged broccoli slaw mix in the produce department of your grocery store. The fine shreds of broccoli stalks, which resemble shredded cabbage, need no cooking and are ready to toss into slaws, leaving you more time to tend the barbecue. These four recipes, using the nutritious slaw mix, offer lots of variety.

make ahead • quick & easy

Cilantro Slaw

Prep: 10 min.

¼ cup finely chopped fresh cilantro
¼ cup Dijon mustard
3 Tbsp. mayonnaise
1 Tbsp. white wine vinegar
1 (12-oz.) package broccoli slaw mix

Whisk together first 4 ingredients in a large bowl; add broccoli slaw, tossing to coat. **Makes** 4 cups.

make ahead • quick & easy

Broccoli Slaw

Prep: 20 min.

This is a terrific dish to take to a barbecue after a busy day because you can make it the night before.

1 (12-oz.) package broccoli slaw mix
1 cup seedless red grapes, halved
1 Granny Smith apple, diced
1 cup Vidalia onion dressing or poppy seed dressing
2 oranges, peeled and sectioned
Toasted chopped pecans (optional)

Stir together first 5 ingredients in a large bowl. Top with chopped pecans, if desired. **Makes** 8 servings.

quick & easy

Blue Cheese-Bacon Slaw

Prep: 15 min.

1 (16-oz.) bottle Ranch dressing
1 cup crumbled blue cheese
2 (12-oz.) packages broccoli slaw mix
1 small onion, chopped
6 bacon slices, cooked and crumbled

Stir together Ranch dressing and blue cheese in a large bowl. Rinse slaw mix with cold water; drain well. Combine slaw mix, onion, and bacon; toss. Top with dressing just before serving. **Makes** 8 servings.

make ahead

Broccoli-Squash Slaw

Prep: 20 min., Other: 2 hrs.

¼ cup mayonnaise
¼ cup honey
2 Tbsp. fresh lemon juice
1 tsp. salt
½ tsp. black pepper
⅛ to ¼ tsp. ground red pepper
1 (12-oz.) package broccoli slaw mix
2 medium-size yellow squash, cut in half lengthwise and thinly sliced
1 red bell pepper, chopped
½ cup chopped pecans, toasted

Whisk together first 6 ingredients in a small bowl. Combine broccoli slaw, squash, and bell pepper in a large bowl. Add half of mayonnaise mixture (about ¼ cup), tossing to coat. Cover and chill both slaw mixture and remaining mayonnaise mixture at least 2 hours or up to 24 hours.
Drain slaw mixture, just before serving, discarding excess liquid; return to bowl. Add reserved half of mayonnaise mixture and pecans, tossing to coat. **Makes** 4 servings.

'Cue: What type of coleslaw goes best with barbecue?

A: There are two basic types of coleslaw: vinegar based and creamy. Vinegar-based coleslaws mirror the tangy flavors of barbecue sauce for those adventuresome palates that can't get enough. Creamy coleslaws tame the heat of hot sauces—literally if dairy products are in the slaw, and figuratively if the slaws are mayonnaise based. So pick a slaw that complements your preferences.

make ahead

Sweet-and-Tart
Red Cabbage Coleslaw
Prep: 20 min., Other: 1 hr.

Pineapple juice and sugar sweeten this German-style coleslaw.

⅓ cup pineapple juice
¼ cup sugar
¼ cup olive oil
¼ cup lemon or lime juice
¼ cup rice wine vinegar
½ tsp. salt
½ tsp. pepper
⅛ tsp. hot sauce
1 large red cabbage, finely shredded
1 small Granny Smith apple, chopped
1 large carrot, shredded
1 small sweet onion, minced
5 to 6 bacon slices, cooked and crumbled

Whisk together first 8 ingredients in a large bowl until sugar dissolves.
Add cabbage and next 3 ingredients, tossing to coat. Cover and chill at least 1 hour. Sprinkle with bacon before serving. **Makes** 8 cups.

make ahead

Spectacular Overnight Slaw
Prep: 8 min., Cook: 4 min., Other: 8 hrs.

This slaw is true to its name! Chilling the slaw overnight allows the flavors to blend, resulting in a taste sensation.

1 medium cabbage, finely shredded
1 medium-size red onion, thinly sliced
½ cup chopped green bell pepper
½ cup chopped red bell pepper
½ cup sliced pimiento-stuffed olives
½ cup sugar
½ cup vegetable oil
½ cup white wine vinegar
1 tsp. salt
1 tsp. celery seeds
1 tsp. mustard seeds
2 tsp. Dijon mustard

Combine first 5 ingredients in a large bowl; stir well. Combine sugar and remaining 6 ingredients in a small saucepan; bring to a boil. Boil 1 minute. Pour over cabbage mixture; toss well. Cover and chill 8 hours. Toss well. **Makes** 12 servings.

make ahead

Tangy Marinated Coleslaw
Prep: 5 min., Other: 8 hrs.

4 cups coarsely shredded green cabbage
1 medium cucumber, thinly sliced
1 cup coarsely shredded carrot
½ cup diced red onion
½ cup diced green bell pepper
¼ cup cider vinegar
1 Tbsp. sugar
1 Tbsp. Dijon mustard
1 Tbsp. vegetable oil
2 tsp. prepared horseradish
½ tsp. pepper
¼ tsp. salt

Combine first 5 ingredients in a large bowl; toss well.
Combine vinegar and remaining 6 ingredients in a jar. Cover tightly, and shake vigorously. Pour over vegetables; toss gently. Cover and chill 8 hours. Serve chilled or at room temperature. **Makes** 6 cups.

Chinese Cabbage Slaw
Prep: 15 min., Cook: 5 min.

1 head bok choy, shredded
1 bunch green onions, diced
2 Tbsp. butter or margarine
¼ cup sliced almonds
¼ cup sesame seeds
½ cup vegetable oil
¼ cup sesame oil
6 Tbsp. rice wine vinegar
¼ cup sugar
1 tsp. salt
1 tsp. pepper

Place bok choy and green onions in a large bowl.
Melt butter in a skillet. Add almonds and sesame seeds; sauté mixture over medium-high heat 5 minutes or until lightly browned. Drain and cool slightly. Add to bok choy mixture.
Stir together oils and remaining 4 ingredients. Toss with bok choy mixture. Serve immediately. **Makes** 4 servings.

Buttermilk-Dressing Coleslaw
Prep: 15 min., Other: 2 hrs.

½ cup sugar
½ cup mayonnaise
¼ cup milk
¼ cup buttermilk
2½ Tbsp. lemon juice
1½ Tbsp. white vinegar
½ tsp. salt
⅛ tsp. pepper
2 (10-oz.) packages finely shredded cabbage
1 carrot, shredded

Whisk together first 8 ingredients in a large bowl until blended. Add cabbage and carrot, and toss to coat. Cover and chill at least 2 hours. **Makes** 8 to 10 servings.

Memphis-Style Coleslaw
Prep: 8 min., Other: 4 hrs.

2 cups mayonnaise
¼ cup sugar
¼ cup Dijon mustard
¼ cup cider vinegar
1½ to 2 Tbsp. celery seeds
1 tsp. salt
⅛ tsp. pepper
1 medium cabbage, shredded
2 carrots, grated
1 green bell pepper, diced
2 Tbsp. grated onion

Stir together first 7 ingredients in a large bowl; add cabbage and remaining ingredients, tossing gently. Cover and chill 3 to 4 hours; serve with a slotted spoon. **Makes** 12 servings.

Barbecue Slaw
Prep: 5 min., Other: 3 hrs.

Move over, ordinary coleslaw—this easy barbecue-flavored variation is sure to become a favorite in your family.

⅓ cup sugar
⅓ cup ketchup
⅓ cup white vinegar
11 cups shredded cabbage (about 1 medium cabbage)

Combine first 3 ingredients in a small saucepan; bring to a boil, stirring until sugar dissolves. Pour hot vinegar mixture over cabbage; toss well. Cover and chill at least 3 hours. **Makes** 8 servings.

Bacon Potato Salad

Bacon Potato Salad
Prep: 15 min., Cook: 18 min., Other: 1 hr.

6 to 8 medium potatoes (about 3 lb.), peeled and cut
    into 1-inch cubes
½ lb. bacon, cooked and crumbled
6 green onions, chopped
2 celery ribs, finely chopped
2 Tbsp. diced pimiento, drained
¾ tsp. salt
¼ tsp. pepper
½ cup mayonnaise
½ cup sour cream
Garnishes: paprika, celery sticks

Cook potatoes in boiling water to cover in a Dutch
oven over medium heat 15 to 18 minutes or until
tender. Drain and cool slightly.
Place potatoes in a large bowl. Add bacon, chopped
green onions, and next 4 ingredients.
Stir together mayonnaise and sour cream until
blended. Pour over potato mixture, tossing gently to
coat. Cover and chill at least 1 hour. Garnish, if
desired. **Makes** 6 servings.

Southern-Style Potato Salad
Prep: 15 min., Cook: 40 min.

4 lb. potatoes (about 4 large)
3 large hard-cooked eggs, peeled and grated
1 cup mayonnaise
½ cup sour cream
¼ cup celery, finely chopped
2 Tbsp. onion, finely chopped
2 Tbsp. sweet pickle relish
1 Tbsp. mustard
1 tsp. salt
½ tsp. freshly ground pepper
½ lb. bacon, cooked and crumbled

Cook potatoes in boiling water to cover 40 minutes
or until tender; drain and cool. Peel potatoes, and
cut into 1-inch cubes.
Stir together potatoes and egg in a large bowl.
Stir together mayonnaise and next 7 ingredients;
gently stir into potato mixture. Cover and chill.
Sprinkle with bacon just before serving. **Makes** 8
servings.

Lemon-Basil Potato Salad
Prep: 20 min., Cook: 25 min.

2½ lb. small Yukon gold potatoes, cut into eighths*
¼ cup lemon juice
4 garlic cloves, minced
¾ cup chopped fresh basil
1 Tbsp. Dijon mustard
1 tsp. salt
½ tsp. freshly ground pepper
⅔ cup olive oil
½ medium-size red onion, chopped
1 (10-oz.) package leaf spinach, cut into thin strips
10 thick bacon slices, cooked and crumbled

Arrange potato evenly on a lightly greased 15- x 10-
inch jelly-roll pan; coat potato with cooking spray.
Bake at 475°, stirring occasionally, 20 to 25 minutes
or until tender and golden.
Whisk together lemon juice and next 5 ingredients;
whisk in oil in a slow, steady stream. Gently toss
potato and onion with ½ cup vinaigrette.
Arrange spinach evenly in 6 bowls, and drizzle with
remaining vinaigrette. Top with potato mixture;
sprinkle with bacon. **Makes** 6 servings.

*Substitute 2½ lb. small new potatoes, if desired.

Sweet Potato Salad with Rosemary-Honey Vinaigrette
Prep: 10 min., Cook: 35 min.

4½ cups peeled, cubed sweet potato
2 Tbsp. olive oil, divided
¼ cup honey
3 Tbsp. white wine vinegar
2 Tbsp. chopped fresh rosemary
2 garlic cloves, minced
½ tsp. salt
½ tsp. freshly ground pepper

Line a 15- x 10-inch jelly-roll pan with aluminum
foil. Coat foil with vegetable cooking spray.
Toss together sweet potato and 1 Tbsp. oil in pan.
Bake at 450° for 35 minutes or until tender.
Whisk together remaining 1 Tbsp. oil, honey, and
next 5 ingredients in a large bowl. Add sweet potato;
toss well. Cool. **Makes** 6 servings.

Brunswick Stew
Prep: 40 min.; Cook: 2 hrs., 40 min.

1 (4½-lb.) pork roast
1 (4½-lb.) hen
3 (16-oz.) cans whole tomatoes, undrained and chopped
1 (8-oz.) can tomato sauce
3 large onions, chopped
2 small green bell peppers, chopped
¾ cup white vinegar
¼ cup sugar
¼ cup all-purpose flour
1 cup water
1 tsp. salt
½ tsp. pepper
½ tsp. ground turmeric
2 Tbsp. hot sauce
1 (16-oz.) package frozen white shoepeg corn

Place pork roast, fat side up, on a rack of a roasting pan. Insert meat thermometer, being careful not to touch bone or fat. Bake at 325° for 2 hours or until thermometer registers 160°. Cool. Trim and discard fat; cut pork into 2-inch pieces.

Meanwhile, place hen in a Dutch oven, and cover with water. Bring to a boil; cover, reduce heat, and simmer 2 hours or until tender. Remove hen from broth, and cool. (Reserve broth for another use.) Bone hen, and cut meat into 2-inch pieces.

Coarsely grind pork and chicken in food processor or with meat grinder. Combine ground meat, tomatoes, and next 5 ingredients in a large Dutch oven.

Combine flour and water in a bowl, stirring until smooth; stir into meat mixture. Stir in salt and next 3 ingredients. Cook over medium heat 30 minutes, stirring occasionally. Add water, if needed, to reach desired consistency. Stir in corn, and cook 10 more minutes. **Makes** 22 cups.

Note: This stew freezes well in individual-size containers.

Chicken Brunswick Stew
Prep: 30 min; Cook: 4 hrs., 55 min.

2 (2½-lb.) whole chickens
2 qt. water
1 Tbsp. salt
1½ cups ketchup, divided
2 Tbsp. light brown sugar
1½ tsp. dry mustard
1½ tsp. grated fresh ginger
½ lemon, sliced
1 garlic clove, minced
1 Tbsp. butter or margarine
¼ cup white vinegar
3 Tbsp. vegetable oil
1 Tbsp. Worcestershire sauce
¾ tsp. hot sauce
½ tsp. pepper
2 (28-oz.) cans crushed tomatoes
2 (15.25-oz.) cans whole kernel corn, undrained
2 (14¾-oz.) cans cream-style corn
1 large onion, chopped
¼ cup firmly packed light brown sugar
1 Tbsp. salt
1 Tbsp. pepper

Bring first 3 ingredients to a boil in a large heavy stockpot; cover, reduce heat, and simmer 45 minutes or until chicken is tender. Drain chicken, reserving 1 qt. broth in pot; skin, bone, and shred chicken, and return to pot.

Cook ½ cup ketchup and next 11 ingredients in a small saucepan over medium heat, stirring occasionally, 10 minutes.

Stir ketchup mixture, remaining 1 cup ketchup, tomatoes, and next 6 ingredients into chicken and broth; simmer, stirring often, 4 hours or until thickened. **Makes** 3½ qt.

Pecan-Chocolate Chip
Cookies, page 270

Sweet
Tooth

The only things possibly more

irresistible than succulent barbecue

are crunchy cookies, juicy cobblers,

and fruit-speckled ice creams.

These and more delightful desserts

are sure to cure your most insatiable

sugar craving.

Melt-in-Your-Mouth
Iced Sugar Cookies
Prep: 45 min., Cook: 9 min. per batch

1 cup butter, softened
1½ cups sugar
1 large egg
3 cups all-purpose flour
½ tsp. baking soda
½ tsp. salt
1 tsp. cream of tartar
2 tsp. vanilla extract
Royal Icing
Assorted colors food coloring paste
Decorator sprinkles

Beat butter in a large bowl at medium speed with an electric mixer 2 minutes or until creamy. Gradually add sugar, beating well. Add egg, and beat well. Combine flour and next 3 ingredients. Add to butter mixture, beating at low speed just until blended. Stir in vanilla.

Roll dough to ¼-inch thickness on a lightly floured surface. Cut with 3-inch cookie cutters. Place 1-inch apart on ungreased baking sheets. Bake at 350° for 9 minutes. Cool completely on wire racks.

Spoon about ⅔ cup white Royal Icing into a decorating bag fitted with decorating tip #3 (small round tip). Pipe white icing to outline cookies and detail as desired.

Divide remaining Royal Icing into a separate bowl for each color of icing desired; color as desired with food coloring paste. Slowly stir just enough water into each bowl of icing to make "flow-in icing" that is still thick but flows into a smooth surface after stirring. (Add water a little at a time; if flow-in icing is too watery, it may not dry properly and may run under outline into another color area.)

Fill decorating bags (using no tips) about half full of flow-in icing. Snip off small tip of each cone. Pipe desired colors of icing to cover areas between the Royal Icing outline; spread icing into corners and hard-to-reach areas using wooden picks, as necessary.

Add flow-in icing 1 color at a time, allowing icing to dry before changing colors. Avoid using excess icing to prevent spilling over into another color area. If air bubbles form in icing, use a sterilized straight pin to remove them.

Decorate with decorator sprinkles while icing is still wet. **Makes** 3½ dozen.

Royal Icing
Prep: 10 min., Cook: 9 min.

This icing dries very quickly, so keep it covered with a damp cloth at all times while in the bowl to help keep it moist.

3 egg whites
1 (16-oz.) package powdered sugar, sifted and divided
½ tsp. cream of tartar

Combine egg whites, 1 cup powdered sugar, and cream of tartar in top of a double boiler. Place over simmering water. Cook, stirring constantly with a wire whisk, 9 minutes or until mixture reaches 160°. Remove from heat. Transfer to a large mixing bowl, and add remaining powdered sugar.

Beat at high speed with an electric mixer 5 to 8 minutes or until stiff peaks form. **Makes** 2 cups.

Gingersnaps
Prep: 10 min., Cook: 8 min. per batch

¾ cup shortening
1 cup sugar
1 large egg
¼ cup molasses
2 cups all-purpose flour
2 tsp. baking soda
¼ tsp. salt
1 Tbsp. ground ginger
1 tsp. ground cinnamon
Additional sugar

Beat shortening in a large bowl at medium speed with an electric mixer; gradually add 1 cup sugar, beating well. Add egg and molasses; mix thoroughly.

Combine flour and next 4 ingredients; add flour mixture one-fourth at a time to creamed mixture, mixing after each addition.

Shape dough into ¾-inch balls, and roll in sugar. Place on ungreased baking sheets, and bake at 350° for 8 minutes. (Tops will crack.) Remove to wire racks to cool. **Makes** 8 dozen.

Note: To make larger gingersnaps, shape cookie dough into 1-inch balls, and bake 10 minutes; the yield will be 4 dozen.

Molasses Sugar Cookies
Prep: 25 min., Cook: 10 min. per batch, Other: 40 min.

If you can't find whole wheat pastry flour, increase the all-purpose flour to 1¾ cups and use ¼ cup whole wheat flour.

½ cup applesauce
1¼ cups sugar, divided
6 Tbsp. butter, softened
¼ cup dark molasses
1 large egg
1 cup all-purpose flour
1 cup whole wheat pastry flour
2 tsp. baking soda
1 tsp. ground cinnamon
½ tsp. salt
½ tsp. ground ginger
½ tsp. ground cloves

Spoon applesauce onto several layers of heavy-duty paper towels; spread to ½-inch thickness. Cover with additional paper towels; let stand 5 minutes. Scrape into a bowl using a rubber spatula.

Combine applesauce, 1 cup sugar, and butter; beat at medium speed with an electric mixer until well blended (about 3 minutes). Add molasses and egg; beat well.

Combine flours and remaining 5 ingredients, stirring well with a whisk. Gradually add flour mixture to sugar mixture, beating until blended. Cover and freeze dough 30 minutes or until firm.

With moist hands, shape dough into 32 (1-inch) balls. Roll balls in remaining ¼ cup sugar. Place 3 inches apart on baking sheets coated with cooking spray. Bake at 375° for 8 to 10 minutes. Cool on pans 5 minutes. Remove from pans; cool completely on wire racks. **Makes** 32 cookies.

Old-Fashioned Peanut Butter Cookies

Prep: 25 min., Cook: 8 min. per batch, Other: 3 hrs.

1 cup butter or margarine, softened
1 cup creamy peanut butter
1 cup granulated sugar
1 cup firmly packed brown sugar
2 large eggs
2½ cups all-purpose flour
2 tsp. baking soda
¼ tsp. salt
1 tsp. vanilla extract
Additional granulated sugar

Beat butter and peanut butter at medium speed with an electric mixer until creamy; gradually add sugars, beating well. Add eggs, beating well.

Combine flour, soda, and salt in a medium bowl; add to butter mixture, beating well. Stir in vanilla. Cover and chill 3 hours.

Shape into 1¼-inch balls; place 3 inches apart on ungreased baking sheets. Dip a fork in additional sugar; flatten cookies in a crisscross design. Bake at 375° for 7 to 8 minutes. Remove to wire racks to cool.

Makes 6 dozen.

Peanut Butter Turtle Cookies

Prep: 25 min., Cook: 24 min., Other: 2 min.

½ cup unsalted butter, softened
½ cup granulated sugar
½ cup firmly packed light brown sugar
⅔ cup creamy peanut butter
1 large egg
2 cups all-purpose baking mix
⅔ cup almond toffee bits
⅔ cup coarsely chopped peanuts
⅔ cup milk chocolate morsels
10 oz. vanilla caramels
2 to 3 Tbsp. whipping cream
½ tsp. vanilla extract
⅔ cup milk chocolate morsels, melted

Beat first 4 ingredients at medium speed with an electric mixer until creamy. Add egg, beating until blended. Add baking mix, beating at low speed just until blended. Stir in toffee bits, chopped peanuts, and ⅔ cup chocolate morsels.

Drop dough by rounded tablespoonfuls onto ungreased baking sheets; flatten dough with hand.

Bake at 350° for 10 to 12 minutes or until golden brown. Cool cookies on baking sheets 1 minute; remove cookies to wire racks.

Microwave caramels and 2 Tbsp. cream in a glass bowl at HIGH 1 minute; stir. Continue to microwave at 30-second intervals, stirring until caramels melt and mixture is smooth; add remaining cream, if necessary. Stir in vanilla. Spoon mixture evenly onto tops of cookies; drizzle evenly with chocolate. **Makes** 3 dozen.

Brown Sugar-Oatmeal Cookies

Prep: 10 min., Cook: 14 min. per batch, Other: 2 min.

1 cup butter or margarine, softened
2 cups firmly packed brown sugar
2 large eggs
½ tsp. baking soda
¼ cup hot water
2 cups all-purpose flour
1 tsp. baking powder
½ tsp. salt
4 cups uncooked regular oats
1 cup sweetened flaked coconut
1 cup chopped pecans

Beat butter at medium speed with an electric mixer until creamy; gradually add brown sugar, beating well. Add eggs; beat well.

Combine soda and water, stirring well. Combine flour, baking powder, salt, and soda mixture; gradually add to butter mixture, beating well. Stir in oats and remaining ingredients.

Drop dough by heaping teaspoonfuls onto greased baking sheets. Bake at 350° for 14 minutes or until lightly browned. Cool 2 minutes on sheets; remove to wire racks to cool completely. **Makes** about 6 dozen.

Clear-the-Cupboard Cookies

Prep: 20 min., Cook: 10 min. per batch

1 cup shortening
1 cup granulated sugar
1 cup firmly packed light brown sugar
2 large eggs
2 cups all-purpose flour
1 tsp. baking soda
1 tsp. baking powder
1 tsp. salt
1 cup uncooked regular oats
1 cup sweetened flaked coconut
1 cup crisp rice cereal
1 tsp. vanilla extract
1 cup chopped pecans, toasted (optional)

Beat shortening at medium speed with an electric mixer until fluffy; add sugars, beating well. Add eggs, beating until blended.

Combine flour and next 4 ingredients; gradually add to sugar mixture, beating after each addition. Stir in coconut, cereal, vanilla, and, if desired, pecans.

Drop by tablespoonfuls onto baking sheets.

Bake at 350° for 10 minutes or until lightly golden. Remove to wire racks to cool. **Makes** 4½ dozen.

COOKIES AND 'CUE—A GREAT PAIR

Cookies are terrific post-barbecue treats—they can be made ahead and make plenty to feed a crowd. They also make crisp partners for another summertime favorite: homemade ice cream!

Oatmeal-Raisin Cookies

Prep: 11 min., Cook: 8 min. per batch

1 cup butter or margarine, softened
1 cup granulated sugar
1 cup firmly packed brown sugar
2 large eggs
1 Tbsp. vanilla extract
2 cups all-purpose flour
1 tsp. baking soda
½ tsp. baking powder
½ tsp. salt
1½ cups quick-cooking oats, uncooked
1 cup raisins
1½ cups chopped pecans

Beat butter at medium speed with an electric mixer until creamy; gradually add sugars, beating well. Add eggs and vanilla; beat well.

Combine flour and next 3 ingredients; gradually add to butter mixture, beating well. Stir in oats, raisins, and pecans.

Drop dough by heaping teaspoonfuls onto greased baking sheets.

Bake at 375° for 8 minutes or until lightly browned. Cool slightly on baking sheets; remove to wire racks to cool completely. **Makes** 7 dozen.

Nutty Oatmeal-Chocolate Chunk Cookies

Prep: 10 min., Cook: 8 min. per batch

2½ cups uncooked regular oats
1 cup butter or margarine, softened
1 cup granulated sugar
1 cup firmly packed brown sugar
2 large eggs
1 Tbsp. vanilla extract
2 cups all-purpose flour
1 tsp. baking powder
1 tsp. baking soda
½ tsp. salt
3 (1.55-oz.) milk chocolate candy bars, chopped
1½ cups chopped pecans

Process oats in a blender or food processor until ground.

Beat butter and sugars at medium speed with an electric mixer until fluffy. Add eggs and vanilla; beat until blended.

Combine ground oats, flour, and next 3 ingredients. Add to butter mixture, beating until blended. Stir in chocolate and pecans.

Drop dough by tablespoonfuls onto ungreased baking sheets.

Bake at 375° for 7 to 8 minutes or until golden brown; remove to wire racks to cool. **Makes** 6 dozen.

Orange-Macadamia Nut Cookies

Prep: 15 min., Cook: 10 min. per batch, Other: 2 hrs.

Macadamia nuts and white chocolate pair up for a taste sensation in this delicious drop cookie.

¾ cup butter or margarine, softened
½ cup granulated sugar
½ cup firmly packed brown sugar
1 large egg
1 Tbsp. grated orange rind
¾ tsp. vanilla extract
¼ tsp. orange extract
1⅓ cups all-purpose flour
½ cup quick-cooking oats, uncooked
¾ tsp. baking powder
½ tsp. baking soda
1 (3.5-oz.) jar lightly salted macadamia nuts, coarsely chopped
1 cup white chocolate morsels or chunks

Beat butter at medium speed with an electric mixer 2 minutes or until creamy. Gradually add sugars, beating well. Add egg, orange rind, and flavorings.

Combine flour and next 3 ingredients in a medium bowl. Add to butter mixture, beating at low speed just until blended. Stir in nuts and white chocolate morsels. Cover and chill 2 hours.

Drop dough by rounded tablespoonfuls onto ungreased baking sheets.

Bake at 350° for 9 to 10 minutes or just until edges are golden. Cool 1 minute on baking sheets; remove to wire racks, and cool completely. **Makes** about 3 dozen.

White Chocolate-Macadamia Nut Cookies

Prep: 10 min., Cook: 10 min. per batch

½ cup butter or margarine, softened
½ cup shortening
¾ cup firmly packed brown sugar
½ cup granulated sugar
1 large egg
1½ tsp. vanilla extract
2 cups all-purpose flour
1 tsp. baking soda
½ tsp. salt
1 (6-oz.) package white chocolate baking bars, cut into chunks
1 (7-oz.) jar macadamia nuts, chopped

Beat butter and shortening at medium speed with an electric mixer until creamy; gradually add sugars, beating well. Add egg and vanilla; beat well.
Combine flour, soda, and salt; gradually add to butter mixture, beating well. Stir in white chocolate and nuts.
Drop dough by rounded teaspoonfuls 2 inches apart onto lightly greased baking sheets. Bake at 350° for 8 to 10 minutes or until lightly browned. Cool slightly on baking sheets; remove to wire racks to cool completely. **Makes** 5 dozen.

Cranberry-White Chocolate Cookies

Prep: 15 min., Cook: 12 min. per batch

2½ cups all-purpose flour
1 tsp. baking powder
¼ tsp. salt
⅛ tsp. baking soda
½ cup butter, softened
1⅓ cups sugar
2 large eggs
1½ cups white chocolate morsels
1 (6-oz.) package sweetened dried cranberries (we tested with Craisins)

Combine flour and next 3 ingredients; set aside. Beat butter at medium speed with an electric mixer until creamy; gradually add sugar, beating well. Add eggs, 1 at a time, beating until blended after each addition.

Add flour mixture to butter mixture gradually, beating at low speed until blended. Stir in white chocolate morsels and cranberries.
Drop cookie dough by heaping tablespoonfuls onto lightly greased baking sheets.
Bake at 350° for 10 to 12 minutes or until lightly browned on bottom. Remove to wire racks to cool completely. **Makes** about 3 dozen.

Heavenly Chocolate Chunk Cookies

Prep: 15 min., Cook: 14 min.

Megamorsels give a big chocolate taste to every bite of these deluxe chocolate chip cookies.

2 cups plus 2 Tbsp. all-purpose flour
½ tsp. baking soda
½ tsp. salt
¾ cup butter or margarine
2 Tbsp. instant coffee granules
1 cup firmly packed brown sugar
½ cup granulated sugar
1 large egg
1 egg yolk
1 (11.5-oz.) package semisweet chocolate megamorsels
1 cup walnut halves, toasted

Combine first 3 ingredients in a medium bowl; stir well.
Combine butter and coffee granules in a small saucepan or skillet. Cook over medium-low heat until butter melts and coffee granules dissolve, stirring occasionally. Remove from heat, and cool to room temperature (don't let butter resolidify).
Combine butter mixture, sugars, egg, and egg yolk in a large bowl. Beat at medium speed with an electric mixer until blended. Gradually add flour mixture, beating at low speed just until blended. Stir in megamorsels and walnuts.
Drop dough by heaping tablespoonfuls 2 inches apart onto ungreased baking sheets. Bake at 325° for 12 to 14 minutes. Cool slightly on baking sheets. Remove to wire racks to cool completely. **Makes** 20 cookies.

Chocolate-Chocolate Chip Cookies
Prep: 10 min., Cook: 10 min. per batch

½ cup butter
4 (1-oz.) unsweetened chocolate baking squares, chopped
3 cups (18 oz.) semisweet chocolate morsels, divided
1½ cups all-purpose flour
½ tsp. baking powder
½ tsp. salt
4 large eggs
1½ cups sugar
2 tsp. vanilla extract
2 cups chopped pecans, toasted

Combine butter, unsweetened chocolate, and 1½ cups chocolate morsels in a large heavy saucepan. Cook over low heat, stirring constantly, until butter and chocolate melt; cool. Combine flour, baking powder, and salt in a small bowl; set aside.
Beat eggs, sugar, and vanilla in a medium mixing bowl at medium speed with an electric mixer. Gradually add flour mixture to egg mixture, beating well. Add chocolate mixture; beat well. Stir in remaining 1½ cups chocolate morsels and pecans.
Drop dough by 2 tablespoonfuls 1 inch apart onto parchment paper- or wax paper-lined baking sheets. Bake at 350° for 10 minutes. Cool slightly on baking sheets; remove to wire racks to cool completely. **Makes** about 2½ dozen.

kids love it
Ultimate Chocolate Chip Cookies
Prep: 30 min., Cook: 14 min. per batch

¾ cup butter, softened
¾ cup granulated sugar
¾ cup firmly packed dark brown sugar
2 large eggs
1½ tsp. vanilla extract
2¼ cups plus 2 Tbsp. all-purpose flour
1 tsp. baking soda
¾ tsp. salt
2 cups (12-oz. package) semisweet chocolate morsels

Beat butter and sugars at medium speed with an electric mixer until creamy. Add eggs and vanilla, beating until blended.

Combine flour, soda, and salt in a small bowl; gradually add to butter mixture, beating well. Stir in morsels.
Drop by tablespoonfuls onto lightly greased baking sheets. Bake at 350° for 8 to 14 minutes or until desired degree of doneness. Remove to wire racks to cool completely. **Makes** about 5 dozen.

Peanut Butter-Chocolate Chip Cookies: Decrease salt to ½ tsp. Add 1 cup creamy peanut butter with butter and sugars. Increase flour to 2½ cups plus 2 Tbsp. Proceed as directed. (Dough will look a little moist.)

Oatmeal-Raisin-Chocolate Chip Cookies: Reduce flour to 2 cups. Add 1 cup uncooked quick-cooking oats to dry ingredients and 1 cup raisins with morsels. Proceed as directed.

Pecan-Chocolate Chip Cookies: Add 1½ cups chopped, toasted pecans with morsels. Proceed as directed.

Toffee-Chocolate Chip Cookies: Reduce morsels to 1 cup. Add ½ cup slivered toasted almonds and 1 cup toffee bits (we tested with Hershey's Heath Bits O'Brickle Toffee Bits). Proceed as directed.

Dark Chocolate Chip Cookies: Substitute 2 cups (12-oz. package) dark chocolate morsels (we tested with Hershey's Special Dark Chips) for semisweet chocolate morsels. Proceed as directed.

Chunky Cherry-Double Chip Cookies: Microwave 1 Tbsp. water and ½ cup dried cherries in a glass bowl at HIGH 30 seconds, stirring once. Let stand 10 minutes. Substitute 2 cups (11.5-oz. package) semisweet chocolate chunks for morsels. Add 1 cup white chocolate morsels, ⅓ cup slivered toasted almonds, and cherries with chocolate chunks. Proceed as directed.

Coconut-Macadamia Chunk Cookies: Substitute 2 cups (11.5-oz. package) semisweet chocolate chunks for morsels. Add 1 cup white chocolate morsels, ½ cup sweetened flaked coconut, and ½ cup macadamia nuts with chocolate chunks. Proceed as directed.

Pecan-Chocolate
Chip Cookies

Millionaire Shortbread
Prep: 15 min., Cook: 55 min., Other: 45 min.

1½ cups butter, softened and divided
2 cups all-purpose flour
¾ cup white rice flour*
½ cup granulated sugar
1 (14-oz.) can sweetened condensed milk
¼ cup light corn syrup
1 cup firmly packed light brown sugar
1½ cups semisweet chocolate morsels

Pulse 1 cup butter, flours, and granulated sugar in a food processor 10 to 15 times or until crumbly. Press mixture evenly into a 15- x 10-inch jelly-roll pan coated with cooking spray for baking.
Bake at 350° for 18 to 20 minutes or until light golden brown.
Stir together remaining ½ cup butter, condensed milk, and corn syrup in a 2-qt. heavy saucepan over low heat 4 minutes or until butter is melted and mixture is blended. Add brown sugar, and cook, stirring constantly, 25 to 30 minutes or until caramel colored and thickened. Pour evenly over baked cookie in pan, and spread into an even layer. Chill 30 minutes or until caramel is set.
Microwave morsels in a small glass bowl at HIGH 1 minute or until almost melted. Stir until smooth. Spread over caramel layer in pan. (The chocolate layer will be thin.) Chill 15 minutes or until chocolate is firm. Cut into 2-inch squares; if desired, cut each square into 2 triangles. **Makes** about 3 dozen squares or 6 dozen triangles.

*Substitute ¾ cup all-purpose flour, if desired.

Butter-Mint Shortbread
Prep: 10 min., Cook: 25 min., Other: 10 min.

1 cup butter, softened
¾ cup powdered sugar
½ tsp. mint extract
½ tsp. vanilla extract
2 cups all-purpose flour
Additional powdered sugar

Beat butter and ¾ cup powdered sugar at medium speed with an electric mixer until light and fluffy.

Add extracts, beating until blended. Gradually add flour, beating at low speed until blended. Press dough into an ungreased 15- x 10-inch jelly-roll pan.
Bake at 325° for 25 minutes or until golden. Cool in pan on a wire rack 10 minutes. Cut into squares; sprinkle with additional powdered sugar. Remove from pan; cool on wire rack. **Makes** 3 dozen.

Peanut Butter Shortbread
Prep: 10 min., Cook: 12 min. per batch

⅔ cup creamy peanut butter
½ Basic Butter Cookie Dough recipe
36 milk chocolate kisses

Knead peanut butter into Basic Butter Cookie Dough until smooth and well blended.
Shape dough into 1-inch balls, and place on lightly greased baking sheets. Make an indentation in center of each ball with thumb or spoon handle.
Bake at 350° for 12 minutes or until lightly browned. Immediately press chocolate kiss in center of each cookie. Remove to wire racks to cool. **Makes** 3 dozen.

Basic Butter Cookie Dough
Prep: 20 min.

1 cup butter or margarine, softened
½ cup firmly packed brown sugar
½ cup granulated sugar
1 large egg
3½ cups all-purpose flour
2 tsp. baking powder
½ tsp. salt
2 Tbsp. milk
2 tsp. vanilla extract

Beat butter in a large mixing bowl at medium speed with an electric mixer until creamy. Gradually add sugars, beating well. Add egg, beating well.
Combine flour, baking powder, and salt; add to butter mixture alternately with milk, beginning and ending with flour mixture. Beat at low speed after each addition until mixture is blended. Stir in vanilla.
Divide dough into 2 equal portions; wrap each portion in plastic wrap. Chill. **Makes** 2¼ pounds.

Note: Cookie dough may be frozen up to 1 month.

Marble-Topped Hazelnut Shortbread

Prep: 15 min., Cook: 41 min., Other: 40 min.

½ cup chopped hazelnuts or macadamia nuts
2 cups cake flour
¾ cup powdered sugar
¼ tsp. salt
1 cup butter, softened
4 (1-oz.) semisweet chocolate baking squares
1 (2-oz.) vanilla bark coating square

Bake hazelnuts in a shallow pan at 350°, stirring occasionally, 5 to 10 minutes or until toasted; set aside.
Reduce temperature to 325°.
Combine flour, sugar, and salt in a large mixing bowl; add butter, and beat at low speed with an electric mixer until blended. Press dough into an aluminum foil-lined 10-inch round cakepan.
Bake at 325° for 25 to 30 minutes or until lightly browned.
Microwave chocolate in a small microwave-safe bowl at HIGH, stirring twice, 1 minute or until melted. Spread over shortbread.
Place vanilla bark coating square in a small zip-top freezer bag; seal. Submerge in hot water until bark coating melts. Snip a tiny hole in 1 corner of bag, and drizzle lines ¾ inch apart over chocolate.
Swirl melted coating and chocolate with a wooden pick. Sprinkle with hazelnuts.
Cool in pan on a wire rack 40 minutes. Cut into wedges. **Makes** 16 servings.

Peanut-Toffee Shortbread

Prep: 30 min., Cook: 20 min., Other: 5 min.

1 cup butter, softened
⅔ cup firmly packed light brown sugar
⅓ cup cornstarch
2 cups all-purpose flour
¼ tsp. salt
2 tsp. vanilla extract
2 cups coarsely chopped honey-roasted peanuts, divided
2 cups (12-oz. package) semisweet chocolate morsels

Beat butter at medium speed with an electric mixer until creamy. Combine brown sugar and cornstarch; gradually add to butter, beating well. Gradually add flour and salt to butter mixture, beating at low speed just until blended. Add vanilla and 1 cup peanuts, beating at low speed just until blended.
Turn dough out onto a lightly greased baking sheet; pat or roll dough into an 11- x 14-inch rectangle; leave at least a 1-inch border on all sides of baking sheet.
Bake at 350° for 20 minutes or until golden brown. Remove baking sheet to a wire rack; sprinkle shortbread evenly with chocolate morsels. Let stand 5 minutes; gently spread melted morsels over shortbread. Sprinkle with remaining 1 cup peanuts; cool completely. Cut or break into 2- to 3-inch irregular-shaped pieces. **Makes** about 2½ to 3 dozen pieces.

Peanut-Toffee Shortbread

Banana-Split Brownies

Prep: 10 min., Cook: 45 min.

1 (17.6-oz) package chocolate double-fudge
    brownie mix (we tested with Duncan Hines Chocolate
    Lover's Double Fudge Brownie Mix)
½ cup dried cherries
¼ cup water
1 medium banana, sliced
1 tsp. vanilla extract
½ cup sliced almonds (optional), toasted
Toppings: ice cream, hot fudge, and caramel sauces;
    toasted flaked coconut; grated milk chocolate;
    chopped pecans; candy-coated chocolate pieces;
    whipped cream; maraschino cherries with stems

Prepare brownie mix according to package direc-
tions, following cakelike instructions.
Microwave cherries and ¼ cup water on HIGH 1½
minutes. Drain and cool.
Stir cherries, banana, vanilla, and, if desired, almonds
into batter.
Pour into a lightly greased 8-inch square baking pan.
Bake at 350° for 40 to 45 minutes. Cool and cut
brownies into squares. Serve with desired toppings.
Makes 1 dozen.

Banana-Split Brownies

Mississippi Mud Brownies

Prep: 5 min., Cook: 25 min., Other: 50 min.

1 (20.5-oz.) package low-fat fudge brownie mix
⅔ cup water
1 tsp. vanilla extract
½ cup reduced-fat semisweet chocolate morsels
2 cups miniature marshmallows
1 (16-oz.) container reduced-fat ready-to-spread
    chocolate-flavored frosting

Combine brownie mix, ⅔ cup water, and vanilla; stir
well. Fold in chocolate morsels.
Spread batter in a lightly greased 13- x 9-inch pan.
Bake at 350° for 23 minutes.
Sprinkle marshmallows over hot brownies; return
pan to oven, and bake 2 more minutes. Cool completely (about 20 minutes) in pan on a wire rack.
Spread frosting over brownies; let stand at least
30 minutes. Cut into 24 squares. **Makes** 2 dozen.

Double-Chocolate Brownies

Prep: 10 min., Cook: 35 min.

1 cup butter or margarine, softened
2 cups sugar
4 large eggs
1 cup unsweetened cocoa
1 tsp. vanilla extract
1 cup all-purpose flour
1 cup chopped pecans
⅔ cup white chocolate or semisweet chocolate morsels

Beat butter at medium speed with an electric mixer
until creamy; gradually add sugar, beating well. Add
eggs, 1 at a time, beating just until blended.
Add cocoa and vanilla; beat at low speed 1 minute or
until blended. Gradually add flour, beating well.
Stir in pecans and chocolate morsels. Pour batter into
a greased 13- x 9-inch baking pan.
Bake at 350° for 30 to 35 minutes or until done. Cool
and cut into squares. **Makes** 2 dozen.

Fudge Pie

Prep: 25 min., Cook: 30 min.

Strong brewed coffee brings out the rich, fudgy flavor of this easy chocolate pie—it's a "must try." If you usually use instant coffee granules, use 2 tsp. granules per 1 cup water to make the strong coffee.

2 cups (12-oz. package) semisweet chocolate morsels
¼ cup butter or margarine, softened
¾ cup firmly packed brown sugar
3 large eggs
2 tsp. strong brewed coffee
1 tsp. vanilla extract
1½ cups chopped pecans, divided
¼ cup all-purpose flour
1 unbaked 9-inch pastry shell
1 cup whipping cream, whipped

Microwave chocolate in a 1-qt. glass bowl at HIGH 1½ minutes or until melted, stirring twice.
Beat butter at medium speed with an electric mixer until creamy; gradually add sugar, beating well. Add eggs, 1 at a time, beating after each addition. Stir in melted chocolate, coffee, and vanilla. Gradually add 1 cup pecans and flour, stirring well.
Spoon chocolate mixture into pastry shell; sprinkle with remaining ½ cup pecans. Bake at 375° for 30 minutes or until a knife inserted in center comes out almost clean. Cool completely on a wire rack. Serve with whipped cream. **Makes** 8 to 10 servings.

Chocolate Sauce

Prep: 5 min., Cook: 3 min.

If you have chocolate fever, this sauce makes a satisfying topping for any chocolate or nut pie or for simply drizzling over ice cream.

1 cup (4 oz.) semisweet chocolate morsels
¼ cup whipping cream
2 Tbsp. butter

Stir together all ingredients in a small saucepan over low heat, and cook, stirring constantly, until chocolate and butter melt and sauce is warm. **Makes** 1 cup.

Bourbon-Chocolate-Pecan Pie

Prep: 10 min., Cook: 1 hr.

½ (15-oz.) package refrigerated piecrusts
4 large eggs
1 cup light corn syrup
6 Tbsp. butter or margarine, melted
½ cup granulated sugar
¼ cup firmly packed light brown sugar
3 Tbsp. bourbon
1 Tbsp. all-purpose flour
1 Tbsp. vanilla extract
1 cup coarsely chopped pecans
1 cup (6-oz. package) semisweet chocolate morsels

Fit piecrust into a 9-inch pieplate according to package directions; fold edges under, and crimp.
Whisk together eggs and next 7 ingredients in a large bowl until mixture is smooth; stir in chopped pecans and morsels. Pour into piecrust.
Bake on lowest oven rack at 350° for 1 hour or until set. **Makes** 8 servings.

Coconut-Macadamia Nut Pie

Prep: 10 min.; Cook: 1 hr., 8 min.; Other: 15 min.

½ (15-oz.) package refrigerated piecrusts
1 cup sugar
3 large eggs
1 cup light corn syrup
¼ cup whipping cream
1 Tbsp. butter or margarine, melted
1 tsp. vanilla extract
¾ cup coarsely chopped macadamia nuts
1 cup sweetened flaked coconut
Garnishes: whipped cream, chopped macadamia nuts, toasted sweetened flaked coconut

Fit piecrust into a 9-inch pieplate according to package directions; fold edges under, and crimp. Freeze 15 minutes. Bake at 425° for 6 to 8 minutes or until golden; cool on a wire rack.
Whisk together sugar and next 5 ingredients in a medium bowl; stir in nuts and coconut. Pour into prepared piecrust.
Bake at 350° for 55 minutes to 1 hour. Cool on a wire rack. Garnish, if desired. **Makes** 8 servings.

Spiked Strawberry-Lime Ice-Cream Pie

Prep: 30 min.; Cook: 10 min.; Other: 3 hrs., 30 min.

This pie softens quickly due to the alcohol content, which lowers the freezing temperature of the ice cream.

4 cups pretzel twists
½ cup butter, melted
2 Tbsp. granulated sugar
1 (½-gal.) container premium strawberry ice cream
    (we tested with Blue Bell Ice Cream)
1 (16-oz.) container fresh strawberries, stemmed
½ cup powdered sugar
1 (6-oz.) can frozen limeade concentrate, partially
    thawed
½ cup tequila
¼ cup orange liqueur (we tested with Triple Sec)
Garnishes: lime rind curls, fresh whole strawberries,
    pretzels

Process first 3 ingredients in a food processor until pretzels are finely crushed. Firmly press mixture into a lightly greased 10-inch springform pan.

Bake at 350° for 10 minutes. Cool completely in pan on a wire rack.

Let strawberry ice cream stand at room temperature 20 minutes or until slightly softened.

Process strawberries and powdered sugar in food processor until pureed, stopping to scrape down sides.

Place ice cream in a large bowl; cut into large (3-inch) pieces. Fold strawberry mixture, limeade concentrate, tequila, and orange liqueur into ice cream until well blended. Spoon mixture into prepared crust in springform pan. Freeze 3 hours or until firm. Let stand 10 minutes at room temperature before serving. Garnish, if desired. **Makes** 10 to 12 servings.

Strawberry-Lime Ice-Cream Pie: Omit tequila and orange liqueur, and add 1 (6-oz.) can frozen orange juice concentrate, partially thawed. Proceed with recipe as directed. Let stand 15 minutes at room temperature before serving. Garnish, if desired.

Strawberry Smoothie Ice-Cream Pie

Prep: 50 min.; Cook: 10 min.; Other: 5 hrs., 5 min.

1 (7-oz.) package waffle cones, broken into pieces
6 Tbsp. butter, melted
1 Tbsp. granulated sugar
2 (1-qt.) containers premium vanilla ice cream, divided
    (we tested with Häagen-Dazs)
1 (16-oz.) container fresh strawberries, stemmed
¼ cup powdered sugar, divided
1 pt. fresh blueberries
2 ripe bananas
Garnishes: waffle cone pieces, fresh whole strawberries,
    fresh blueberries

Process first 3 ingredients in a food processor until finely crushed. Firmly press mixture onto bottom of a lightly greased 10-inch springform pan.

Bake at 350° for 10 minutes. Cool completely in pan on a wire rack.

Let vanilla ice cream stand at room temperature 20 minutes or until slightly softened.

Process strawberries and 2 Tbsp. powdered sugar in a food processor until pureed, stopping to scrape down sides. Remove strawberry mixture; set aside.

Process blueberries and 1 Tbsp. powdered sugar in food processor until pureed, stopping to scrape down side; set aside.

Mash bananas with a fork in a large bowl; stir in remaining 1 Tbsp. powdered sugar. Set aside.

Place 1 qt. ice cream in a large bowl; cut into large (3-inch) pieces. Fold strawberry mixture into ice cream until blended. Freeze until slightly firm.

Divide remaining 1 qt. ice cream in half, placing halves in separate bowls. Stir blueberry mixture into half and mashed banana mixture into remaining half. Place bowls in freezer.

Spread half of strawberry mixture evenly into prepared crust in springform pan. Place pan and remaining strawberry mixture in freezer. Freeze 30 minutes or until strawberry layer in pan is slightly firm. Spread banana mixture evenly over strawberry layer in pan; return pan to freezer, and freeze 30 minutes or until banana layer is slightly firm. Repeat procedure with blueberry mixture. Spread remaining strawberry mixture over blueberry layer in pan, and freeze 3 hours or until all layers are firm. Let pie stand at room temperature 15 minutes before serving. Garnish, if desired. **Makes** 10 to 12 servings.

Strawberry Smoothie Ice-Cream Pie

Layered Fruit Congealed Salad

Prep: 30 min.; Cook: 50 min.; Other: 4 hrs., 15 min.

Don't cover bowls or glasses during each chill time (except at the very end). This shortens the required time in the refrigerator as you move through the steps.

1 small navel orange
2 cups water
2½ cups sugar, divided
2 (3-oz.) packages peach-flavored gelatin
4 cups boiling water, divided
½ cup half-and-half
¼ cup cold water
2 tsp. unflavored gelatin
½ (8-oz.) package cream cheese
¼ tsp. vanilla extract
2 (3-oz.) packages raspberry-flavored gelatin
2 cups fresh raspberries

Cut orange into thin (⅛-inch-thick) slices, discarding ends.

Stir together 2 cups water and 2 cups sugar in a large saucepan over medium-high heat. Bring to a boil, and stir until sugar dissolves. Gently stir in orange slices, and bring to a simmer; reduce heat to low, and simmer, occasionally pressing orange slices into liquid, 40 minutes. Remove orange slices using a slotted spoon, and place in a single layer on wax paper; cool completely. Discard liquid in pan.

Place 1 orange slice in bottom of each of 6 (1½- to 2-cup) water glasses, discarding or reserving remaining orange slices for another use. (Orange slices will not lie flat against bottoms of glasses.) Set aside.

Remove and discard 2 Tbsp. peach-flavored gelatin from 1 package. Stir together remaining peach-flavored gelatin and 2 cups boiling water in a bowl 1 to 2 minutes or until gelatin dissolves. Pour about ⅓ cup peach-flavored gelatin mixture over orange slice in each glass. Chill 1 hour or until firm.

Stir together half-and-half and ¼ cup cold water in a medium saucepan. Sprinkle with 2 tsp. unflavored gelatin, and stir.

Place pan over medium heat; stir in remaining ½ cup sugar, and cook, stirring often, 3 to 5 minutes or until sugar and gelatin dissolve. (Do not boil.) Remove pan from heat.

Microwave cream cheese at MEDIUM (50% power) 45 seconds or until very soft; stir until smooth. Whisk cream cheese into half-and-half mixture until smooth; whisk in vanilla extract, and chill 30 minutes or until slightly cool. Spoon about 3 Tbsp. cream cheese mixture in an even layer over firm peach layer in each glass; chill.

Remove and discard 2 Tbsp. raspberry-flavored gelatin from 1 package. Stir together remaining raspberry-flavored gelatin and remaining 2 cups boiling water 1 to 2 minutes or until gelatin dissolves.

Chill 45 minutes or until consistency of unbeaten egg white.

Stir in fresh raspberries, and spoon about ½ cup raspberry mixture in an even layer over cream cheese mixture in each glass. Cover and chill at least 2 hours or up to 24 hours before serving. **Makes** 6 servings.

FOR THE LOVE OF LAYERS

- Use clear glass or acrylic bowls or other see-through containers to show off layers.
- Think outside the round bowl. Go for a fun and unexpected shape, such as a square, rectangle, or scallop-edged bowl; a trifle bowl is also a good option. With so much from which to choose, don't forget glassware for some unique individual serving possibilities.

Strawberry-Sugar Biscuit Trifle

Prep: 35 min., Cook: 50 min., Other: 4 hrs.

When prepping for this recipe, make the custard first; then bake the biscuits, and prepare the fruit.

Sugar Biscuits
6 Tbsp. orange liqueur or orange juice, divided
2½ lb. fresh strawberries, halved
Trifle Custard
1½ cups whipping cream
¼ cup plus 2 Tbsp. powdered sugar
Garnishes: strawberries, mint leaves

Cut Sugar Biscuits in half; brush cut sides evenly with 5 Tbsp. orange liqueur.
Line bottom of a 4-qt. bowl or trifle bowl with 8 Sugar Biscuit halves.
Arrange strawberry halves around lower edge of bowl.
Spoon one-third of Trifle Custard evenly over Sugar Biscuit halves; top with one-third of remaining strawberry halves. Repeat layers as shown in photo below.
Drizzle remaining 1 Tbsp. orange liqueur evenly over top. Cover and chill 3 to 4 hours.
Beat whipping cream until foamy; gradually add powdered sugar, beating until soft peaks form.
Spread whipped cream over trifle, and serve immediately. Garnish, if desired. **Makes** 10 to 12 servings.

Sugar Biscuits

Prep: 10 min., Cook: 20 min.

1 (12-count) package frozen buttermilk biscuits
2 Tbsp. whipping cream
1 Tbsp. sugar
¼ tsp. ground cinnamon

Brush tops of frozen biscuits with whipping cream; sprinkle evenly with sugar and ground cinnamon. Place biscuits on a lightly greased baking sheet.
Bake at 350° for 20 minutes. Cool. **Makes** 1 dozen.

Trifle Custard

Prep: 5 min., Cook: 8 min., Other: 2 hrs.

1 cup sugar
⅓ cup cornstarch
6 egg yolks
2 cups milk
1¾ cups half-and-half
1 tsp. vanilla extract

Whisk together all ingredients in a heavy saucepan. Bring to a boil over medium heat; whisk constantly. Boil, whisking constantly, 1 minute or until thickened. Remove from heat. Place pan in ice water; whisk occasionally until cool. Chill 2 hours. **Makes** 4 cups.

Peaches 'n' Cream Trifle

Prep: 35 min.; Other: 8 hrs., 20 min.

3 Tbsp. sugar
7 fresh ripe peaches, peeled and sliced (4 cups)
1¾ cups whipping cream
¼ cup sifted powdered sugar
Crème Anglaise
6 cups pound cake, cut into 1-inch cubes
½ cup amaretto liqueur
¼ cup sliced almonds, toasted

Sprinkle sugar over peaches; toss and let stand 20 minutes or until juicy.

Combine whipping cream and powdered sugar in a chilled mixing bowl. Beat at medium speed with an electric mixer until soft peaks form. Fold half of whipped cream into Crème Anglaise.

Place half of cake cubes in a 3-qt. trifle bowl. Sprinkle ¼ cup liqueur over cubes. Top with half each of Crème Anglaise mixture and peaches. Repeat layers.

Spread remaining Crème Anglaise mixture on top of trifle. Cover and chill 8 hours. Sprinkle with almonds before serving. **Makes** 14 servings.

Crème Anglaise

Prep: 4 min., Cook: 14 min., Other: 10 min.

2 cups milk, or 1 cup milk and 1 cup half-and-half
½ cup sugar
5 egg yolks
1 tsp. vanilla extract

Bring milk to a simmer over medium heat. Beat sugar and egg yolks at high speed with an electric mixer until pale and mixture forms a ribbon.

Gradually add hot milk to egg yolk mixture, whisking until blended; return to saucepan. Cook over low heat, stirring constantly, until custard thickens and coats a spoon. Remove from heat; pour through a wire-mesh strainer into a bowl, and cool 10 minutes. Stir in vanilla. Cover and chill. **Makes** 2 cups.

THE CLASSIC TRIFLE

Full of fruit, cream, and tender cake or biscuit layers, trifles end a spicy barbecue meal on a cool and creamy note.

Jumbleberry Trifle

Jumbleberry Trifle

Prep: 45 min., Other: 50 min.

1 (10-oz.) package frozen unsweetened raspberries, thawed
1 (18-oz.) jar seedless blackberry jam or preserves, divided
1 (10.75-oz.) frozen pound cake, thawed
2 Tbsp. cream sherry
1½ cups whipping cream
1 (10-oz.) jar lemon curd
Garnishes: whipped cream, fresh raspberries and blackberries, fresh mint sprigs, lemon rind strips

Stir together raspberries and 1 cup jam. Press mixture through a wire-mesh strainer into a bowl; discard seeds. Cover sauce, and chill 20 minutes.

Cut pound cake into ¼-inch-thick slices. Spread remaining jam on 1 side of half of slices; top with remaining slices. Cut sandwiches into ½-inch cubes; drizzle with sherry, and set aside.

Beat whipping cream and lemon curd at low speed with an electric mixer until blended. Gradually increase mixer speed, beating until medium peaks form. Cover and chill 30 minutes.

Spoon 1 Tbsp. berry sauce into 8 large wine glasses; top with about ¼ cup each of cake cubes and lemon curd mixture. Repeat layers once, ending with berry sauce. Serve immediately, or chill until ready to serve. Garnish, if desired. **Makes** 8 servings.

Very Berry Sundaes

Warm Cookie Sundaes

Prep: 5 min., Cook: 30 min., Other: 5 min.

We liked the cookie cups soft, but for a more crisp cookie increase the bake time.

6 packaged refrigerated ready-to-bake peanut butter
    cookie dough rounds with mini peanut butter cups
    (we tested with Pillsbury Ready to Bake Peanut
    Butter Cup Cookies)
Vanilla ice cream
Toppings: hot fudge sauce, whipped cream, chopped
    peanuts

Place each cookie dough round into a lightly greased 8-oz. ramekin or individual soufflé dish.
Bake at 350° for 25 to 30 minutes or until cookies are lightly browned. Cool 5 minutes. Scoop vanilla ice cream into each ramekin; top sundaes with desired toppings. Serve immediately. **Makes** 6 servings.

Note: For testing purposes only, we used half of an 18-oz. package of Pillsbury Ready to Bake Peanut Butter Cup Cookies.

Very Berry Sundaes

Prep: 10 min., Other: 2 hrs.

We used blueberries, blackberries, and raspberries for mixed fresh berries.

2¼ cups fresh strawberries, halved
2¼ cups mixed fresh berries
3 Tbsp. sugar
2 Tbsp. orange liqueur
2 tsp. grated orange rind
½ tsp. chopped mint
3 cups fruit sorbet
Garnishes: orange zest, fresh mint sprigs

Combine strawberries and next 5 ingredients, tossing lightly to combine. Cover and chill up to 2 hours.
Scoop ½ cup sorbet into each of 6 serving dishes.
Spoon ⅔ cup berries over sorbet in each dish. Garnish, if desired. Serve immediately. **Makes** 6 servings.

S'mores Sundaes

Prep: 10 min., Other: 1 hr.

2 cups low-fat chocolate chunk ice cream, slightly
    softened (we tested with Healthy Choice Chocolate
    Chocolate Chunk Premium Low Fat Ice Cream)
20 graham cracker sticks, crushed (we tested with Honey
    Maid Grahams Honey Sticks)
¼ cup marshmallow crème
4 tsp. semisweet chocolate mini-morsels
8 whole graham cracker sticks

Stir together softened ice cream and crushed graham crackers in a small bowl. Freeze 1 hour or until firm.
Spoon ice-cream mixture into 4 bowls; top evenly with marshmallow crème and chocolate mini-morsels. Serve each with 2 graham cracker sticks. **Makes** 4 servings.

Chocolate Pudding

Prep: 15 min., Cook: 10 min.

4 cups whipping cream
6 Tbsp. cornstarch
1 cup sugar
1 cup (6-oz. package) semisweet chocolate morsels
1 tsp. vanilla extract

Stir together 6 Tbsp. whipping cream and cornstarch, stirring until a paste forms.
Bring remaining whipping cream to a simmer in a 2-qt. saucepan over medium heat. Stir in cornstarch mixture, sugar, chocolate morsels, and vanilla; cook, stirring constantly, until chocolate melts.
Cook mixture, stirring often, 8 minutes or until thick and creamy. Serve warm or cool. **Makes** 5 cups.

Bittersweet Chocolate Pudding

Prep: 10 min., Cook: 14 min.

3½ cups milk, divided
1 cup Dutch process or unsweetened cocoa
3 Tbsp. cornstarch
¼ tsp. salt
1 cup sugar
1 egg, lightly beaten
1 large egg yolk, lightly beaten
2 (1-oz.) bittersweet chocolate baking squares, coarsely chopped
1 Tbsp. vanilla extract

Combine 1 cup milk, cocoa, cornstarch, and salt in a large bowl; stir well with a whisk. Set aside.
Cook remaining 2½ cups milk in a large, heavy saucepan over medium-high heat to 180° or until tiny bubbles form around edge (do not boil). Remove from heat; stir in sugar with a whisk until sugar dissolves. Add cocoa mixture to pan, stirring until blended. Bring to a boil over medium heat; cook 2 minutes, stirring constantly.
Combine egg and egg yolk in a medium bowl, stirring well with a whisk. Gradually add milk mixture to egg mixture, stirring constantly. Return mixture to pan. Cook over medium heat until thick (about 2 minutes); stir constantly. Remove from heat. Stir in chocolate and vanilla; stir until chocolate melts. Serve warm or chilled. **Makes** 8 servings.

Best-Ever Banana Pudding

Prep: 25 min., Cook: 25 min.

⅔ cup sugar
¼ cup all-purpose flour
Dash of salt
1 (14-oz.) can sweetened condensed milk
2½ cups milk
4 large eggs, separated
2 tsp. vanilla extract
1 (12-oz.) package vanilla wafers
6 large bananas
⅓ cup sugar
½ tsp. banana extract or vanilla extract

Combine first 3 ingredients in a heavy saucepan. Whisk together milks and egg yolks; stir into dry ingredients.
Cook over medium heat, whisking constantly, until smooth and thickened. Remove from heat; stir in vanilla.
Arrange one-third of wafers in bottom of a 3-qt. baking dish. Slice 2 bananas; layer over wafers. Pour one-third of pudding mixture over bananas. Repeat layers of sliced bananas and pudding twice; arrange remaining wafers around edge of dish.
Beat egg whites at high speed with an electric mixer until foamy.
Add ⅓ cup sugar, 1 Tbsp. at a time, beating until soft peaks form and sugar dissolves. Fold in banana extract; spread over pudding, sealing to edge.
Bake at 325° for 25 minutes or until golden brown.
Makes 8 to 10 servings.

> **❝**While all things barbecue tend to fall squarely along regional and state lines, desserts are all over the map.**❞**
>
> ——Scott Jones, *Southern Living* Staff